鑑賞
ポケット
ガイド
Pocket Guide

Understanding
Japanese Buddhist Sculpture
through
Visual Comparison

対比でみる 日本の仏像

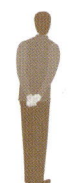

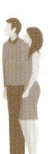

鈴木喜博

Yoshihiro Suzuki

Translation: Michael Jamentz

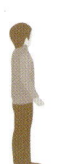

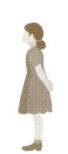

Understanding Japanese Buddhist Sculpture through Visual Comparison

Text by Yoshihiro Suzuki
Translated by Michael Jamentz
Designed by Yoko Hayashi (Sparrow Design)
Drawings by Chika Shibata (@shibatachi)
Vector graphics by Freepik.com (@macrovector)
Edited by Eriko Hara (PIE International)

Published by PIE International Inc.

PIE International Inc.
2-32-4 Minami-Otsuka, Toshima-ku, Tokyo
170-0005 Japan
international@pie.co.jp
http://pie.co.jp/english/

2019 © Yoshihiro Suzuki / PIE International
English text © Michael Jamentz
ISBN 978-4-7562-5238-8 (outside Japan)
Printed in Japan

目 次

Contents

仏像をよく見る

　「仏像をよく見る」ことは、なんども仏像の前に足を運ぶことです。たとえば歴史のあるお寺に出かけるとしましょう。うす暗い堂内に安置された仏像を、すこし離れた場所から拝むと、今日もなお信仰の対象であるとあらためて納得することと思います。このときに、写真では実感できない仏像の大きさや、重量感が記憶に残ることでしょう。

仏像の展示に通う

　こうして仏像に関心を持ったら次の段階があります。めぐり合わせた博物館・美術館の仏像展示に、足しげく通ってみることです。展示会場では、明るい照明のなかで仏像と間近に対面できます。このとき、仏像を横からも後ろからも見ることを私はすすめます。近年の仏像展示は、こうした「ぐるっと見る」ニーズに応えるものが多くなっています。そのようにして得られた仏像の立体感の記憶は、その仏像の個性や優れた表現、あるいはその信仰の心に気づくのに重要なヒントを与えてくれると思います。

　さらに、こうした展示会場では、興味のある仏像の前に立ち、頭の中でその隣に他の仏像を思い浮かべるのも面白いと思います。前よりも少し分かったという気分になるからです。

比べて見る

　このようなプロセスを机上で実践してみたのが本書です。2つの仏像写真を見開きに並べ、様々な角度から双方を比べられるようにしました。実際には大きさの異なる仏像を、写真ではほぼ同じ高さにそろえて並べています。すると、1つの仏像を見るだけでは気づかなかった特徴が見えてくることでしょう。

　このような本書のねらいが、「仏像をよく見ること」をさらに充実させるものとなり得るかどうか——是非、構えすぎずにページをめくっていただけたら幸いです。

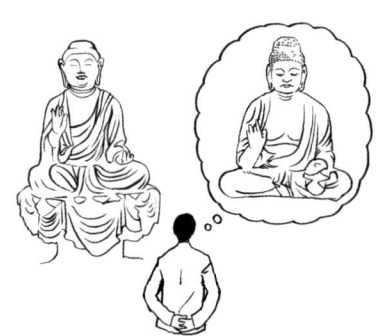

Really Seeing Buddhist Sculpture

"Really seeing Buddhist sculpture" entails making repeated visits to view Buddhist statues. You may, for example, choose to travel to a historic temple. When you revere a statue in a darkened temple hall from a certain distance, you will be reminded why such works are still objects of veneration today. The sense of the icon's size and volume, which cannot be captured in any photograph, will likely remain imprinted upon your memory.

Visiting Exhibitions of Buddhist Sculpture

Once you have developed an interest in Buddhist sculpture, you are ready for the next step. That step involves frequent visits to exhibitions of Buddhist sculpture at the various museums that host such displays. In a museum setting you can view Buddhist sculpture from close range under proper lighting. On such occasions, I recommend that you view the sculpture from the sides and the back. It is a wonderful fact that many modern-day exhibitions of Buddhist sculpture meet the needs of serious viewers and allow visitors to circle around the statues. I believe that the mental impression of the three-dimensionality of these Buddhist sculptures obtained this way will surely provide important hints helping you realize the individuality of the sculpture, its unexcelled artistic representation, and the spiritual core of faith behind it.

When you are at such an exhibit and standing in front of a Buddhist sculpture that is particularly interesting, it is a useful exercise to conjure up the image of another Buddhist statue for comparison. This will give you a sense of being able to comprehend the statue better than before.

Contrasting Views

This book allows you go through this process at home. I have arranged facing photographs of Buddhist sculptures so the statues can be easily compared from various angles. Two Buddhist statues that are in fact of different sizes appear in the photographs as nearly the same size. By doing this, you will undoubtedly be able to see characteristics that you would not have noticed viewing a single Buddhist statue.

My aim in writing this book is to help you make the leap to "really seeing Buddhist sculpture," but, whether or not we reach this goal, I hope you find pleasure in casually flipping through its pages and enjoy the many images contained within.

視点
正面・斜め・側面・背面など、仏像を見るときに意識したい視点を紹介しています。

Perspectives
From the front, an angle, the sides, and the back — these are the perspectives you should keep in mind when viewing Buddhist sculpture.

背面
から見る

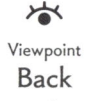

Viewpoint
Back

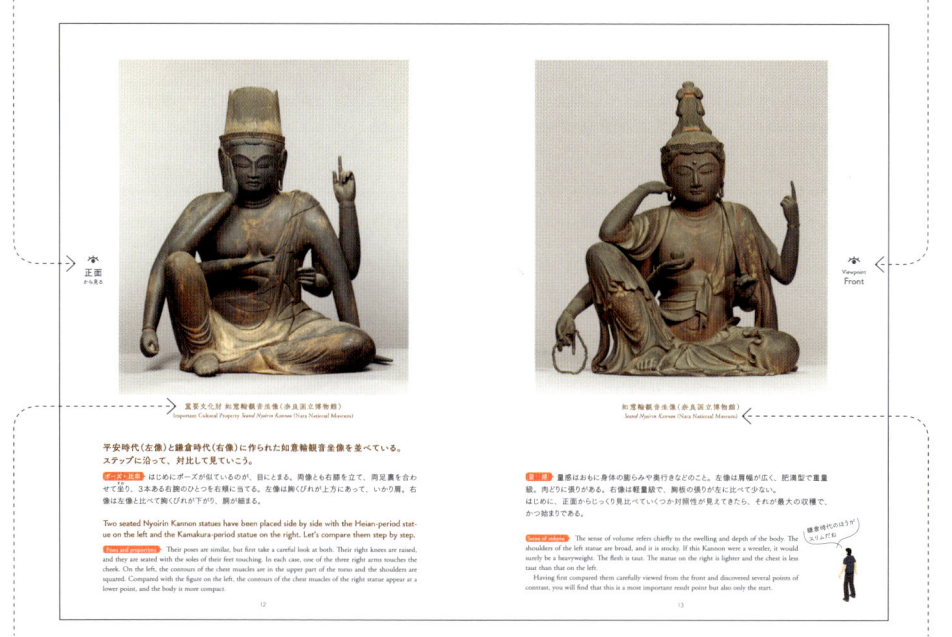

正面
から見る

Viewpoint
Front

重要文化財 如意輪観音坐像（奈良国立博物館）
Important Cultural Property *Seated Nyoirin Kannon* (Nara National Museum)

平安時代（左像）と鎌倉時代（右像）に作られた如意輪観音坐像を並べている。ステップに沿って、対比して見ていこう。

Two seated Nyoirin Kannon statues have been placed side by side with the Heian-period statue on the left and the Kamakura-period statue on the right. Let's compare them step by step.

12

如意輪観音坐像（奈良国立博物館）
Seated Nyoirin Kannon (Nara National Museum)

13

仏像の名称

Names of the statue

第1章では、手引きとして対比ステップを紹介しています。
The first chapter guides you through the steps needed to see contrasts.

対比ステップ → p.8-9参照
より理解と鑑賞が深まるように考えられた着眼点と、その順番です。

Comparative Perspectives → see pp.8-9
Listed below are the focal points and the order needed to develop deeper understanding and appreciation.

① ポーズ・比率
② 量 感
③ 彫刻の空間
④ 動 静
⑤ 衣 文
⑥ 着 衣
⑦ 顔の表情

① Poses and proportions
② Sense of volume
③ Sculptural space
④ Movement
⑤ Pattern of the folds and creases in the robe
⑥ Clothing
⑦ Facial expression

仏像を見るときに役立つポイント
Some points for observing Buddhist icons as statues

博物館・美術館の仏像展示では、仏像を一周して見ること。仏像の背中側が
展示ケースの壁になっていることも多いかもしれないが、側面や斜めからも見よう。

When attending exhibitions of Buddhist sculpture held in various museums, be sure to
view the statues from all angles. Unfortunately, it is often the case that the back of a statue
will be concealed by a wall, but try to at least view the statue from the side or from an angle.

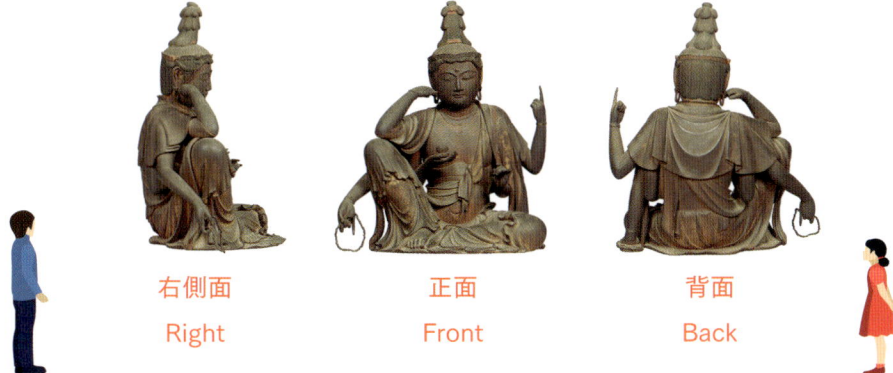

右側面　　　　　　　　　正面　　　　　　　　　背面

Right　　　　　　　　　Front　　　　　　　　　Back

よく見ようと仏像に近づいて、細かな部分を見るのも大事だが、意識して一歩
遠ざかって、仏像の全身の姿をしっかりと見ることも同様に大切だ。

Although it is important to see a Buddhist statue close up and look carefully at the details,
it is equally vital to deliberately take a step back and view the entire sculpture as a whole.

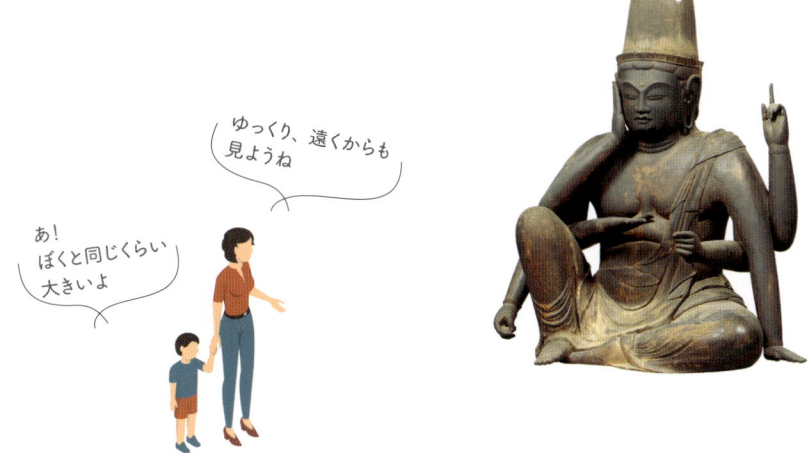

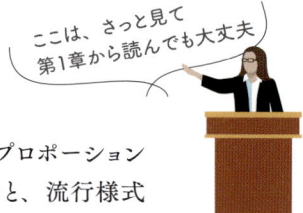

ここは、さっと見て
第1章から読んでも大丈夫

① ポーズ・比率

全身を見るときには、頭部と体部との比率、つまり、プロポーション
に注目してみよう。そのとき、膝頭の位置に注意を払うと、流行様式
の時代の傾向が見えてくる。

① Poses and proportions

When viewing the entire statue as a whole, pay attention to the relative proportions of the head and the body. If you take special note of the location of the kneecaps, you'll be able to see trends that were popular in the style of the historical period when the statue was made.

② 量 感

側面から見ると、仏像の量感に意識がまわる。おなじ肥満型でも、肉とりが引き締ま
って豊かなのか、ゆるんでいるのか。正面だけでなく、ぐるりと回ってみると、そのボリ
ュームを実感できる。

② Sense of volume

When viewing a statue from the side, your attention will turn to the sense of volume. Even if two statues are both stout figures, you can see whether the full flesh is tight or flabby. When you circle the statue instead of just viewing it head-on, you will be able to feel the volume.

③ 彫刻の空間

遠く彼方をみるか、顎を引いて目を下に落とすか。上体が後ろに反るか、前に傾くか。
左右の肘や膝の張りが大きく広がるか、窮屈に狭まるか。さらに手首や足の動き（坐
像ならば足の組み方）などによって構築される「彫刻の空間」を意識して見よう。そ
れが仏像を立体彫刻としてみる最も重要なポイントだ。

③ Sculptural space

Is the statue looking off into the distance, or is the chin pulled inward and the eyes downcast? Is the upper body curved backward or leaning forward? Are the elbows or knees pulled in tightly or spread widely? Does it feel cramped? What about the movement of the wrists and legs? Or, if the statue is seated, how are the legs arranged? These give us a sense of the "sculptural space" in which the works were constructed. This is the most important point in seeing Buddhist statues as three-dimensional sculptures.

④ 動 静

仏像を前にして、姿勢や腰のひねり、腕や脚の開きぐあい、さらに指先の印相（ポー
ズ）までを、同じように自ら真似てみる。すると、対面している仏像の動きが文字通り
手に取るように分かってくる。それは仏像のオーラが、見る者に乗り移ってくる気分に
似ている。よく見るための大切な瞬間だ。

④ Movement

When you are standing in front of a Buddhist statue, you should try to mimic its pose adopting the same twist of the hips, the stretching of arms and legs, even the symbolic hand gesture. If you do this, you can truly grasp the movement of the Buddhist statue in front of you. It is similar to the feeling of having the aura of a Buddhist icon transferred onto oneself. That is critical instant for "really seeing."

⑤ 衣文

衣文（衣の皺）の数を数えることは、平安時代の仏師の調査項目にも入っていた。布の皺が心地よく整うか、不規則に乱れるか、彫り口が深いか浅いか。特に肌に密着して皺を作らない箇所に気がつけば、布の質感表現に敏感になるだろう。

⑤ Pattern of the folds and creases in the robe

Counting the folds and creases in the robes was a routine for Heian-period Buddhist sculptors. They paid attention to whether the folds were satisfyingly regular or were irregular and disordered and whether the carving was deep or shallow. If you are particularly careful in checking how the folds and creases cling to the body, you will likely become sensitive to the feel of the fabric.

⑥ 着衣

仏像は何をまとうか、あるいはまとわないか、その着付け方は、つじつまが合うか否か。それぞれの仏像の服制に注意しながら観察すると、その仏像が作られるときに手本とした仏像や仏画からの「写し崩れ」に気づくことがあるかもしれない。そこからは、仏像や仏画の影響関係を探る、仏教美術史の面白い世界に踏み込むことになるだろう。

⑥ Clothing

How is a Buddhist sculpture clad or unclad? What is it wearing and how? Is the clothing consistent? If you pay attention to the clothing of each Buddhist statue, you may be able to understand how the statue varies from the iconographic image that served as its model. Exploring the relationship between Buddhist paintings and Buddhist sculpture can often be a step into the fascinating world of Buddhist art history.

⑦ 顔の表情

仏像が発する威力は、顔の表情に端的にあらわれている。それを直観的な印象として、より深くとらえることが大事である。これまでの6つのポイントは、そのような直観を磨くための心得と考えてもよい。それぞれの仏像だけにしかないオリジナルな個性、あるいは優れた表現に気づくための視点だ。

⑦ Facial expression

The majesty radiated by a Buddhist sculpture is represented directly in its facial expression. It is vital to grasp this more deeply as an intuitive impression. The previous six points can be understood as lessons to sharpen this capacity for intuitive observation. Assuming such a vantage point will help you become aware of the unique character of each statue and its unexcelled manner of representation.

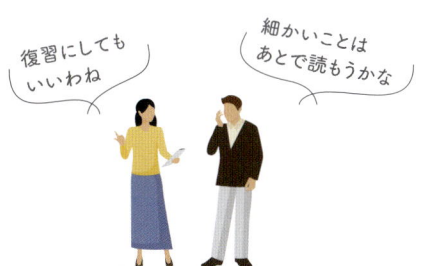

復習にしてもいいわね

細かいことはあとで読もうかな

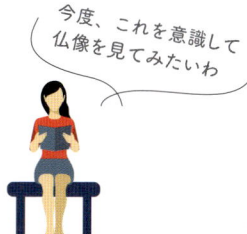

今度、これを意識して仏像を見てみたいわ

【凡例】
・本書で扱う仏像の様式の時代区分は次の通り。
　奈良時代（710〜794年）、平安時代（794〜1185年）、鎌倉時代（1185〜1333年）
・仏像の造形の鑑賞を主眼とするため、基本情報（制作年代、所蔵者、作者等）は、各章扉と各章末および巻末に掲載し、解説文中では最小限の記述とした。
・◉は国宝、◎は重要文化財を意味する。
・仏像を数える単位は「軀」を用いた。
・解説文中の「左像」または「右像」の表記はそれぞれ、見開きの「左頁の像」、「右頁の像」を意味する。
・解説文中の「左」および「右」の表記は、仏像じしんから見た視点である。
・「世紀」は「c.」と略した箇所もある。

Notes
- The chronological divisions of the Buddhist sculptural styles dealt with in this book are the Nara period (710–794), Heian period (794–1185), and Kamakura period (1185–1333).
- In order to concentrate on the appreciation of sculptural form, I have confined basic information on each statue (for example the year of production, the owner, and the name of the sculptor) to the introduction and conclusion of each chapter and avoided such details in the explanatory portions as much as possible.
- References to left and right in the text are from the point of view of the statue.
- Names of the deities below are written throughout in Japanese.
　Skt. Bodhisattva Cintāmaṇi-cakra: Jp. Nyoirin Kannon
　Skt. Bodhisattva Ekadaśamukha: Jp. Jūichimen Kannon
　Skt. Vajrapāṇi: Jp. Kongō Rikishi

Abbreviations
c.: century
◉: National Treasure
◎: Important Cultural Property

【画像提供（五十音順。敬称略）】　Photo Credits (in Japanese alphabetical order, without honorifics)
株式会社 飛鳥園　Askaen inc.
金井杜道 Morio Kanai
佐々木香輔 Kyosuke Sasaki
鈴木喜博 Yoshihiro Suzuki
奈良国立博物館 佐々木香輔 Kyosuke Sasaki, Nara National Museum
公益財団法人 美術院 Bijyutsuin
山本勉 Tsutomu Yamamoto

【謝辞】
本書の制作にあたり多くの方のご協力を賜りました。心より厚く御礼申し上げます。

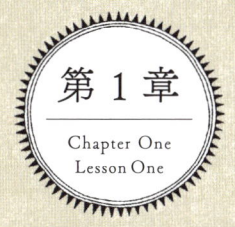

レッスン1

2つの時代の仏像を比べよう

平安仏と鎌倉仏　同じ如意輪観音坐像でも、こんなにちがう

ここでは、2つの時代の如意輪観音坐像を「対比」して見ていく。実物は大きさがだいぶ違うが、比べるために写真では高さを揃えている。[対比ステップ]をもとに具体的に仏像の特徴をつかもう。（2軀ともに奈良国立博物館所蔵）

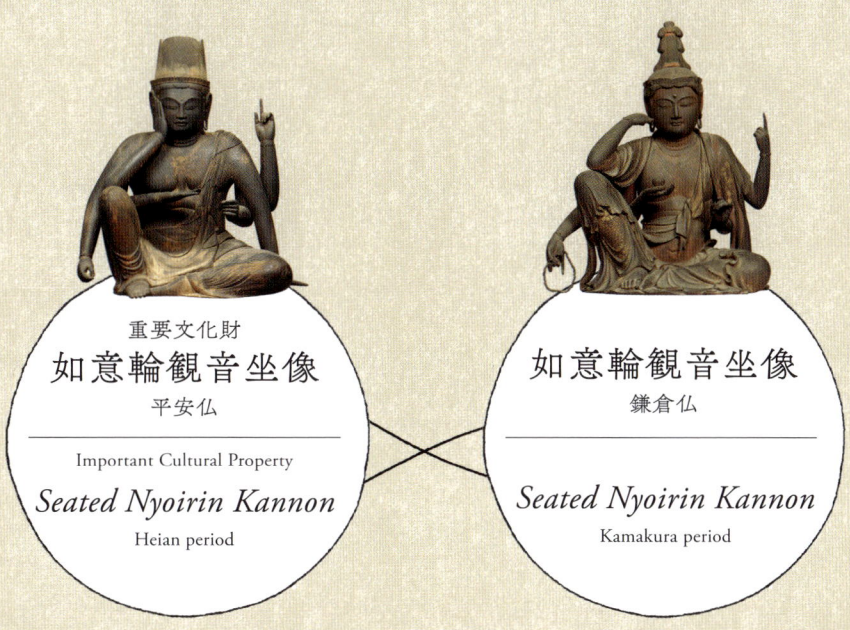

重要文化財
如意輪観音坐像
平安仏

Important Cultural Property
Seated Nyoirin Kannon
Heian period

如意輪観音坐像
鎌倉仏

Seated Nyoirin Kannon
Kamakura period

Two Statues of the Same Divinity from Different Time Periods

Let's compare Nyoirin Kannon statues from the Heian and Kamakura periods.

The sizes of actual statues are quite different, but for the sake of comparison, their heights in the photographs have been aligned. Let's use the following steps to compare the specific characteristics of these Buddhist statues. (Both statues are from the collection of the Nara National Museum)

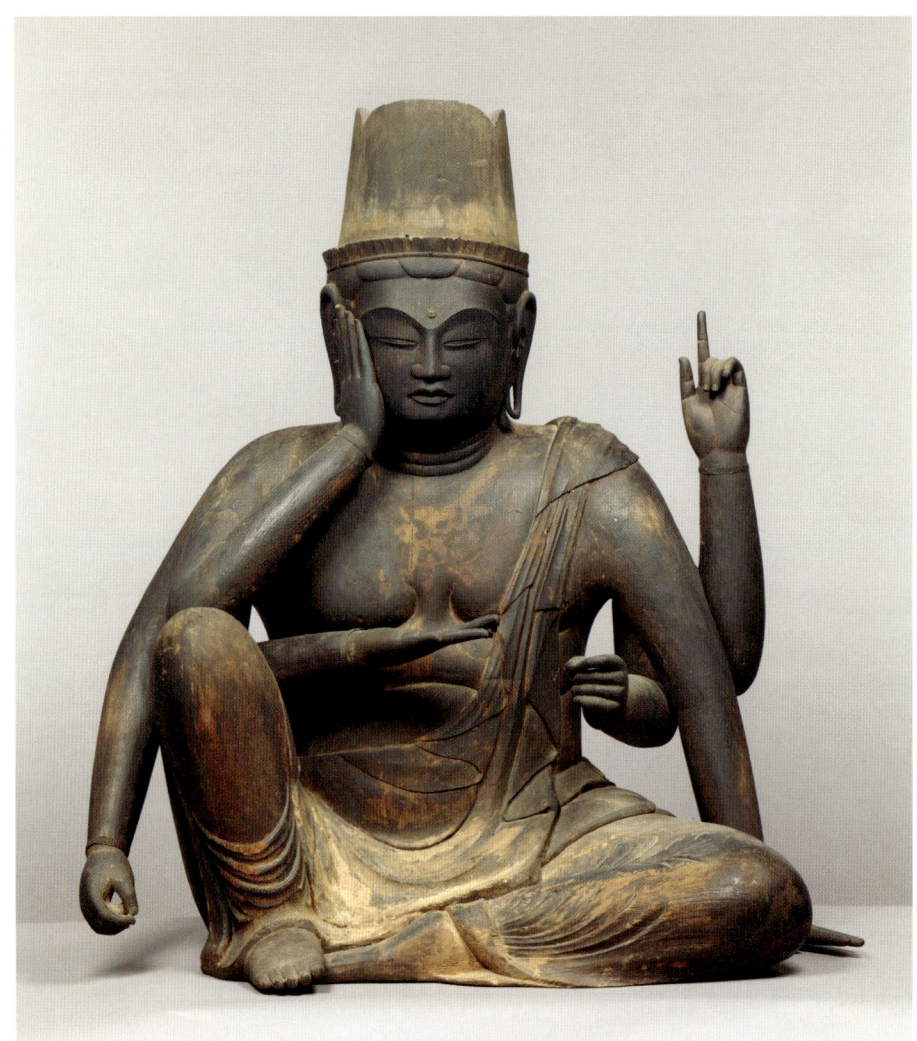

重要文化財 如意輪観音坐像（奈良国立博物館）
Important Cultural Property *Seated Nyoirin Kannon* (Nara National Museum)

平安時代（左像）と鎌倉時代（右像）に作られた如意輪観音坐像を並べている。
ステップに沿って、対比して見ていこう。

ポーズ・比率 はじめにポーズが似ているのが、目にとまる。両像とも右膝を立て、両足裏を合わ
せて坐り、3本ある右腕のひとつを右頬に当てる。左像は胸くびれが上方にあって、いかり肩。右
像は左像と比べて胸くびれが下がり、胴が細まる。

Two seated Nyoirin Kannon statues have been placed side by side with the Heian-period statue on the left and the Kamakura-period statue on the right. Let's compare them step by step.

Poses and proportions Their poses are similar, but first take a careful look at both. Their right knees are raised,
and they are seated with the soles of their feet touching. In each case, one of the three right arms touches the
cheek. On the left, the contours of the chest muscles are in the upper part of the torso and the shoulders are
squared. Compared with the figure on the left, the contours of the chest muscles of the right statue appear at a
lower point, and the body is more compact.

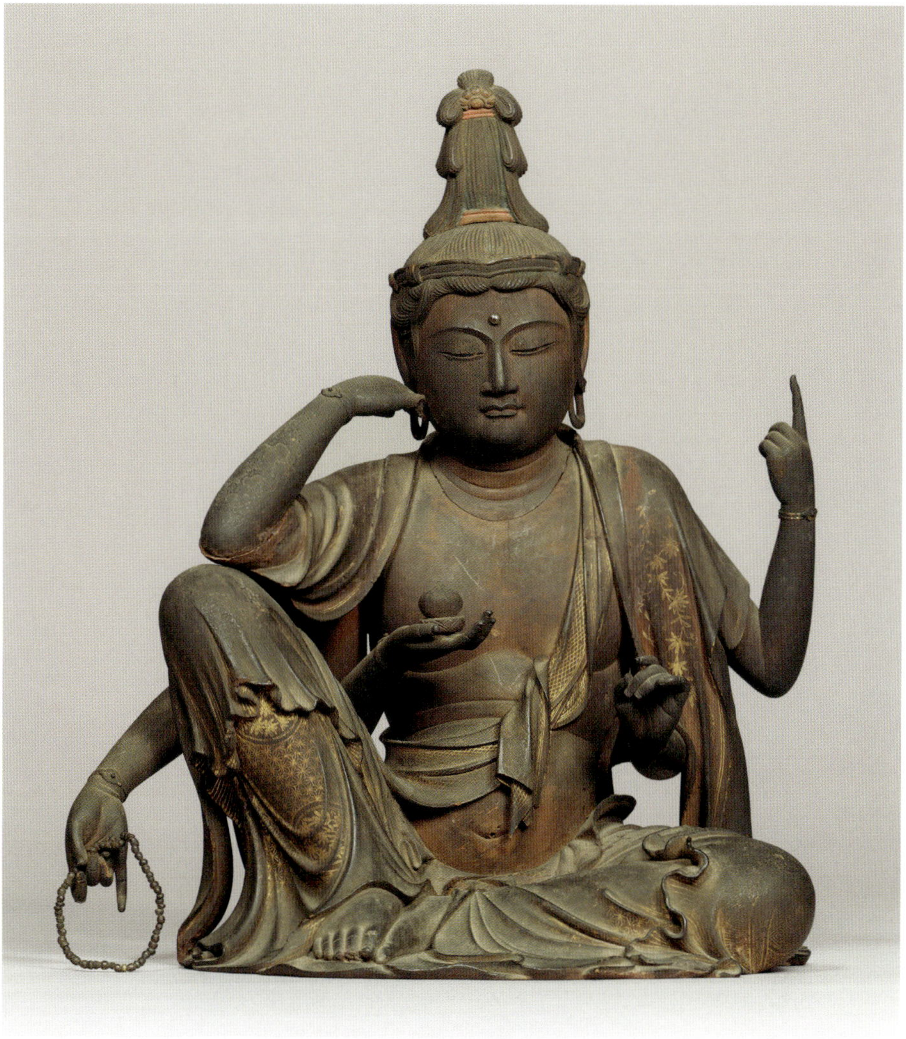

Viewpoint
Front

如意輪観音坐像（奈良国立博物館）
Seated Nyoirin Kannon (Nara National Museum)

量　感　量感はおもに身体の膨らみや奥行きなどのこと。左像は肩幅が広く、肥満型で重量級。肉どりに張りがある。右像は軽量級で、胸板の張りが左に比べて少ない。
はじめに、正面からじっくり見比べていくつか対照性が見えてきたら、それが最大の収穫で、かつ始まりである。

Sense of volume　The sense of volume refers chiefly to the swelling and depth of the body. The shoulders of the left statue are broad, and it is stocky. If this Kannon were a wrestler, it would surely be a heavyweight. The flesh is taut. The statue on the right is lighter and the chest is less taut than that on the left.

Having first compared them carefully viewed from the front and discovered several points of contrast, you will find that this is a most important result point but also only the start.

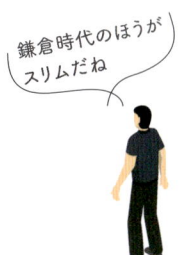

鎌倉時代のほうがスリムだね

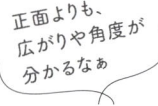

斜め
から見る

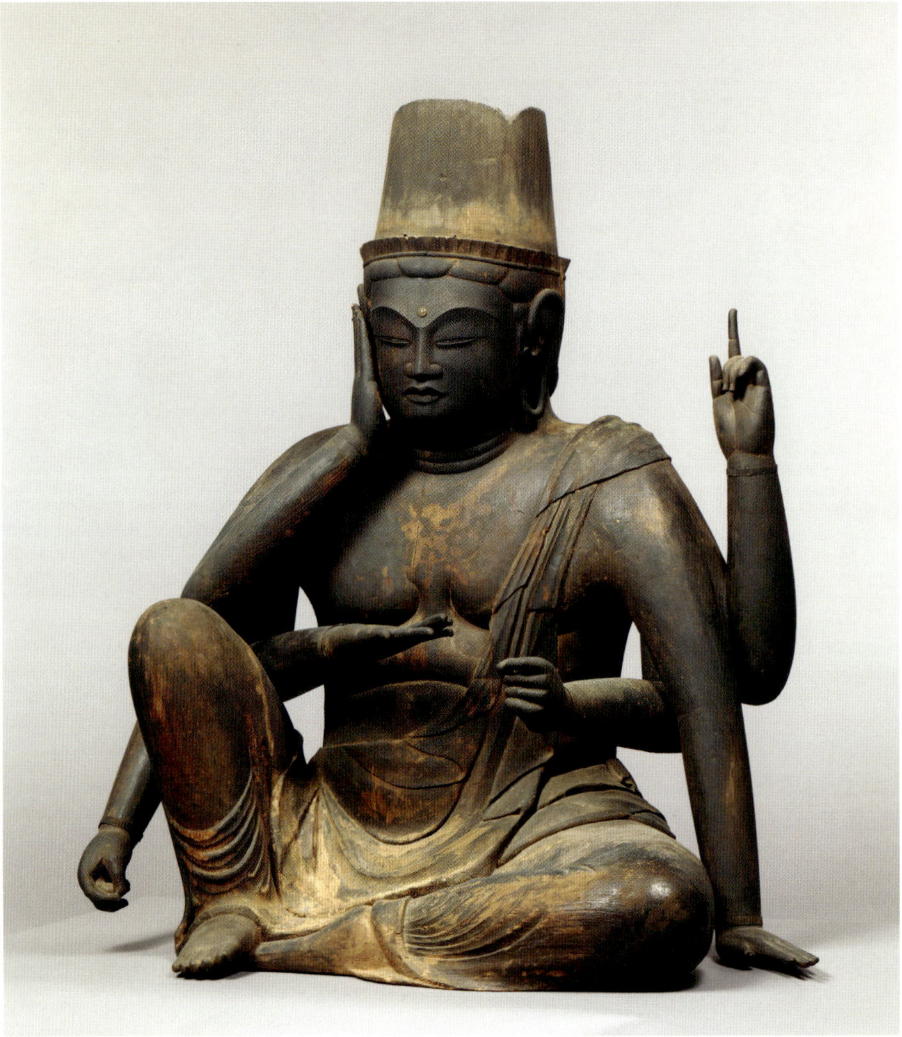

平安仏（左像）
Heian period (Left)

正面をじっくり見比べたら、少し斜めに視点を変えて見よう。
そしてもう一度、ステップ1から意識して見よう。

正面よりも、
広がりや角度が
分かるなぁ

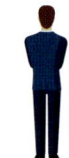

ポーズ・比率 頬に手を当てるポーズが、大きく違う。左像は手のひら全体、
右像は指先が頬に触れる程度である。首は、左像はまっすぐに立てて、右
像は傾ける。立て膝とする右脚は、左像は垂直に近く、右像は外に大きく開く。

After comparing them thoroughly from the front, let's change the perspective to view them from
a slight angle. But, let's keep step one in mind when viewing them again.

Poses and proportions The pose of the hand to the cheek differs greatly. The entire palm of the statue on the
left touches the cheek, but only the fingertips do so in the statue on the right. As for the neck and head, they
are held erect on the left, but tilted to the side on the right. The right leg with the raised knee is nearly vertical
on the left, but widely inclined to the side on the right.

14

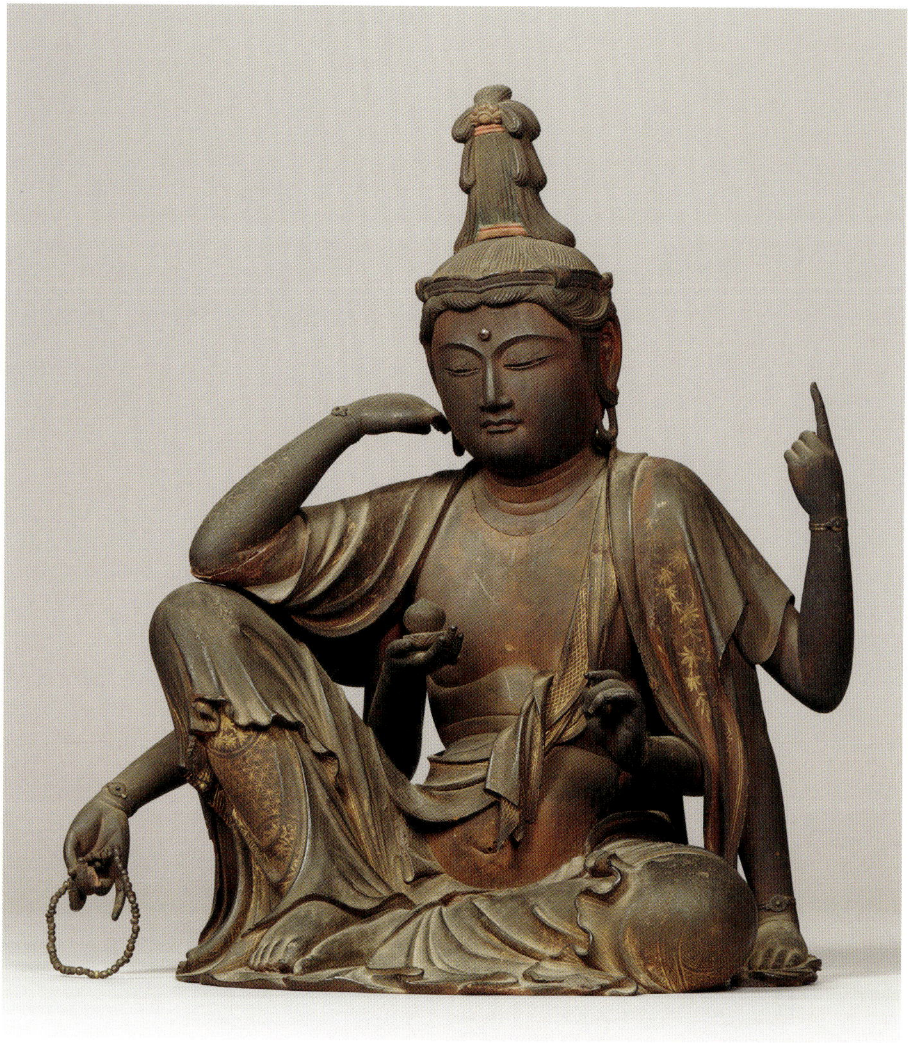

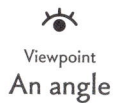

Viewpoint
An angle

鎌倉仏（右像）
Kamakura period (Right)

量　感 ▶ 正面からは気づきにくい胸腹部の張りと膨らみ、肩まわりの肉どりが左右の仏像で異なることがよく分かる。

彫刻の空間 ▶ 視点が変わることで、顔の傾きや６本の腕、そして足組みの広がりで構築される「彫刻の空間」が見えてくる。正面から見たときよりも一層、空間を意識できたなら、仏像を立体彫刻として見る核心に迫ったといえる。

Sense of volume ▶ The differences of the Buddhist statues on the left and right are readily apparent in the swelling and tension of the chest and midsection as well as the fleshiness around the shoulders, which are difficult to notice when viewed from the front.

Sculptural space ▶ By switching perspectives, the "sculptural space" created by the angle of the head, the six arms and the extension of the folded legs become clearly visible. If you have thus gained a greater sense of "sculptural space" than when you viewed it frontally, you are approaching an understanding of the essence of how to see Buddhist statues as three-dimensional sculpture.

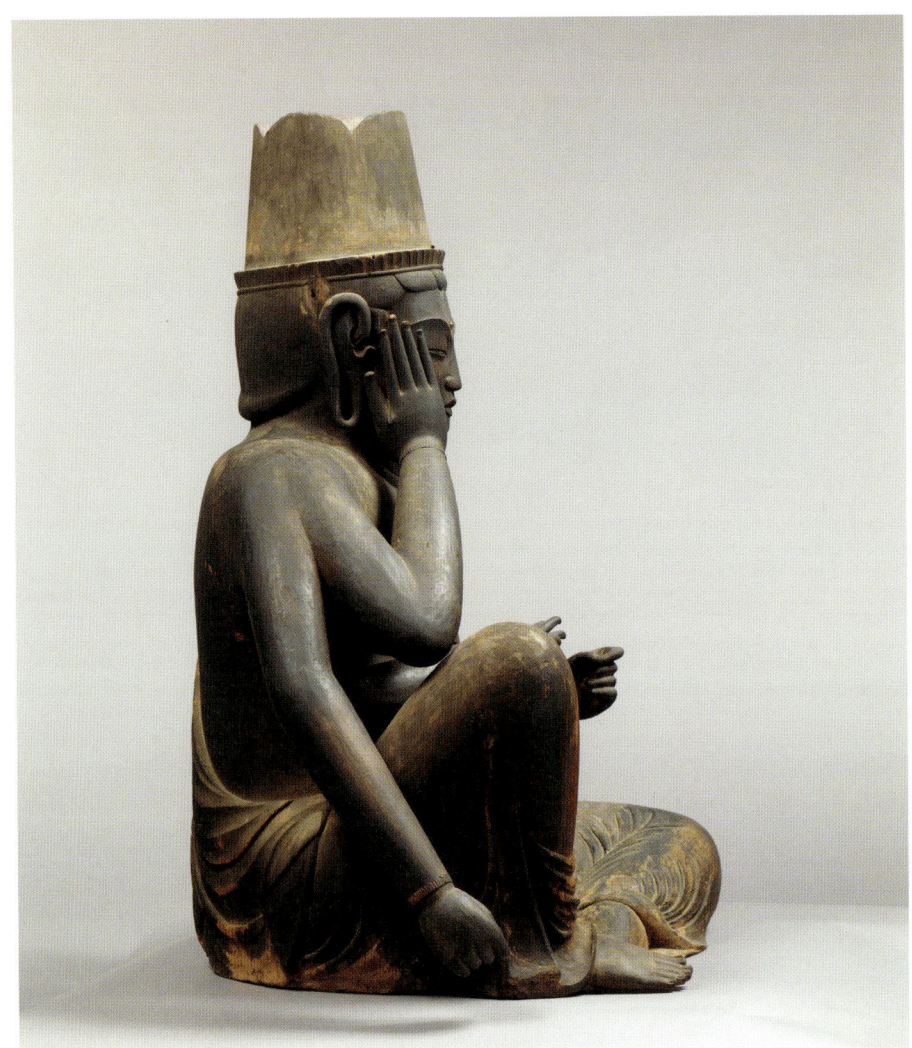

平安仏（左像）
Heian period (Left)

続いて、側面から見よう。
頭の前後の傾きや背中の緊張感がよく見えてくるだろう。

ポーズ・比率 左像は顔を正面に向け、背筋をピンと伸ばし、頬に当てる右手は上腕を前方に出して肘を急角度にまげている。右像は顎を引き、背中を丸め、頬に当てた右手は肘をひざにのせ、楽な姿勢である。

Continuing the process, let's next view them from the side.
The tilt of the head and the sense of tension in the back now become perfectly clear.

Poses and proportions The head on the left faces forward, the back muscles are stretched tight, the right hand is held to the cheek, the upper arm is pushed forward with the elbow bent at a sharp angle. The chin on the right is pulled inward, the back is rounded, and the elbow of right arm whose hand touches the face rests on the knee in a relaxed pose.

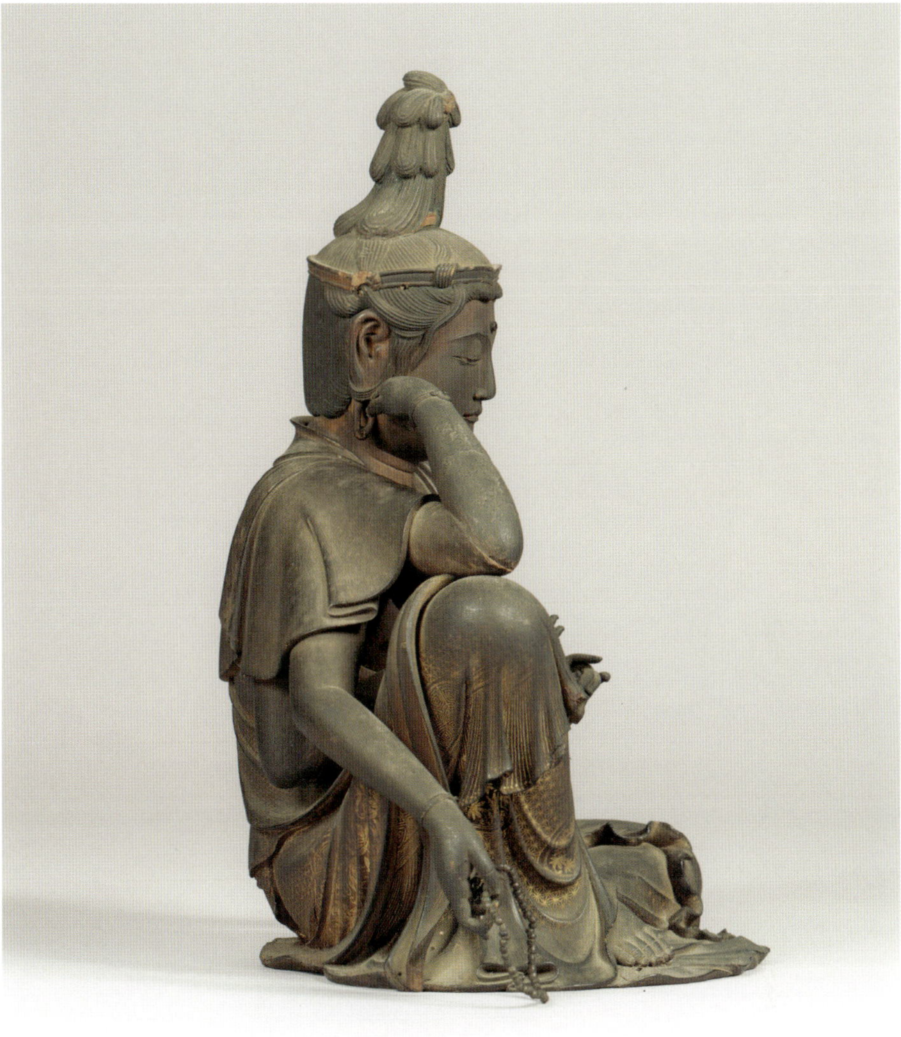

Viewpoint
Side

鎌倉仏（右像）

Kamakura period (Right)

量　感 ▶ 左像は面奥（頭の奥行き）が右像よりもことさらに深く、重厚な感じである。

動　静 ▶ 左像は手足の構えが緊張して気張った感じで、肉どりが充実し、威圧的でもある。右像は緊張を解いた手の動きであり、威圧感はほとんどない。

Sense of volume ▶ The depth of the head of the statue on the left is considerably deeper than that on the right and evokes a strong sense of volume.

Movement ▶ The arrangement of the arms and legs of the statue on the left are taut conveying a sense of tension, and its fleshiness is fully developed and striking. The movement of arms of the statue on the right is relaxed without tension and not at all oppressive.

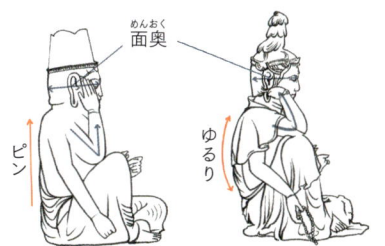

17

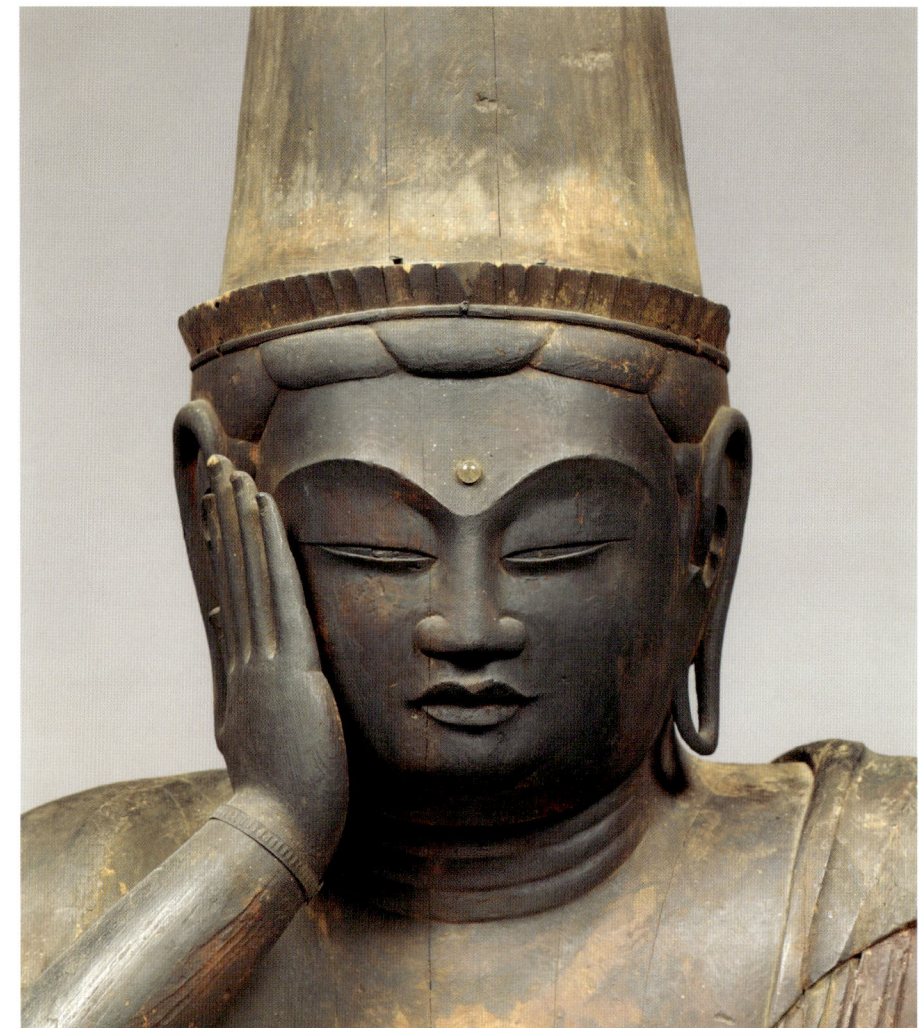

平安仏（左像）
Heian period (Left)

顔の正面をよく見てみよう。

顔の表情 ➤ 左像は面幅（顔の幅）が広く、上下から圧縮をかけたかのように、目鼻が顔いっぱいに大きく配され、鼻りょうが太く、短い。眉の弧線は雄勁に立ちあがる。一方、右像では目鼻は顔面に程よく配され、眉は静かな弧線を描く。左像の方が深遠なまなざしである。

Let's look at the face from the front.

Facial expression ➤ The width of the face of the statue on the left is broad and it seems squat, with the eyes and nose arranged so as to fill the entire face; the bridge of the nose is wide, but short. The arcs of the brows are prominently raised. On the other hand, the facial features of the statue on the right are evenly spaced, and the brows display a gentle arc. The statue on the left seems to gaze profoundly off into the distance.

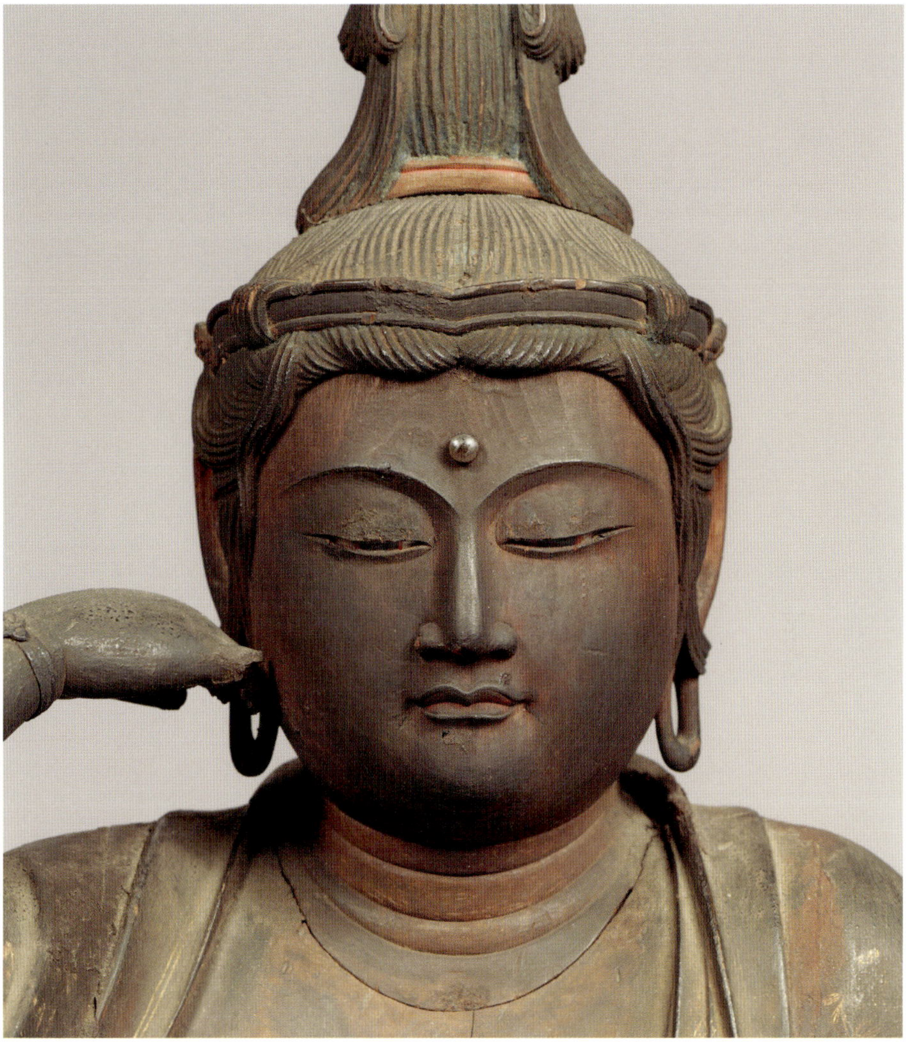

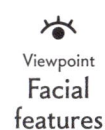

Viewpoint
Facial features

鎌倉仏（右像）
Kamakura period (Right)

唇も、左像は肉厚で、右像は薄く小さい。右像は鼻りょうが細く、鼻筋がまっすぐに通り、知的な
まなざしで、りりしい顔つきである。

The lips are thick and fleshy on the statue on the left, while those on the right are small
and thin. The bridge of the nose on the right is narrow and the ridge of the nose is straight.
The gaze exhibits wisdom, and the expression of the face is dignified.

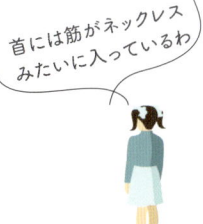

首には筋がネックレス
みたいに入っているわ

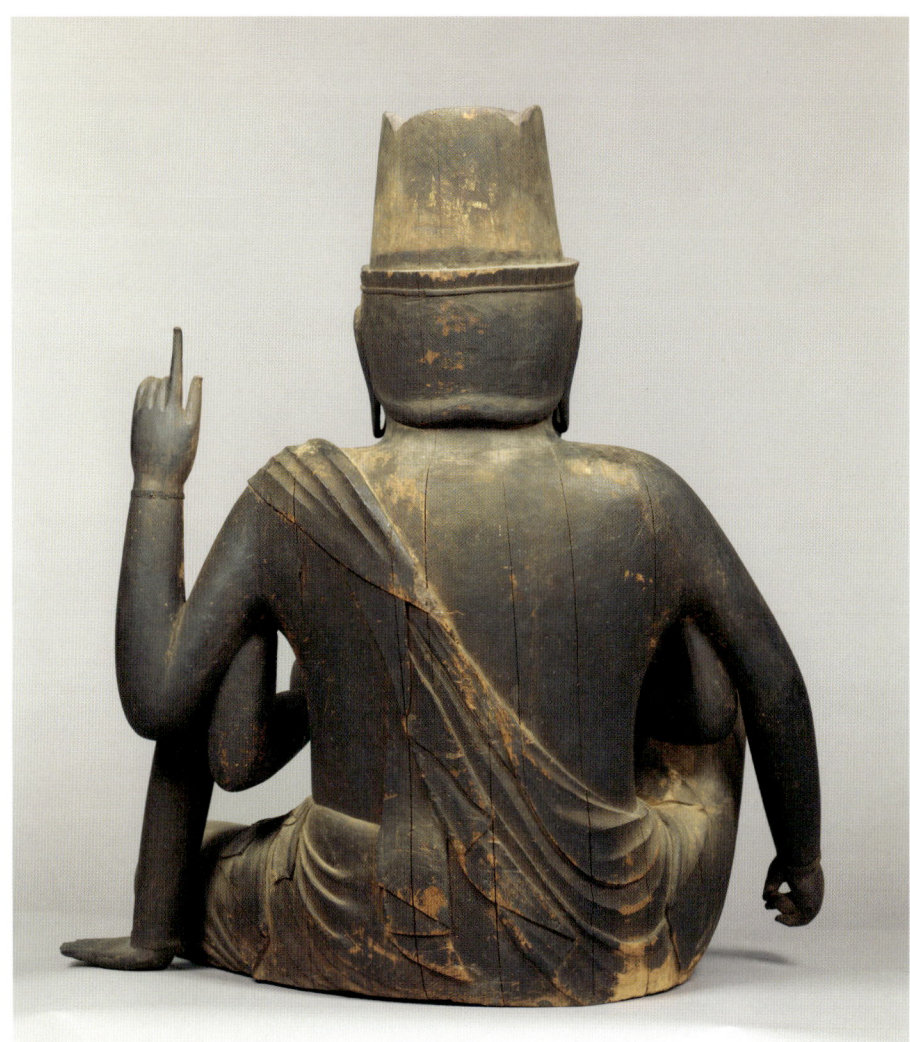

背面
から見る

平安仏（左像）
Heian period (Left)

背面はめったに見られない視点だが、多くの魅力をたたえている。

ポーズ・比率 右腕に着目したい。これまではわからなかったが背面から見ることで、左像は見えているのが1本だけで他の2本は隠れている。右像は3本しっかり見えている。

量感 左像は肩幅が広く、胴部も横幅があって豊かな肉づきである。右像は天衣（肩にかかる布）などに隠れるものの、やや傾けた胴体はスリムである。

The rarely seen back of a Buddhist sculpture has much to offer.

Poses and proportions Please pay attention to the right arm. Looking at the statue from the back, in a view previously unseen, you'll see only one right arm on the statue on the left, and the other two arms are obscured. Three arms can clearly be seen on the statue on the right.

Sense of volume The shoulders of the statue on the left are broad and the torso is also wide and well-muscled. The shawl-like garment conceals the slim torso of the statue on the right, which tilts to the right.

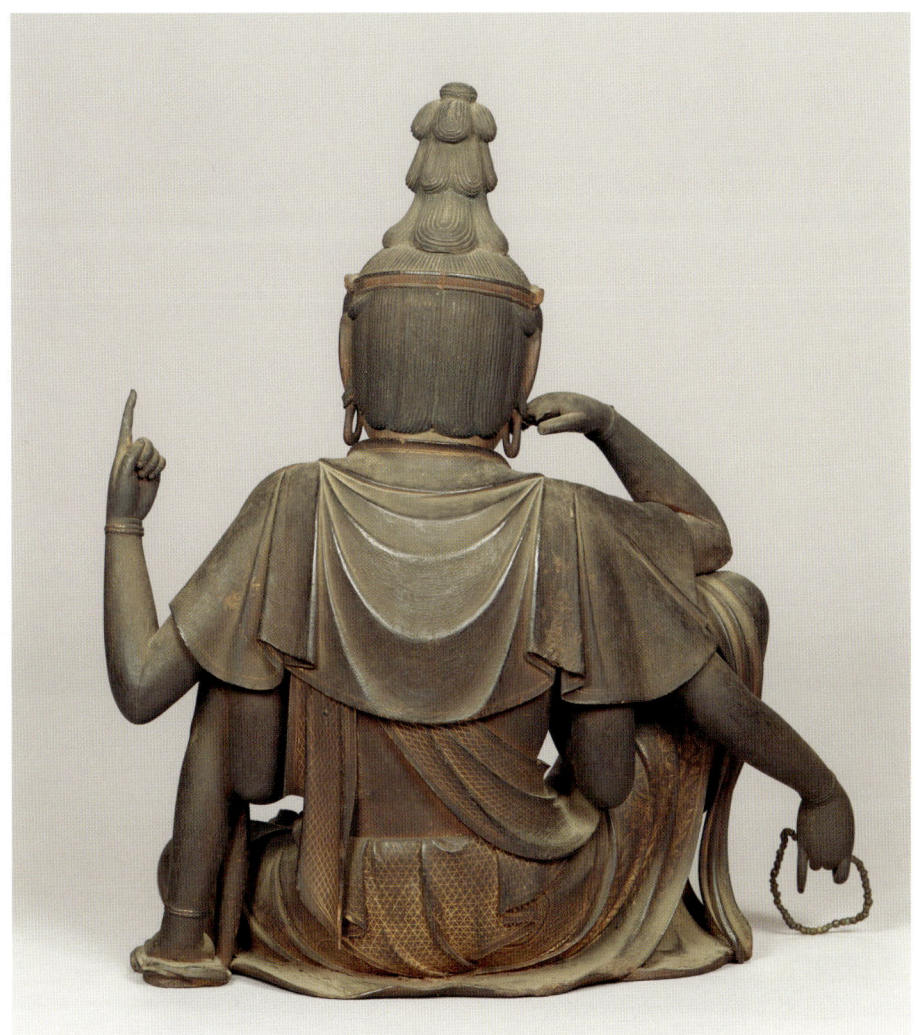

Viewpoint
Back

鎌倉仏（右像）
Kamakura period (Right)

動　静　背中側にまわると、正面で見た正中線が左像は垂直に、右像は右に曲がり、手足もそれに応じた動きをみせている。

衣文と着衣　左像は左肩にかかるたすき（条帛）が背中の中央で折り返し、腰から尻に向かって幅広く垂れる。衣の皺の表現は勢いと強さがある。右像は両肩から天衣を羽織り、左右相称風に衣文が刻まれる。整頓された感覚を好むかのようである。

Movement　Stepping around to the back of the statue, we see that the center line, just as seen from the front, is perpendicular on the left and curved to the right on the statue on the right whose arms and legs show a corresponding sense of movement.

Pattern of the folds and creases in the robe & Clothing　The narrow, scarf-like garment is stretched over the left shoulder of the statue on the left. Folded in the center of the back, it hangs broadly from the hips spreading out over the buttocks. There is strong sense of energy in the expression of the creases in the robe. The shawl-like garment draped over both shoulders on the right displays left-right symmetry in the carving of the pattern of folds in the cloth. A sense of orderliness appears to have been preferred in the statue on the right.

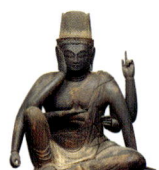

重要文化財 如意輪観音坐像
Important Cultural Property

Seated Nyoirin Kannon

一木造（榧）
現状古色* 像高94.9㎝
平安時代（9c.末～10c.前半）
京都・回向院伝来
*当初の色彩でない、古びた色を呈していること

Carved from a single block of *kaya* (Japanese nutmeg)
with simulated ancient coloring
Height 94.9 cm
Heian period (end of 9c.- first half of 10c.)
from Ekōin Temple in Kyoto

すべて奈良国立博物館所蔵。
Both statues are from the collection of
the Nara National Museum.

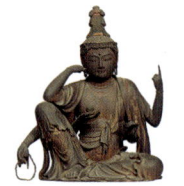

如意輪観音坐像

Seated Nyoirin Kannon

寄木造（榧）
素地・截金 像高32.7㎝
鎌倉時代（13c.） 建治元年（1275）
像内に「般若心経」等を納める
（現在は別保管）
大阪・四天王寺伝来

Assembled-block construction (*kaya*)
unpainted with cut gold leaf
Height 32.7 cm
Kamakura period (13c.), 1275 (Kenji 1)
Deposited within the statue were a transcription of the *Hannyashingyō* (Heart Sutra) and other items, which are now preserved separately
from Shitennōji Temple in Osaka

対比でわかる特徴
Characteristics Gleaned from Comparison

右の仏像にはお経が入っていたんだ

• 正面を向いた顔
• 背筋をまっすぐにした姿勢
• ゆたかな量感
• 張りのある肉どり
• 面幅のひろい深遠な顔つき
• 厳しいまなざし
• 勢いと強さのある衣文の彫り口
• 一見窮屈な、緊張した彫刻空間

• Face looks straight forward
• Spine stretched straight
• Stout
• Taut fleshiness
• Broad facial features and a distant expression
• Stern gaze
• Energetic carving of the folds of the robe
• Clearly cramped, tense sculptural space

• 右に傾けた顔と上半身
• 背中を丸めた姿勢
• 細身で柔軟なからだつき
• しまりのある肉どり
• ととのった目鼻だち
• 理知的なまなざし
• 左右相称風に形式的にまとめた衣文
• 右の立ち膝を外に大きく傾けた、広々とした彫刻空間

• Face and upper body tilted to the right
• Rounded back
• Slim and nimble-looking body
• Firm flesh
• Regular facial features
• Intelligent gaze
• Robes display left-right symmetry
• Broad sculptural space with the raised right knee leaning widely to the side

以上に見た2つの仏像の対比は、そのまま時代の様式の違いを示している。仏像の様式（表現）からその制作年代を推定するのは、各時代の代表的な仏像を数多く見てきて、その理解を積み重ね、かつ深めながら、だんだんと分かってくることである。ここでは必要条件としての情報を次にまとめておこう。

The comparison of the two Buddhist statues above itself demonstrates the stylistic differences of the two historical periods. Estimating the period of a work's production based on the stylistic expression of a Buddhist statue becomes possible only gradually after one has viewed many statues representative of each period and amassed an understanding deepened with repeated viewings. The following does not cover everything, but I would like to provide a summary of the necessary information regarding these periods.

平安時代初期（9世紀）

榧（かや）の一材から彫刻した仏像（一木造）が多い。一木造は頭・体部の主要部を一材で彫るのが主流であり、◎如意輪観音坐像（p.12）もそれに該当する。1本の丸太から彫刻するイメージが本像の重厚な造形感覚のなかに感じられるとしたら、それは木彫の本質を見抜く力となるに違いない。

The early Heian period (9th century)

Many Buddhist statues were carved from a single block of *kaya* wood in a technique called *ichibokuzukuri* in Japanese. Using this technique, the main portions of the statue, the body and head, were usually carved from one block, and the statue (p.12) is an example of this type. If you can sense the weighty feel of the sculptural form of this statue from an image of a single carved log, you undoubtedly have the power to discern the essential character of this sculpture.

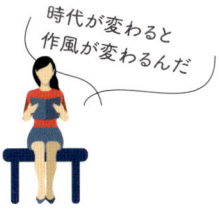

時代が変わると
作風が変わるんだ

鎌倉時代後期（13世紀後半）

初期の運慶・快慶から数えて3～4世代目の仏師たちの活躍時期にあたる。中国の新しい宋風美術の影響を受けながら、前期の現実直視の写実精神から中期以降の穏健な写実的作風が広まった頃にこの如意輪観音坐像（p.13）の制作年代は位置する。なお同像は榧材を用いた寄木造の仏像で、鎌倉時代の檀像*としての意義を持つ。いまだ俗に走らず、理智的な聖なる感性を表しているところはその辺りに理由がある。

*白檀や梅檀などの香木を彫刻した仏像。
奈良時代の仏像に多い。

The Late Kamakura Period (second half of the 13th century)

This is the period of the activity of sculptors who came three or four generations after the early period when the master sculptors Unkei and Kaikei were active. The *Nyoirin Kannon* statue (p.13) can be dated to the period when the spirit of realism, based on actual observation, had waned, and a more-gently realistic style had spread while still under the influence of the new art of the Song dynasty. Moreover, this statue was produced from *kaya* using the assembled-block technique. Its significance resides in its being a Kamakura-period *danzō*, a statue made to resemble those carved from aromatic sandalwood, which were frequently seen in the Nara period. The reason it has not descended into this-worldly banality is that it still evokes a sense of the sacred tinged with a deep rationality.

以上のことから、 レッスン1 で比較して見た仏像は次のようにまとめられる。

Judging from the above, we can summarize the Buddhist statues in Lesson one in the following way.

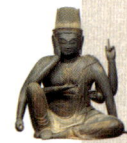

- 平安初期木彫の特色を引き継いだ等身の大きさの木彫。
- 平安時代前期（9c.末～10c.前半）の作。

- A life-sized wooden statue preserving the special characteristics of early Heian period sculpture.
- A work produced in the early Heian-period, from the end of the 9th century to the first half of the 10th century.

- 鎌倉時代後期、13世紀後半の特色をあらわす小品。
- じつは仏像内に納入品があり、建治元年（1275）の作と判明する。
- 鎌倉時代後期の基準作（制作年代の判明する作品）のひとつ。

- A small-scale work that displays the characteristics of the late Kamakura period during the second half of the 13th century.
- Dated items in the statue indicated it was made in 1275 (Kenji 1).
- An example of a signature work that serves as representative of the latter half of the Kamakura period (because the date of its production is certain).

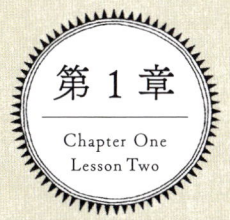

第 1 章

Chapter One
Lesson Two

レッスン2

3躯の十一面観音立像を比べよう

レッスン1では、坐っている仏像を「対比」し、それぞれの時代様式の特徴を見た。
ここでは、3躯の立っている像を比べてみる。レッスン1の坐像とは違った対比
のポイントがあるはずだ。（3躯とも奈良国立博物館所蔵）

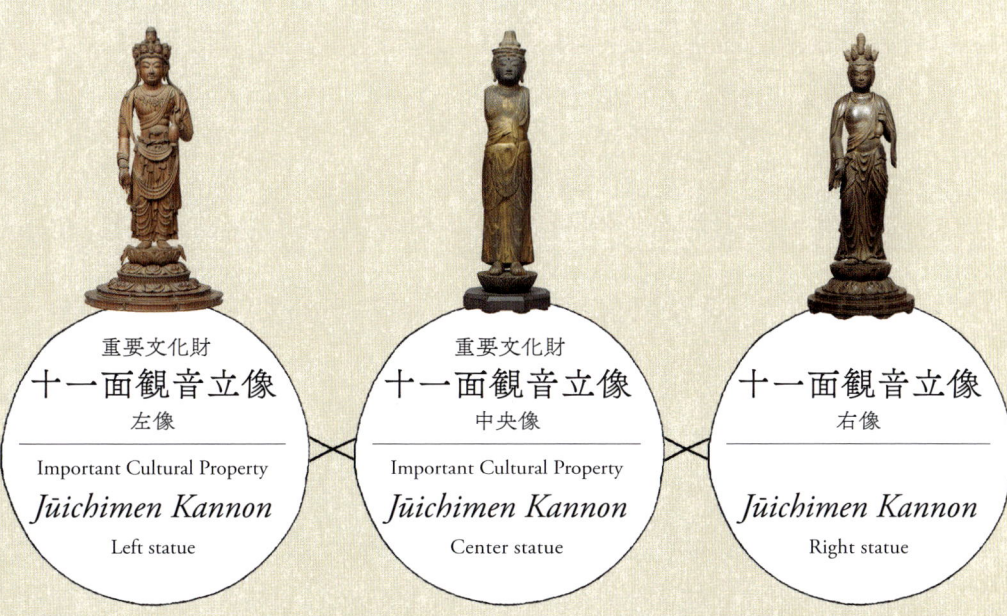

重要文化財
十一面観音立像
左像

Important Cultural Property
Jūichimen Kannon

Left statue

重要文化財
十一面観音立像
中央像

Important Cultural Property
Jūichimen Kannon

Center statue

十一面観音立像
右像

Jūichimen Kannon

Right statue

Comparing three different statues of the same divinity

In Lesson 1 we compared seated Buddhist statues and saw the unique characteristics of the styles of the periods they represent. Here we'll try to compare three standing statues. There are bound to be important points of comparison that are unlike those used to compare the seated statues in Lesson 1.
(All three statues are from the collection of the Nara National Museum)

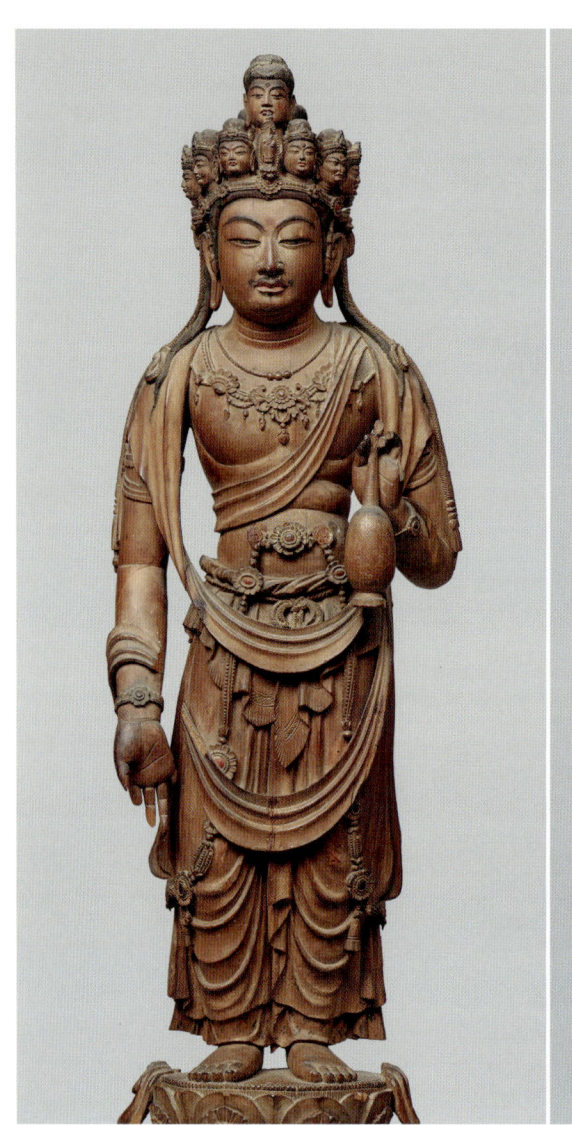

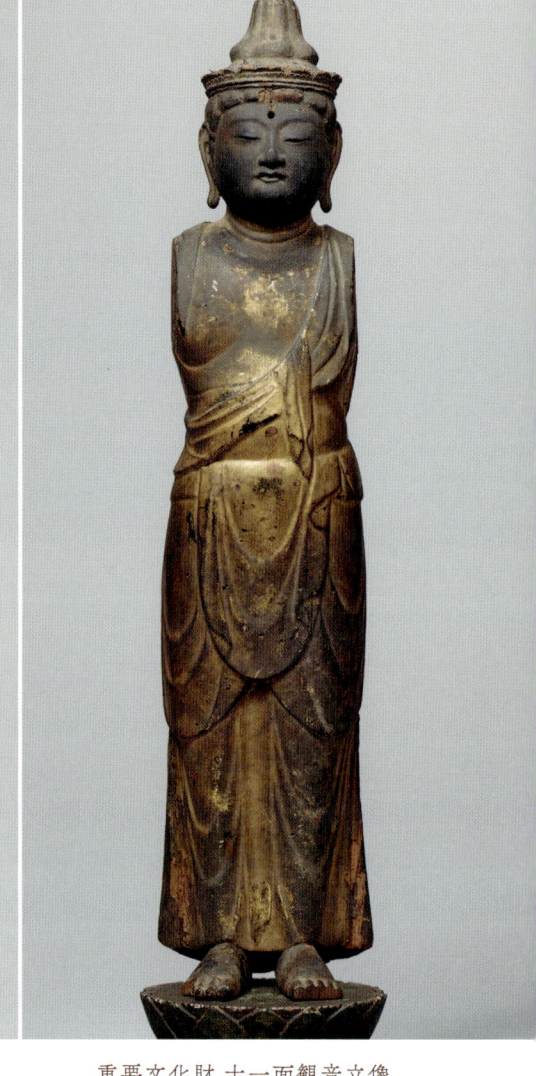

正面
から見る

重要文化財 十一面観音立像
Important Cultural Property *Jūichimen Kannon*

重要文化財 十一面観音立像
Important Cultural Property *Jūichimen Kannon*

まずは基本の正面からプロポーション（比率）をみよう。

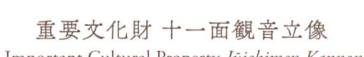 立像は、まず頭・体部の均衡に注目しよう。この3軀は、高さが40〜50cm前後の小さな仏像である。左像は特に、体に比べて頭が大きく、小像なりのインパクトを出す小彫刻特有の造形意識がある。中央像や右像は、頭と体の均衡が人間に近く、大きい仏像のミニチュアサイズの感が強い。

仏像の大小にかかわらず、プロポーションの特徴を見ようとするとき、膝頭がどこにあるかを考えるとよいと思う。均整のとれたプロポーションか、大腿部が異様に長い体形なのか、さまざまなプロポーションに気づくだろう。

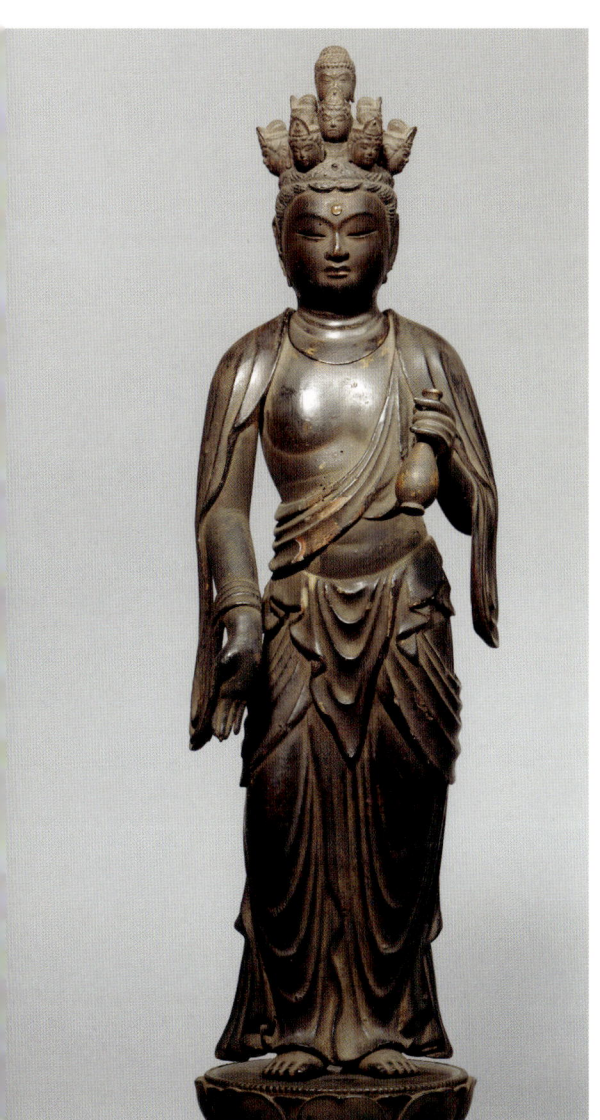

十一面観音立像
Jūichimen Kannon

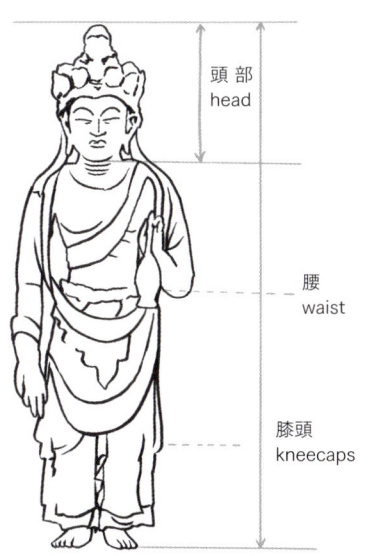

頭部
head

腰
waist

膝頭
kneecaps

Viewpoint
Front

First, let's look at basic proportions from the front.

Pose / ratio ▸ Let's first note the balance of the head and body of these three figures. All three are small-scale Buddhist statues, ranging from 40-50 centimeters in height. The head on the left is quite large in relation to the body, and it displays a formal sculptural consciousness unique to small-scale stat-ues. The balance between the head and body of those in the center and on the right resemble that of an actual human being, and these works convey a strong sense of being miniature versions of large-scale stat-ues. Whether a Buddhist statue is small or large, when you try to examine its proportions, it is a good idea to consider the placement of the kneecaps. When you do, you'll understand much about its propor-tions, such as whether the form is well balanced or not.

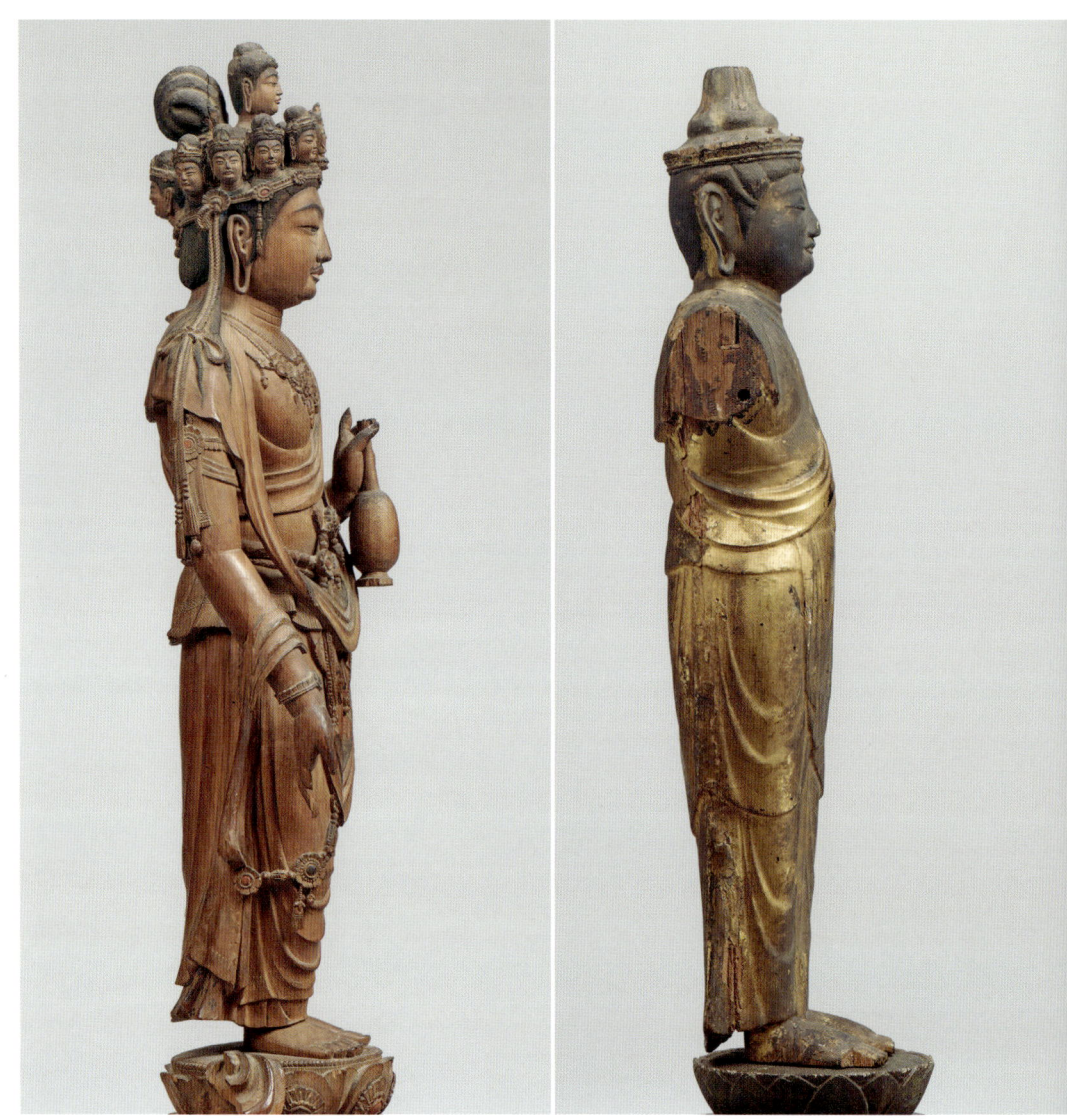

側面
から見る

左像
Left

中央像
Center

つづいて右の側面から見てみよう。

量　感 左像は頭部の奥行き（面奥）が深く、胸は鳩胸のように高まり、厚みがある。中央像と右像は、面奥は正面の顔の幅（面幅）と同じくらいである。中央像は猫背ぎみの丸い背中であるものの、胸から腹の肉どりは抑揚がゆるやかで、前方につき出ている。右像は上体を後ろに反らしぎみに引いており、スリムで、しなやかな動きがともなう。

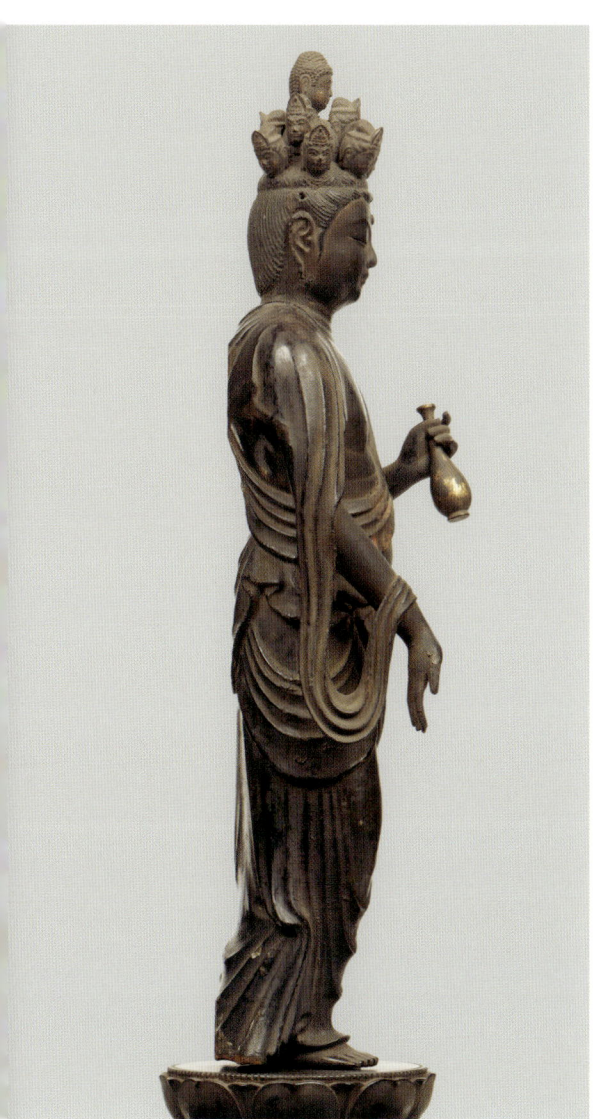

右像
Right

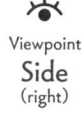

Viewpoint
Side
(right)

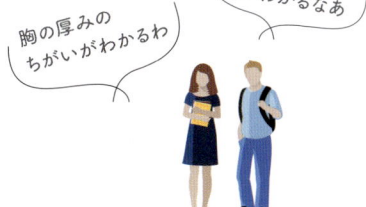

胸の厚みの
ちがいがわかるわ

腹の出っ張りも
よくわかるなあ

Let's continue by looking at them from the right side.

Sense of volume ▸ The depth of the head of the statue on the left is quite pronounced, and the breasts are full, swollen like those of a bird. The depth of those in the center and right are approximately equal to their width. The back of the central statue is rounded and slightly stooped, but the contours of the flesh on the chest and midsection are gentle and protrude only slightly. The slim upper body on the right is drawn backward in a graceful curve.

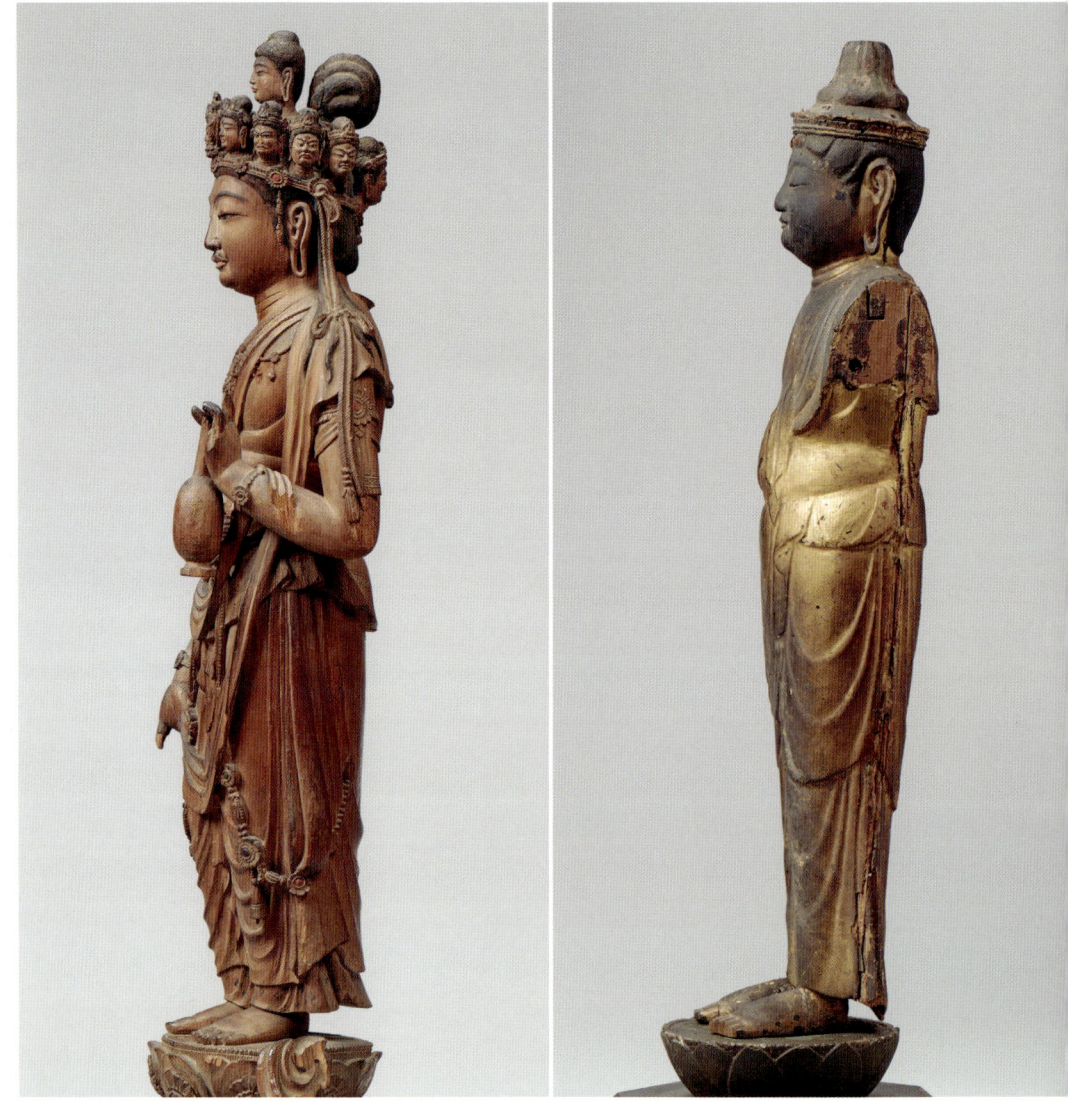

👁
側面
から見る

左像
Left

中央像
Center

次に左側面から3軀を比べてみると、なにが見えてくるだろうか。

動　静 ▶ 左像と右像は右膝が出ており、左足に重心をおいて腰をひねる動きがあることがわかる。中央像は、膝頭をまっすぐに伸ばして立つ。左像は下半身が重厚で、がっしりした体形で、裾が後ろにわずかになびく。中央像は腹や腰の厚みに対して足もとの奥行きが非常に浅く、裾が無風状態のなかで静かに垂れるようだ。右像の下半身は軽快な動きを表し、裙（スカート）が微風を受けてたるむかのような造形である。

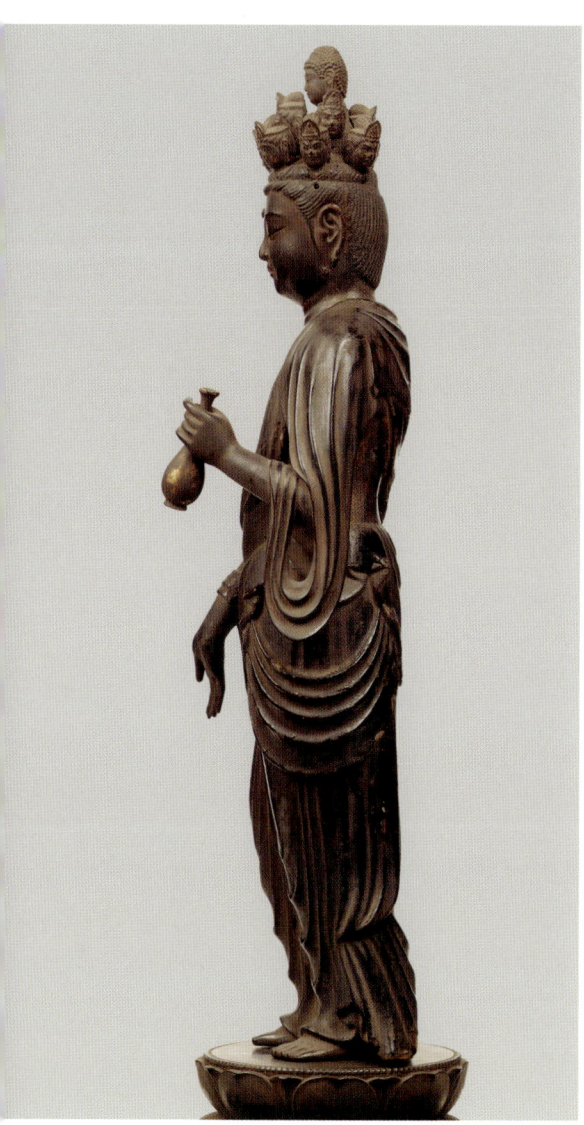

右像
Right

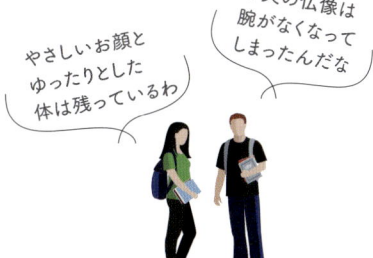

中央の仏像は
腕がなくなって
しまったんだな

やさしいお顔と
ゆったりとした
体は残っているわ

Next, let's compare the three statues viewing them from the left side and see what we can discover.

`Dynamic` → We realize immediately that the right knees of the statues on the left and right are bent forward and the left legs bear the weight of the bodies, and the waists are twisted dynamically. The kneecaps of that in center are locked straight. The lower body on the left is voluminous, with a stout feel and the hems of the robe are drawn slightly to the rear. In contrast to the stockiness of the midsection and hips of the central statue, its legs are extremely shallow and the hems of the robe hang silently motionless without any sign of the wind. The lower body on the right displays a nimble physicality. Its rather limp skirt-like *kun* seems to be ruffled by a mild breeze.

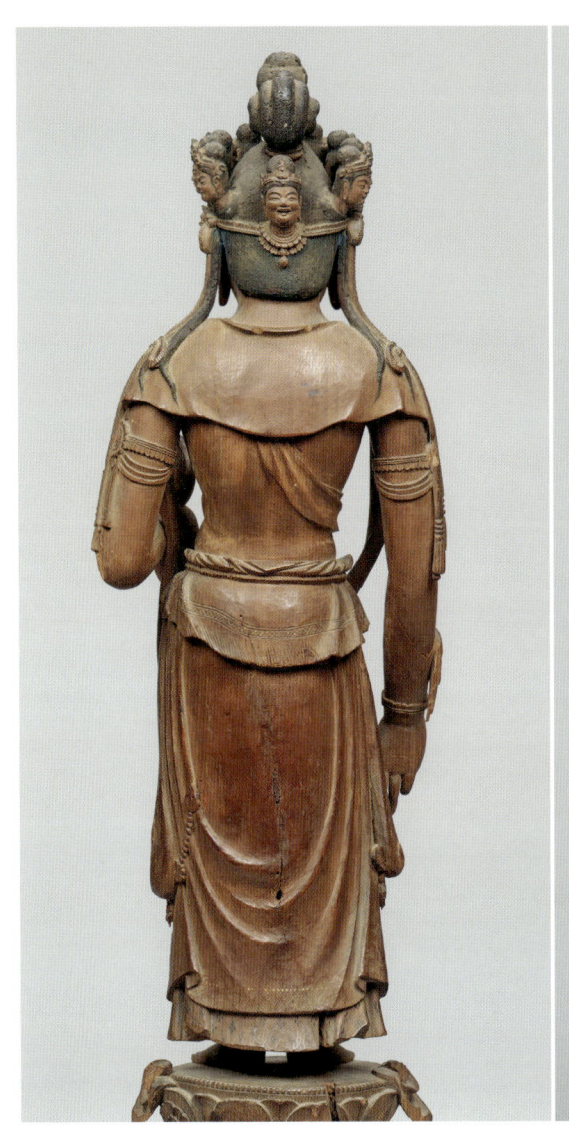

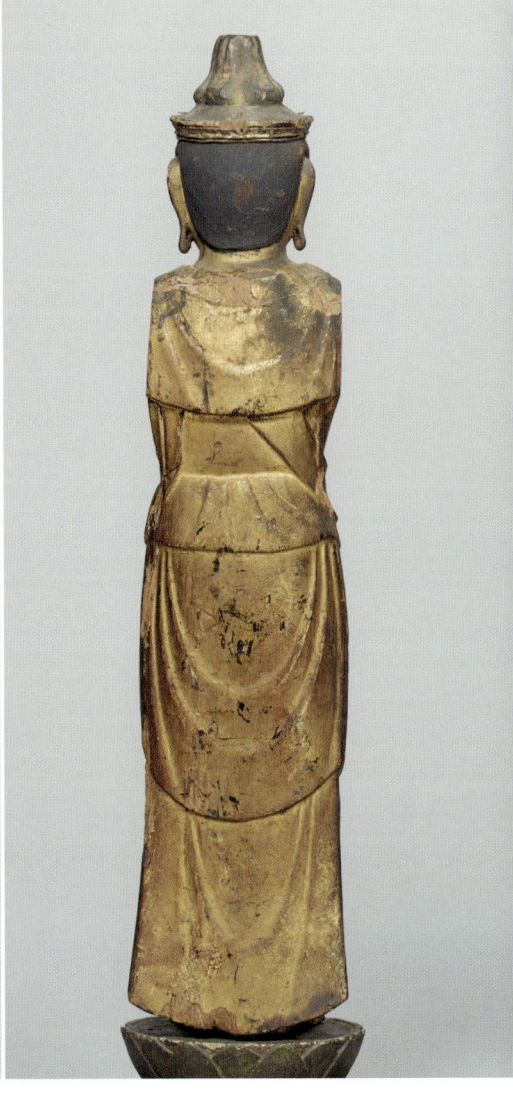

左像
Left

中央像
Center

つづいて背面を見てみよう。

頭部の大きさ、腰のひねり方、衣文(え もん)(衣の皺(し わ))の扱いなど、

三者三様の違いがよくわかる。

衣　文 左像と右像では、肩にかかる天衣(て ん ね)や裙(く ん)の折り返しの縁が波打つが、中央像では体に密着するかのような、薄い布の質感をあらわす。裙の衣文を見ると、左像は茶杓の先のような形が交互に、かつリズミカルに刻まれる。中央像はU字形の衣文が浅くゆるやかで、右像は布の下に空気をはらんだような皺の表現で、布のたるみがよりはっきりと意識されていることが分かる。

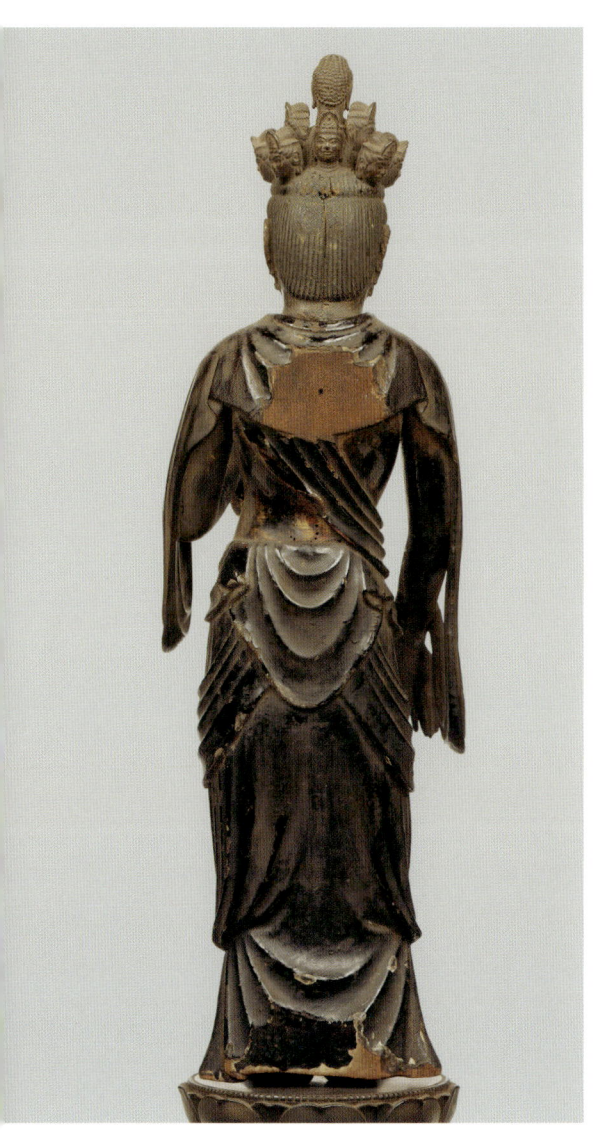

右像
Right

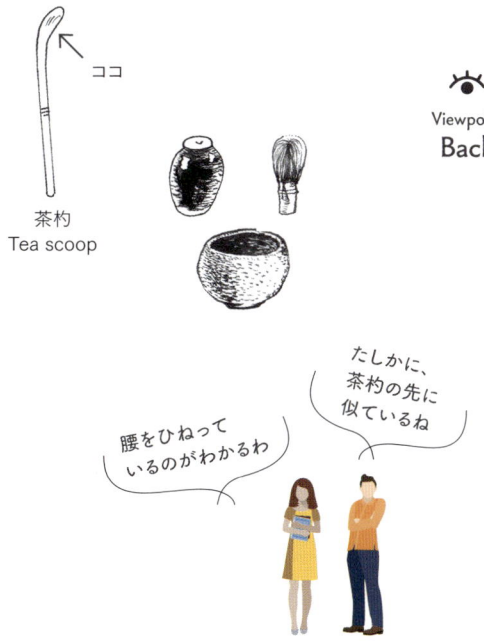

ココ

茶杓
Tea scoop

👁
Viewpoint
Back

たしかに、
茶杓の先に
似ているね

腰をひねって
いるのがわかるわ

Next, let's look at these statues from the back.
The size of the head, how the hips are tilted, and the treatment of pattern of the folds in the robes demonstrate the three different styles.

Pattern of the folds and creases in the robe The turned edges of shawl-like *tenne* draped over the shoulders and hems of the robes on the left and right have a rolling-wave pattern, but the cloth on the central statue appears to cling closely to the body evoking the tactile sense of the sheer cloth. The pattern of the rhythmically alternating folds on the reverse of the skirt on the left resemble the rounded nose of a bamboo tea scoop, and the u-shaped pattern of the robe in the center is shallowly carved, while the folds of the robe on the right appear to be blown away from the body by air beneath the cloth, and the slackness in the drape of the cloth is more obvious.

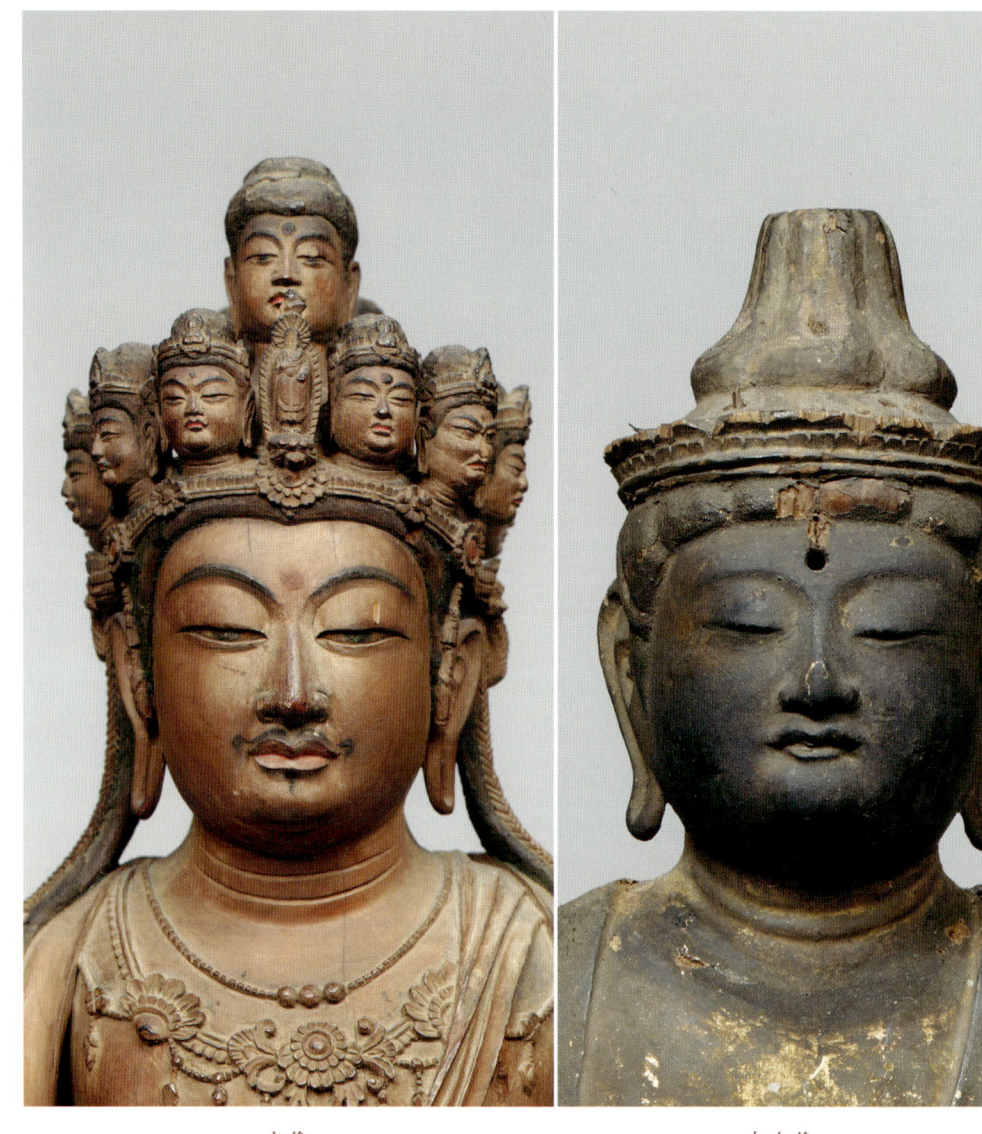

正面_の
表情
_{を見る}

左像
Left

中央像
Center

顔の正面を見てみよう。
（ただし、十一面を象徴する頭上面は現状、左像はオリジナルのもの、中央像は欠失し、右像は現代に作られたものであるから、割愛する。）

顔の表情 目鼻立ちが、左像は顔一杯に大きく、中央像と右像は程よい釣り合いで、配される。
まなざしは、左像は眼の見開きが大きくて意志の強さが、中央像は目を伏せて、慈悲深いやさしさが、右像は目尻が上がり、きりっとした鋭い視線が感じられる。
左像は、丸い頬だが、奥行きの深さが感じられる。中央像は頬から顎にかけて、横への広がりが感じられる丸い肉どりである。右像は、こめかみがやや窪みぎみで、頬それ自体が独立して丸く引き締まる。

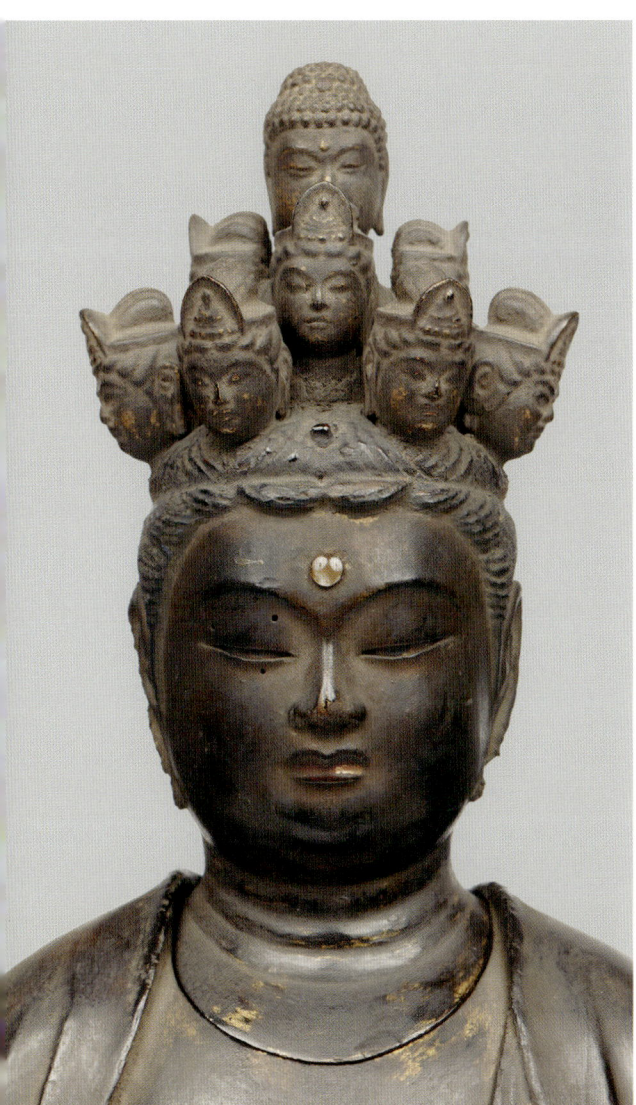

右像
Right

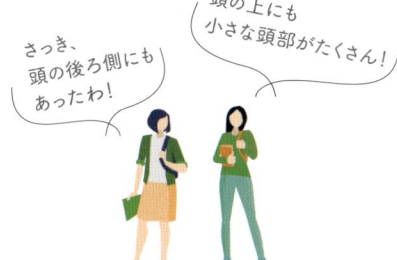

Let's look at the faces from the front.
(The multiple heads above the main head are characteristic of Jūichimen Kannon but because those on the left are original, while those that should be on the center statue are missing entirely, and those on the right are later replacements, I will avoid discussing them.)

Facial expression The prominent facial features fill the face on the left, while those of the other two are arranged in a more well-balanced fashion.

As for the gaze, the statue on the left is wide-eyed and peers outward with strong intent, but the eyes of that in the center are downcast displaying deeply benevolent kindness, and those on the right are drawn up and outward giving the eyes a sharply penetrating glint.

The left has round cheeks that evoke a sense of depth. The rounded contours of the flesh on that in the center extend broadly down both cheeks to the jaw line. The right is slightly dimpled, but the cheeks themselves are both taut and round.

35

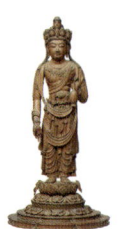

重要文化財

十一面観音立像

Important Cultural Property

Jūichimen Kannon

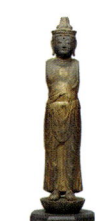

重要文化財

十一面観音立像

Important Cultural Property

Jūichimen Kannon

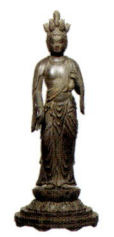

十一面観音立像

Jūichimen Kannon

一木造（白檀）
素地・截金（きじ・きりかね）
像高42.8cm
奈良時代末〜
平安時代初期
（8c.末〜9c.初）

Single-block construction
(sandalwood)
Plain unpainted wood,
cut gold leaf
Height of statue 42.8 cm
Late-Nara to early-Heian
period (end of 8c. to early
9c.)

×

一木割矧造（檜）（わりはぎ）
漆箔（しっぱく）
像高53.0cm
平安時代後期（12c.）
像内に絹本著色「千手観音像」を納める（けんぽんちゃくしょく）
（現在は別保管）

Assembled-block con-
struction (*hinoki*)
Lacquered gilding
Height of statue 53.0 cm
Late Heian period (12c.)
Color on silk painting of
Senju Kannon deposited
within the statue (now
preserved separately)

×

寄木造（檜）　善円作（ぜんえん）
彩色・截金（現状古色*）（きりかね）
像高46.6cm
鎌倉時代（13c.）
承久3年（1221）
像内に「金剛般若波羅蜜経」等を納める（現在は別保管）

Assembled-block con-
struction (*hinoki*)
Colors, cut gold leaf (pres-
ently a simulated archaic
appearance)
Height of statue 46.6 cm
Kamakura period
(13c.,dated 1221, Jōkyū 3)
Deposited within the statue: *Kongō Hannya hara
mitta kyō* (now preserved
separately)
Produced by Zen'en

*当初の色彩でない、古びた色を呈していること

すべて奈良国立博物館所蔵。
All three statues are from the collection of the Nara National Museum.

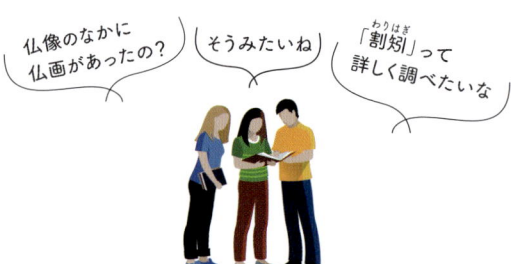

仏像のなかに仏画があったの？　そうみたいね　「割矧」（わりはぎ）って詳しく調べたいな

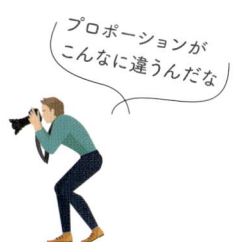

プロポーションが
こんなに違うんだな

対比でわかる特徴
Characteristics gleaned from these comparisons

- 膝頭が低く、大腿部が長いプロポーション。
- 奥行きの深い頭部。
- 厚い胸。
- がっしりした体形。
- 意志的な眼の表情。
- 顔一杯に大きく配された目鼻立ち。
- 波打つ衣の縁。
- 茶杓形の衣文。

- 膝頭が脚の中央に位置する、均整のとれたプロポーション。
- 猫背ぎみの丸い背中。
- 抑揚のゆるやかな胸腹部の肉どり。
- 浅い体奥。
- 慈愛にみちた、やさしいまなざし。
- 身体に密着するような薄い布。
- 浅い彫り口のU字形の衣文。

- 短いひざ下。
- 顔の幅と頭部の奥行きが同じくらいの大きさ。
- しなやかな動きの体つき。
- ゆらめく衣の縁と皺のたるみ。
- 目尻の上がった、きりっとしたまなざし。

- Kneecaps are low, thighs are disproportionally long
- The head is deep
- The chest is thick
- The body is stout
- The expression of the eyes is intent
- The facial features fill the face
- Edges of the robe have a rolling-wave pattern
- Folds in the robe resemble the rounded nose of a bamboo tea scoop

- Kneecaps are in the center of the legs; proportions are balanced
- Stooped, rounded shoulders
- Gentle modulation of the flesh of the chest and midsection
- Shallow body
- Benevolent, kind gaze
- Sheer clothing clings to the body
- Shallowly carved u-shaped pattern of the folds of the robe

- Short shins
- Depth and breadth of head are equal
- Sprightly nimble body
- Rustling edge of the robe with slack drooping folds
- Eyes drawn upward with a penetrating glint

時代の違いによる作風の違い
Differences in styles based on different historical periods

3像のそれぞれの部分的な特徴は、各部位が別個に独立して時代的な特徴をあらわすわけではない。それぞれが相互に呼応し合う関係を保ちながら、全体として各時代の様式的な特徴を形成している。

The unique characteristics of specific parts of the three statues do not signify that the one part has some individual characteristic representative of a certain historical period. The parts have a mutually corresponding relationship, and together as a whole they form the special characteristic of the styles of these historic periods.

奈良時代末期〜平安時代初期（8c.末〜9c.前半）

均整のとれた造形が崩れていくのが奈良時代末期で、体奥の厚みも増す。平安時代初期はさらに強調かつ誇張され、過度に緊迫感が高まる。

Late-Nara to early-Heian period (late 8c. to early 9c.)

In the late Nara period the balanced proportions seen in sculptural forms continued to deteriorate, and the depth of statues increased. This trend became even more pronounced in the early Heian period, leading to an excessive tension.

×

平安時代後期（11c.後半〜12c.後半）

均衡のとれた、安定感のある体形の定朝様式が一世を風靡した。ゆるやかな抑揚の肉取りや、品格の高い、優雅な作風が特徴的。

Late-Heian period (latter half of the 11c. to the latter half of the 12c.)

The style of the sculptor Jōchō with its well-balanced, stable representation of the body predominated. A chief characteristic of the elegant style was its subdued modulation of the flesh and its graceful dignity.

×

鎌倉時代前期（13c.前半）

頭・体部の均衡や姿態の動きに、現実直視の写実的感覚が重視される。初期は充実した量感表現が顕著で、前期は落ち着きのある作風に展開する。

Early-Kamakura period (first half of the 13c.)

Emphasis was placed on a sense of realism based on actual observation in addition to the balance between head and body and a sense of movement. In the initial stage the sense of volume was conspicuous, but it evolved into a more serene style in the latter part of the early period.

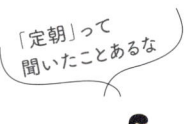

「定朝」って聞いたことあるな

平等院鳳凰堂の阿弥陀如来坐像の作者だ

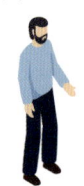
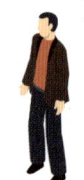

仁王像にみる運慶と快慶
国宝 金剛力士立像 東大寺南大門所在

東大寺南大門の金剛力士立像（以下、仁王像）は、高さがおよそ8mに及ぶ巨像で、阿・吽の力士像の作風が大きく異なっている。従来より、阿形は快慶、吽形は運慶が担当したと説かれている。このことについて、本書の「対比でみる」視点から検証してみよう。

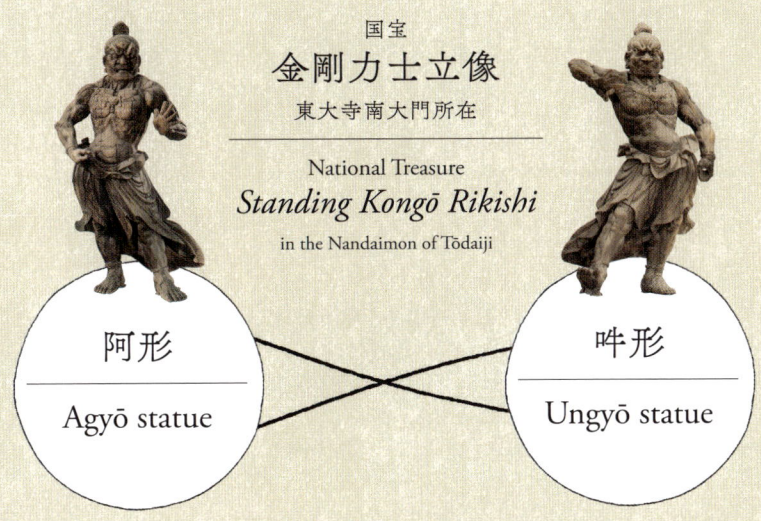

国宝
金剛力士立像
東大寺南大門所在

National Treasure
Standing Kongō Rikishi
in the Nandaimon of Tōdaiji

阿形 — Agyō statue

吽形 — Ungyō statue

Master Sculptors Unkei and Kaikei as Seen in the Niō Statues
The National Treasure *Standing Kongō Rikishi* in the Nandaimon of Tōdaiji

The *Standing Kongō Riksihi* statues in the Nandaimon gate at Tōdaiji, also called the Niō statues, are massive, reaching a height of eight meters. The style of the open-mouthed Agyō statue and the close-mouthed Ungyō statue are very different. It is said that the sculptor Kaikei was in charge of the Agyō statue and Unkei the Ungyō statue. We will test this theory from the perspective of the "comparative viewing" advocated in this book.

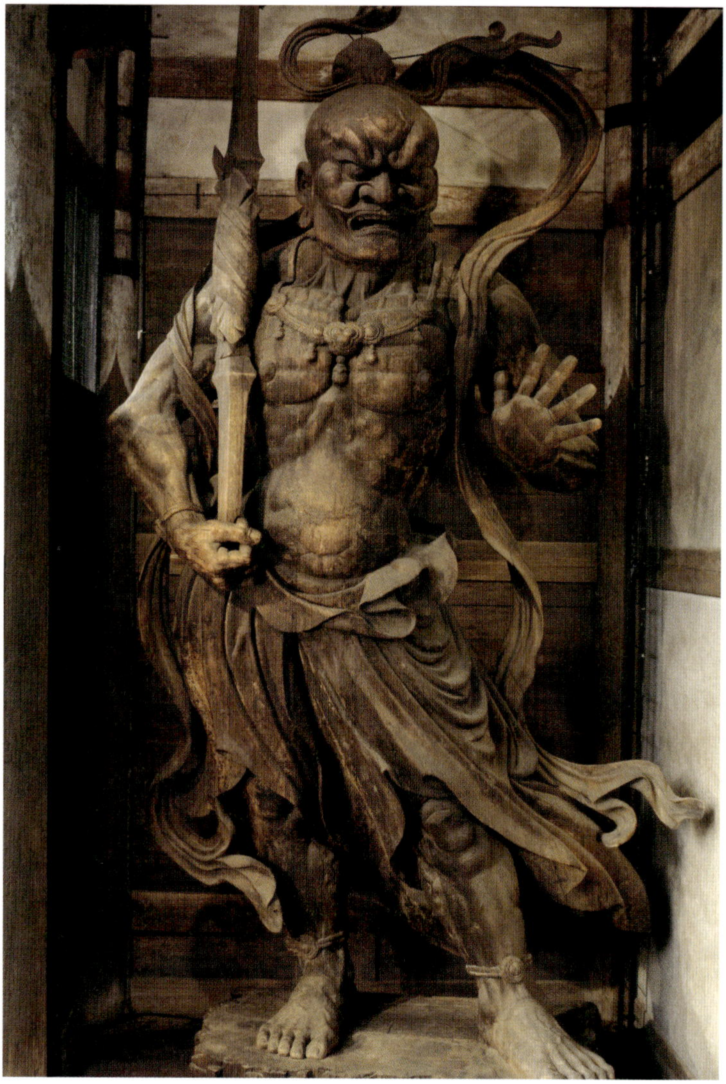

国宝 金剛力士立像 阿形（東大寺 南大門所在）
National Treasure *Standing Kongō Rikishi* Agyō statue (in the Nandaimon of Tōdaiji)

像に正対したアングル。

正面を見る前にまず断っておきたいことがある。上の２つの図版は、撮影時のカメラレンズの位置が仁王像のへそよりやや上にあり、実際に像の前に人が立ったときに下から見上げるアングルとはだいぶ違う。かたちを比較する場合、このように像とカメラレンズの位置が正対した写真の方が分かりやすい。

左右ともに裸身に裙（スカート）をまとうだけの姿で、阿形は口をかっと開いて、金剛杵を右手にのせて肩に当て、吽形は口をへの字に固く結び、金剛杵を左手につかんで前に倒す。ともに強風が全身に吹き付け、天衣が後ろに高く舞い上がる。阿形は左手、吽形は右手が激風を押しとどめるかのように力んでおり、山門の守護神として悪敵退散のオーラを発散させている。

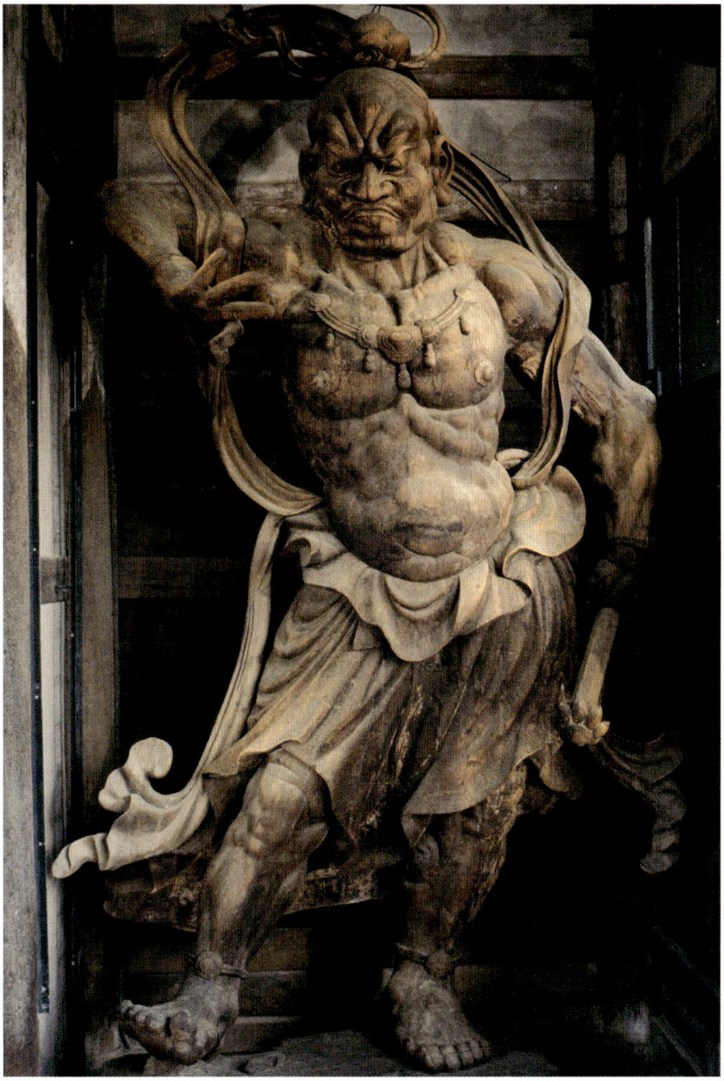

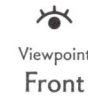

Viewpoint
Front

国宝 金剛力士立像 吽形（東大寺 南大門所在）
National Treasure *Standing Kongō Rikishi* Ungyō statue (in the Nandaimon of Tōdaiji)

The statues seen head-on.

Before we look at the statues head-on, I wish to make something clear. The lens of the camera that took the two photos that appear above was located slightly above the navel of the Niō statues and the angle is in fact very different from that a person would have if he or she stood before the statues in the Nandaimon and looked up at them. When comparing their forms, photographs taken with the camera lens placed directly in front of the statues makes it easier to comprehend differences.

Both the statue on the left and that on the right are semi-clad, wearing only a skirt, and the mouth of Agyō statue is opened wide, and a pestle-shaped vajra is held up in its right hand, touching the shoulder; the mouth of Ungyō is firmly shut and a vajra is held downward in the left hand. In both cases, a strong wind lashes the entire figure and the *tenne* scarves are blown backward and high into the air. The Agyō statue uses its left hand and the Ungyō its right hand to push back against the violent wind, and they both project the aura of a guardian deity of the temple gate repelling evil enemies.

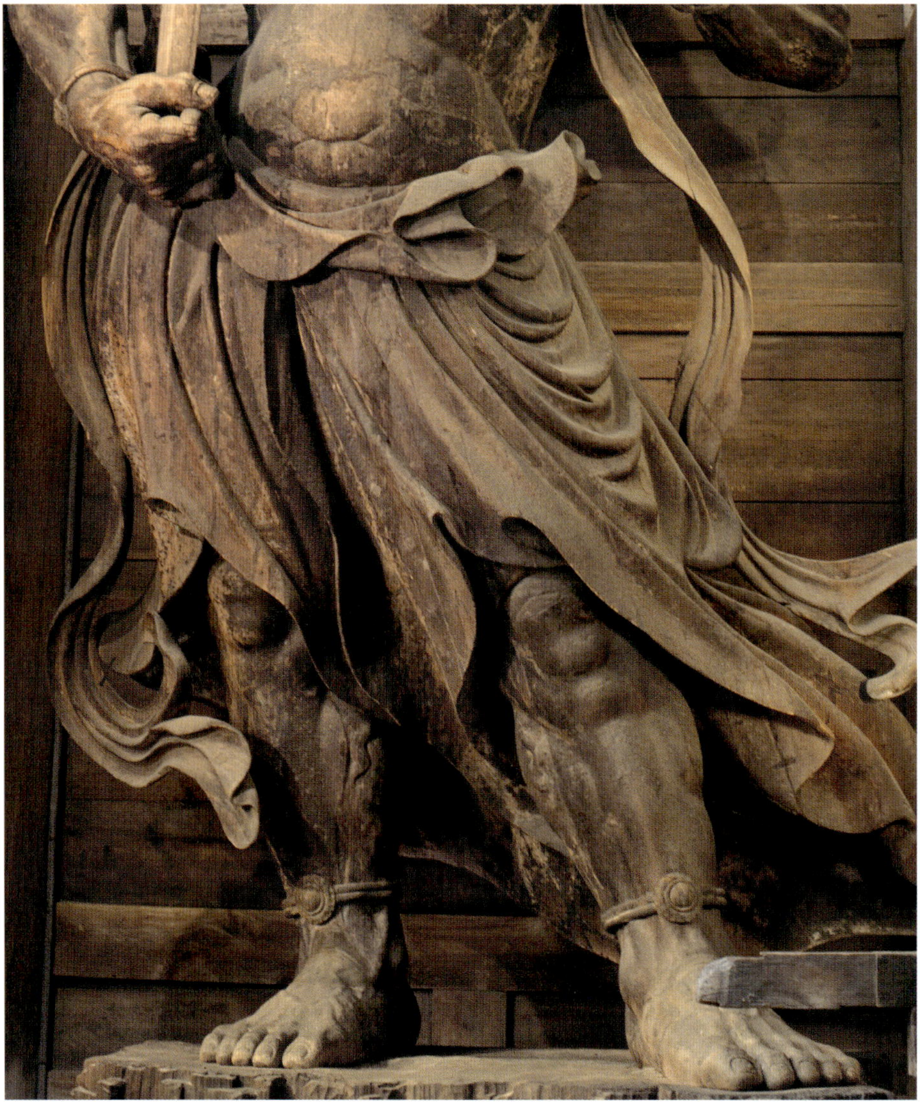

阿形
Agyō

足もとからの表現に注目しよう。

南大門に立つと、上半身や顔に注意がいきがちだが、足もとを見ると
強風に立ちはだかり、あるいは一歩前に出した、たくましい足の筋肉
表現に圧倒される。裙の折り返しが風を受けて、阿形では下腹に密
着し、吽形では衣が激しくゆらめき、ともに股間では密着して裾先が
左右に強くなびく。衣の皺の直線的な強い調子が激風を感じさせるの
に非常に効果的である。

強風を感じる！

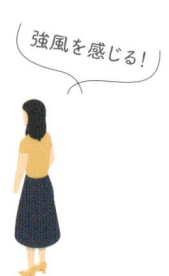

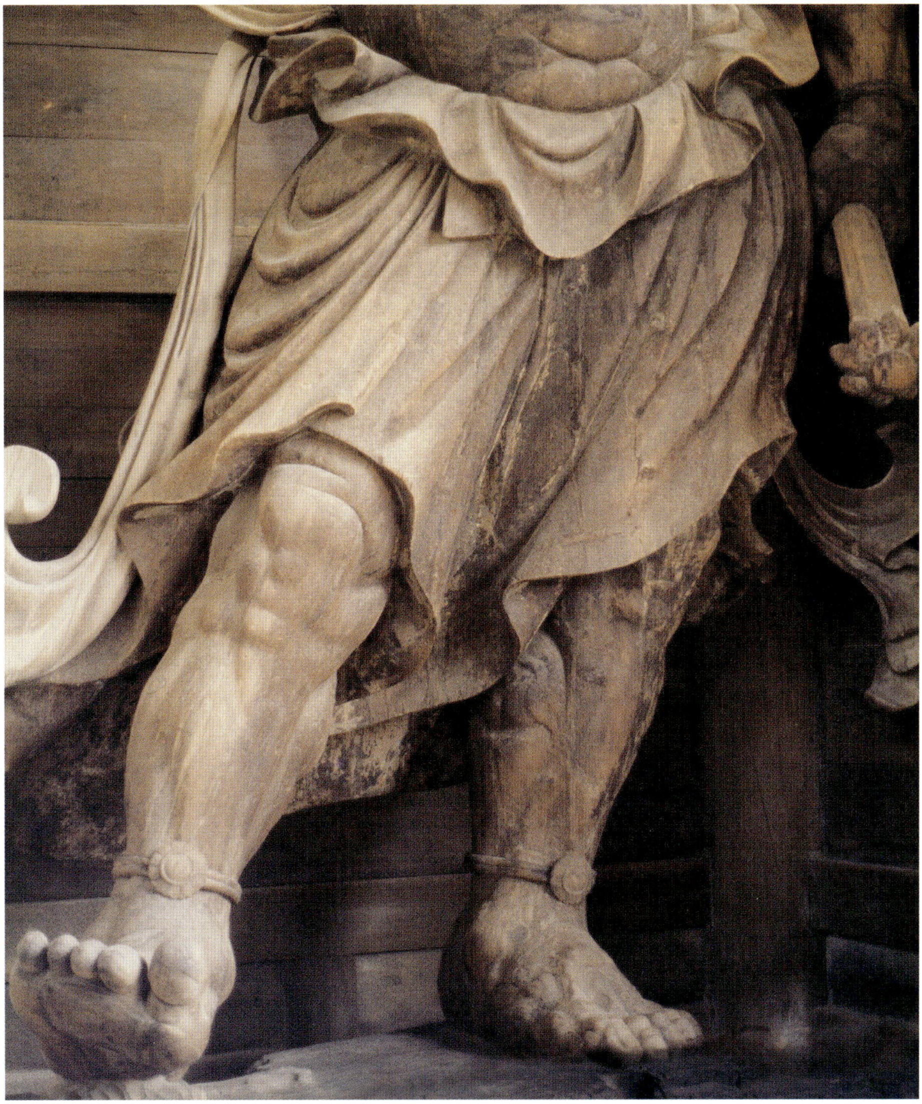

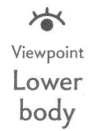

吽形
Ungyō

Let's focus on the representation looking upward from the feet.

One is liable to focus on the upper body and face when standing in the Nandaimon, but by looking at the feet and legs, one cannot help but be impressed by the expressiveness of their robust muscularity, standing firmly against the gale and even stepping forward into the wind. The skirt-like *kun* of the Agyō statue flapping backward in the wind clings to the lower abdomen, and the robe of the Ungyō statue sways violently. The robes also cling to the groins of both statues, and the hems of their skirts are blown strongly backward, trailing off to left and right. The powerfully direct manner of the rendering of the creases in the robes is extremely effective in conveying the power of the gusting wind.

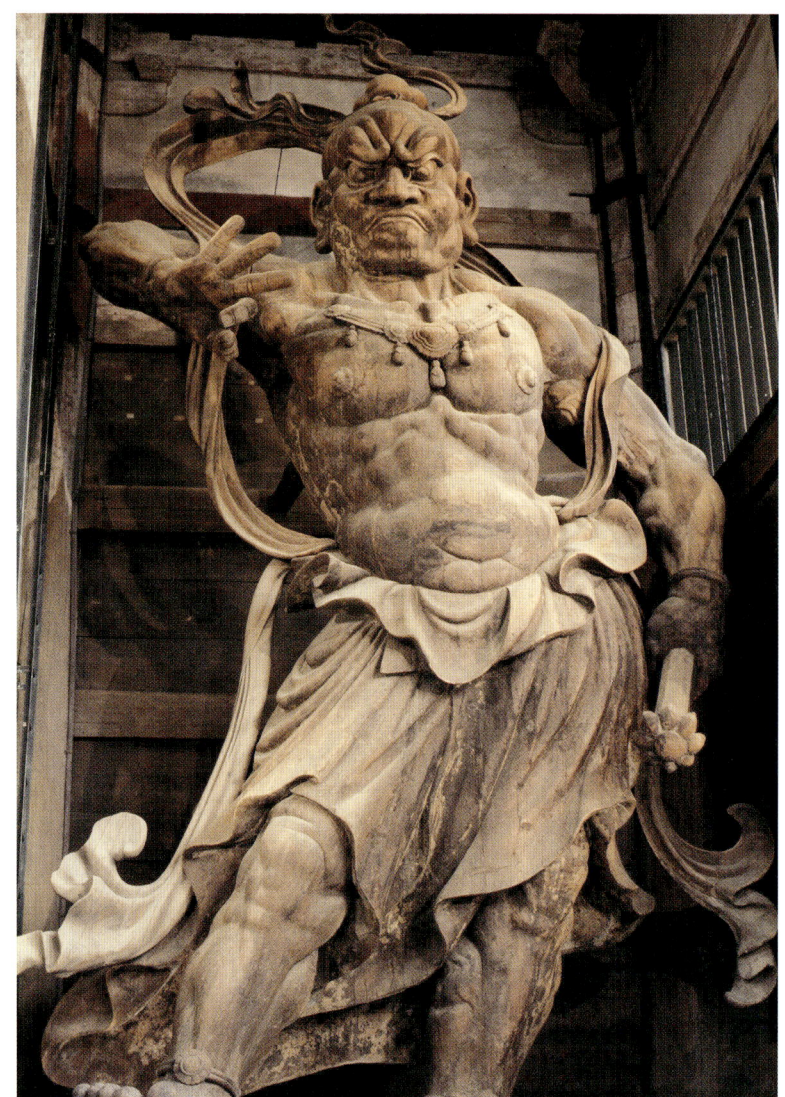

吽形
Ungyō

逆遠近法を駆使。

このような巨像彫刻の造形は、鑑賞者から遠い上方を大きく、下方をやや寸詰まり気味に小さくつくることが基本であり、逆遠近法の原理を応用している。仁王像はこの基本をふまえるだけでなく、振り上げた腕を細く短く、下へおろした腕は長く太くつくる。下から見上げたアングル（左）と正対した写真（右）では、迫力がこれほど大きく異なるのが分かる。

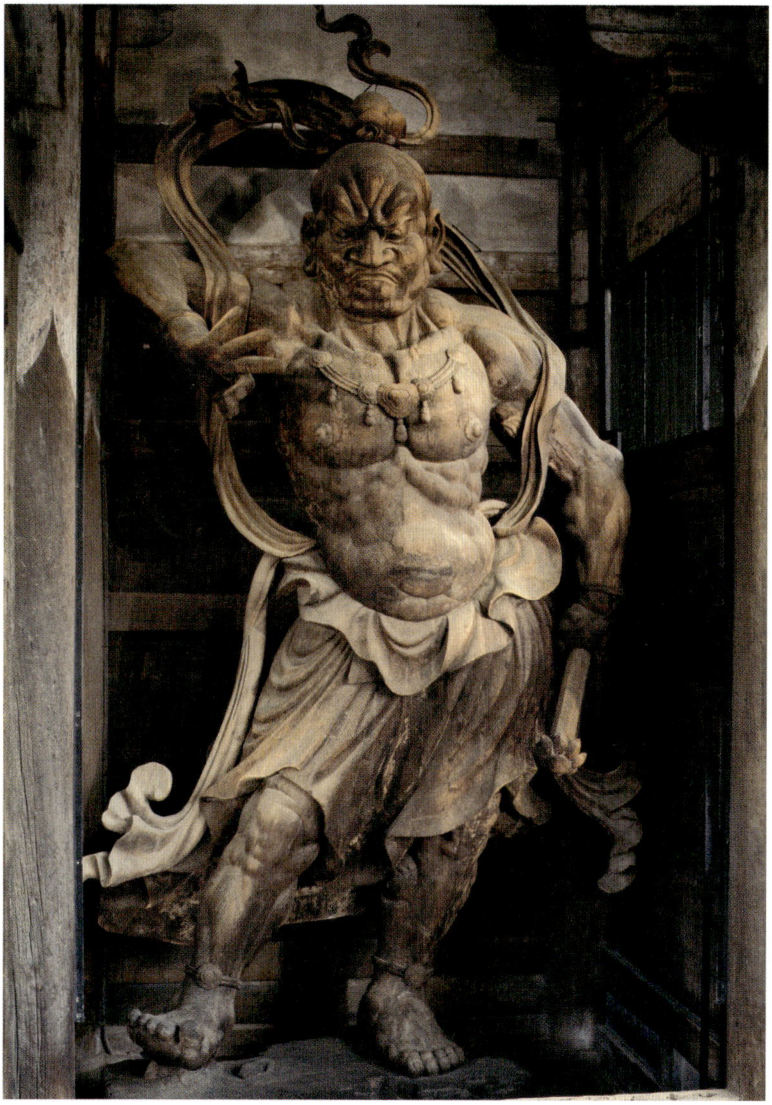

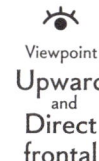

吽形
Ungyō

Using reverse perspective.

A basic principle of the sculptural form of this type of massive work is to make the upper portion, which is more distant from the viewer, larger and make the lower portion that seems rather stout, smaller. This is an example of the application of the principle of reverse perspective. The Niō statues follow this principle, but the raised arms are short and narrow, and the lowered arm is longer and thicker. One realizes just how different the impact is when the angle of sight looking upward from the bottom (on the left) is compared with the direct frontal photography (on the right).

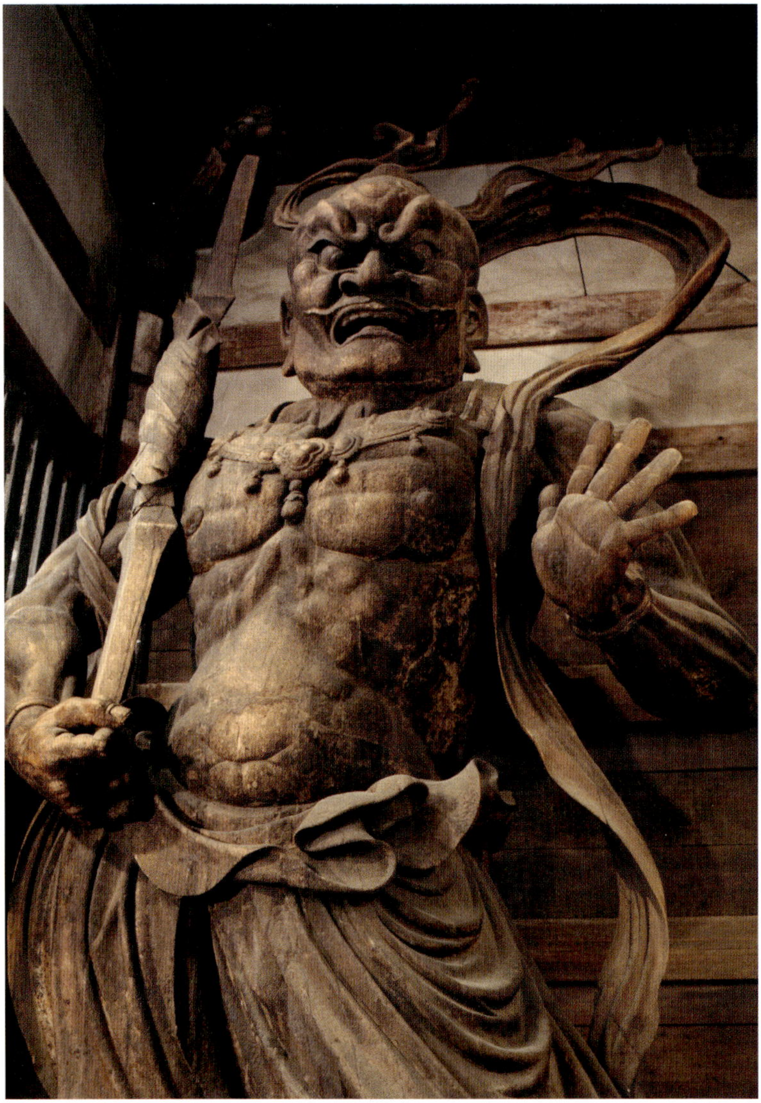

阿形
Agyō

カメラのレンズをへその位置に上げよう。

すると、頭大・短足の特長がよく分かる。それを
下から仰ぎ見れば、その圧倒的な重量感が見る者
を押しつぶすかのように迫ってくる。

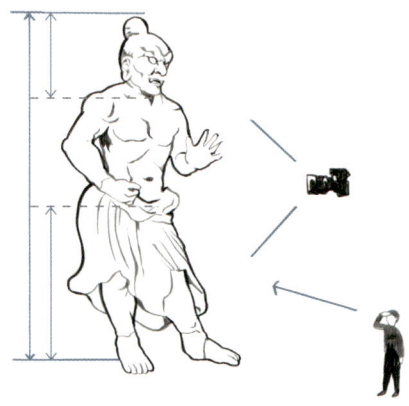

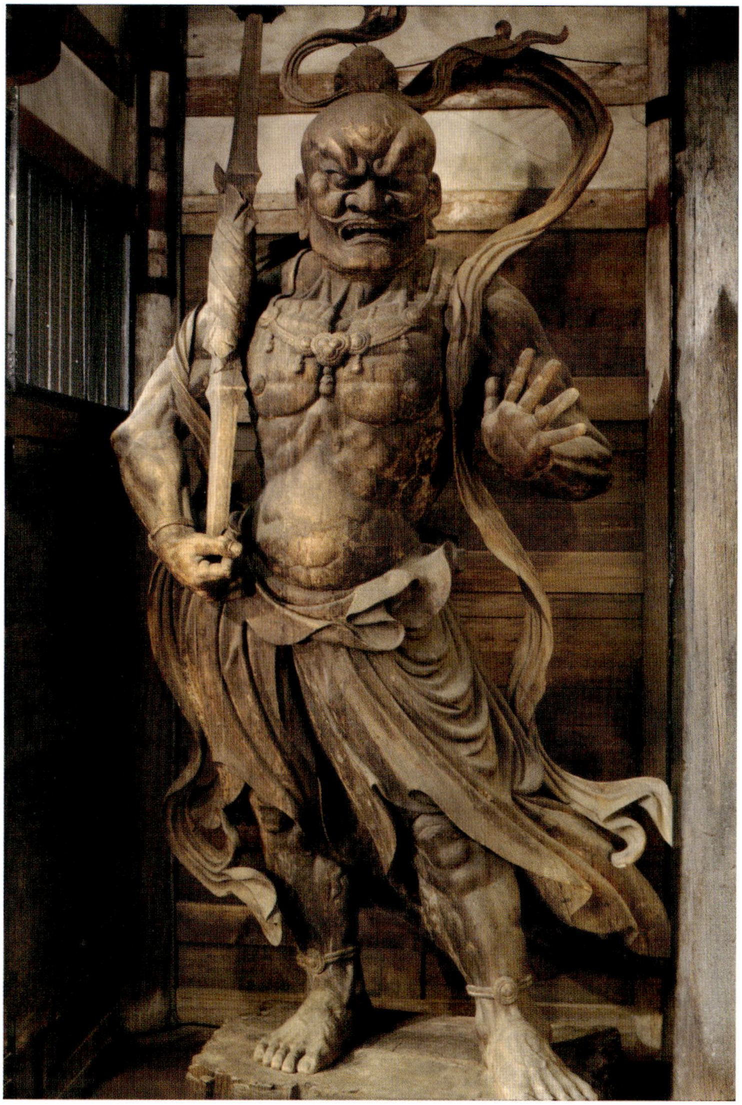

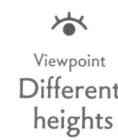

阿形
Agyō

Raising the location of the camera lens to the level of the navel.

If we make this change, as seen on the right, the advantage of a large head and short legs is immediately apparent. However, looking up from below, one feels an almost overwhelming sense of volume that seems to be crushing down on the viewer.

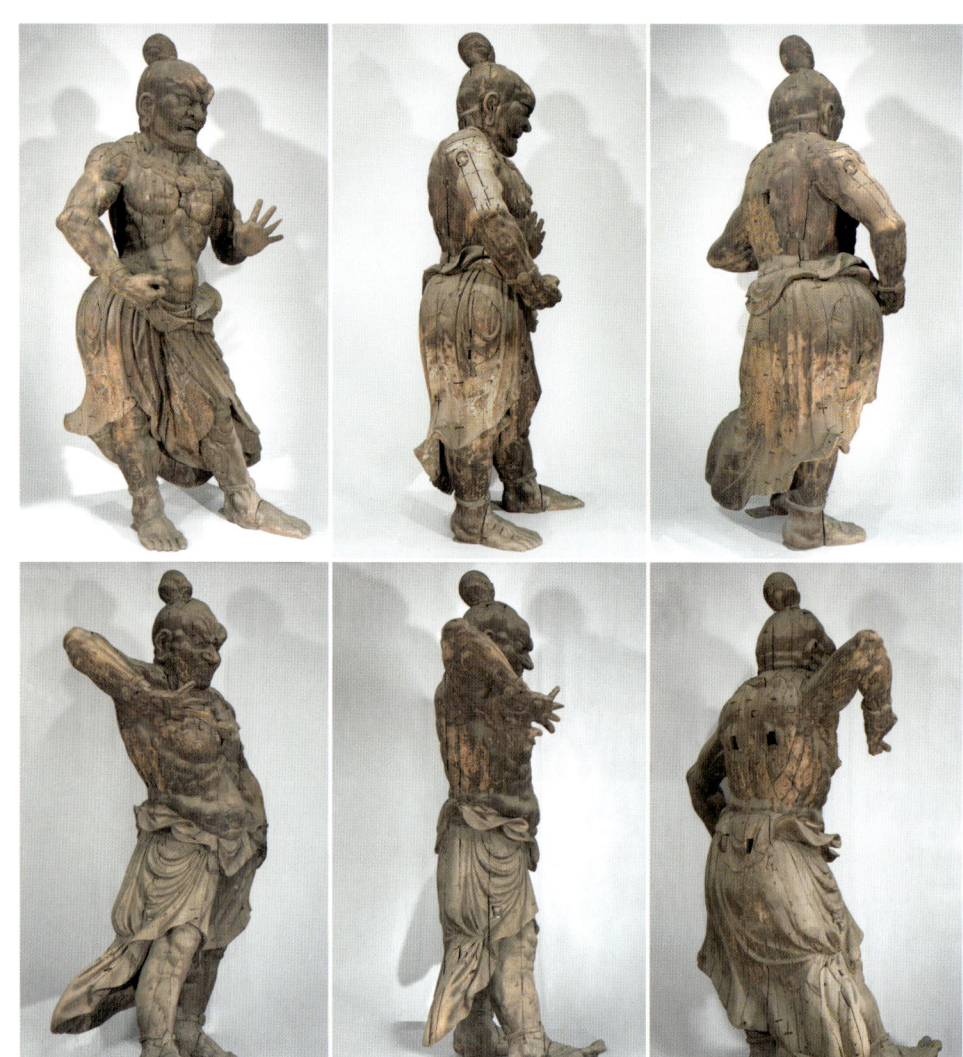

ぐるっと
見る

上段：阿形
Upper images: Agyō

正面からの迫力は、側面・背面になると急に様子が変わる。

仁王像の側面を見ると、阿・吽ともに腕の動きがぎこちない。正面から見ることへの比重が徹底されていたからである。背面は門内の「安置の間」と呼ぶ狭い空間の中で彫刻したと推測され、腰の量感が減じ、裙の裾が重く垂れるなど、両像とも動きのバランスが崩れた感じである。

これら2つの力士像は2軀一具の統一感の原則に従い、像高、目の高さ、上半身の大きさ、乳首やへその位置、裙の上縁や裾先の長さなどに違和感がない。しかし、根気よく、ていねいに対比して見ていくと、作者はひとりではないことが分かる。

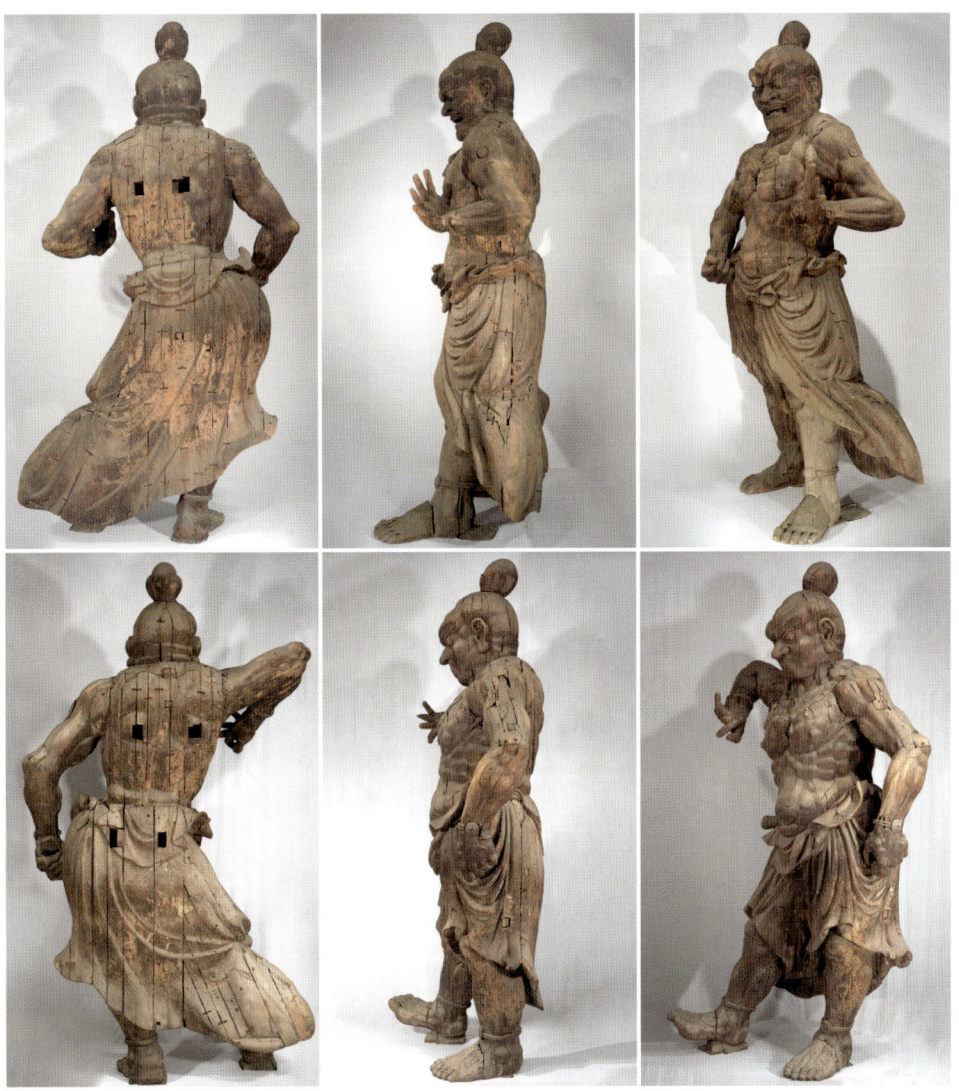

下段：吽形
Lower images: Ungyō

The impact of the direct frontal view changes immediately when viewed from the side or back.

The side views of the Niō statues reveal the awkward movement of the arms of both statues. This is due to the relative importance placed on the frontal view was paramount and thoroughly adhered to. The rear view, reduces the sense of volume of the hips and causes the hems of the skirts to droop heavily. One senses in both statues the balance in their movements has been destroyed. These Niō statues observe the principle of unity that dictates that they form a single set; hence there is no hint of any disparity in the height of the statues, the level of the eyes, the size of the upper bodies, the placement of the nipples and navels, the upper edges or the lengths of the skirts. However, when we compare the two carefully we realize that no single sculptor could have created them both.

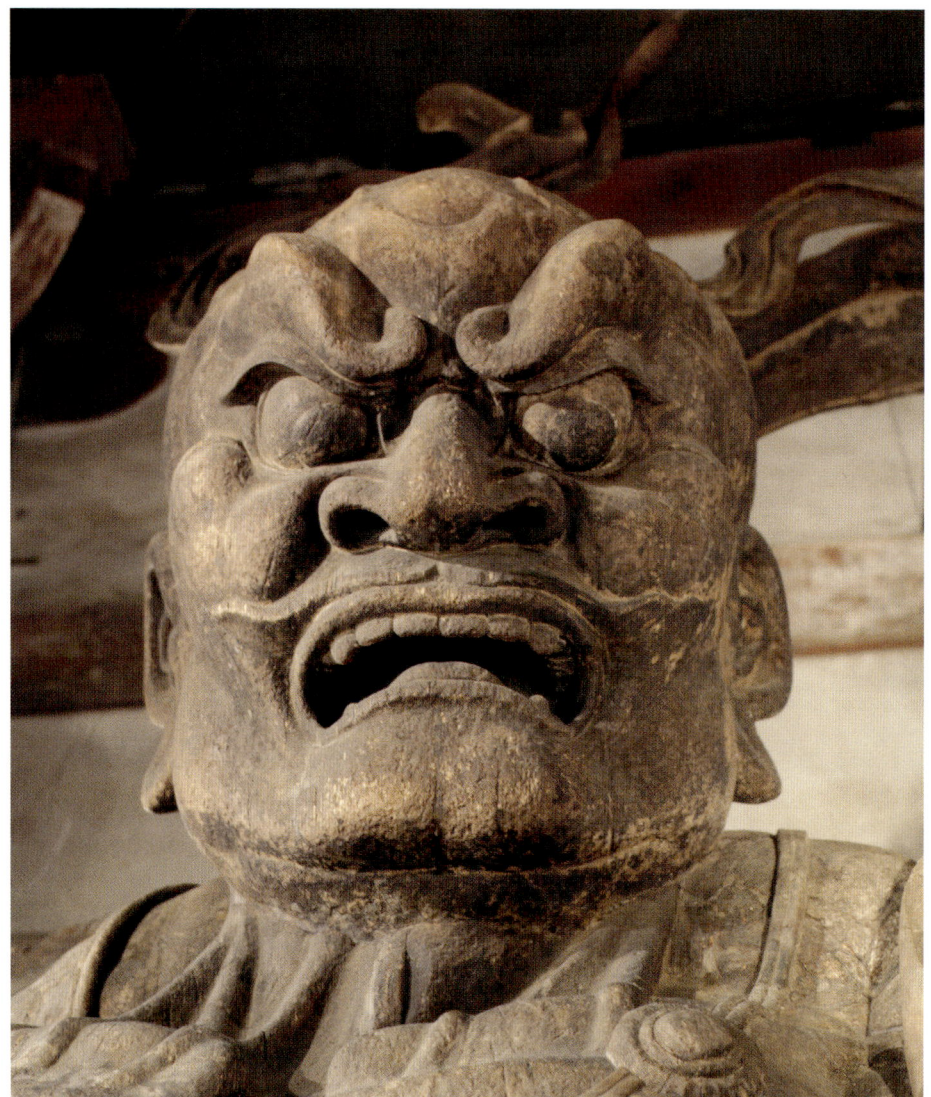

顔の
アップ
を見る

阿形
Agyō

はじめに表情のちがいについて対比してみよう。

阿・吽の顔は、それぞれ骨格が異なる。阿形は顎の鰓が張った四角い顔、吽形は頬の肉どりが引き締まったやや細い顔、といった印象を持つ。しかし、実際の顔の幅は5㎜の差しかない。この感覚の違いは作者の資質の違いを意味すると思う。つまり、阿形は快慶風、吽形は運慶風の顔つきである。

通常の仁王像は顔や体形が双子の兄弟のようによく似ており、ひとりの作者ないしひとつの工房の手によって作られるケースが多い。南大門の仁王像の場合、その点が大きく異なるのである。

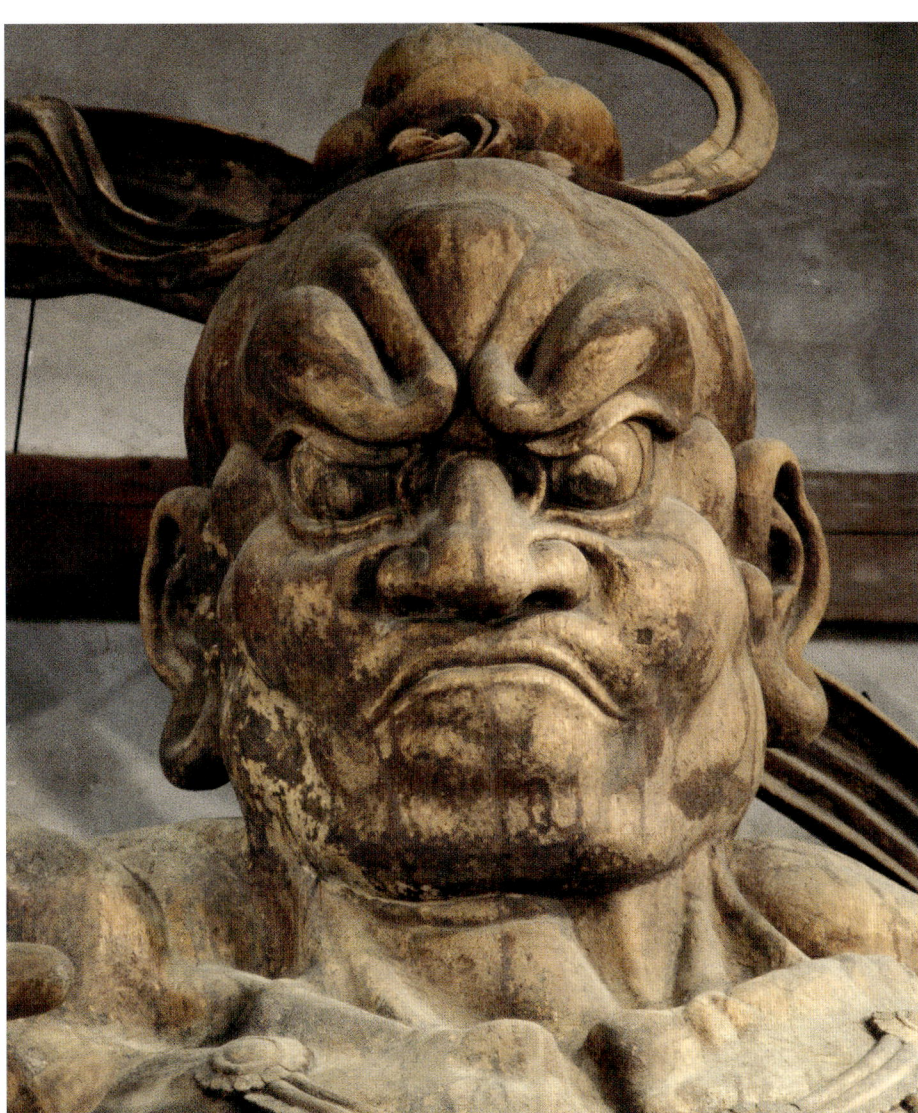

吽形
Ungyō

Let's begin by comparing the differences in the facial expressions.

The faces of the two statues have different structures. One gets the impression that the jaw of the angularly shaped, open-mouthed Agyō statue is tense, and the flesh of the cheeks of the close-mouthed Ungyō statue is firm and the face rather narrow. However, the actual difference in the width of the two faces is merely 5 millimeters. I believe the different impressions are the result of the different personalities of the sculptors. In other words, the face of the Agyō is in the style of Kaikei, and that of the Ungyō is in the style of Unkei.

In the case of typical Niō statues, the faces and bodies often resemble those of identical twin brothers, and in many cases they were produced by a single sculptor or by a single workshop. In the case of the Niō statues at the Nandaimon, it is quite a different matter.

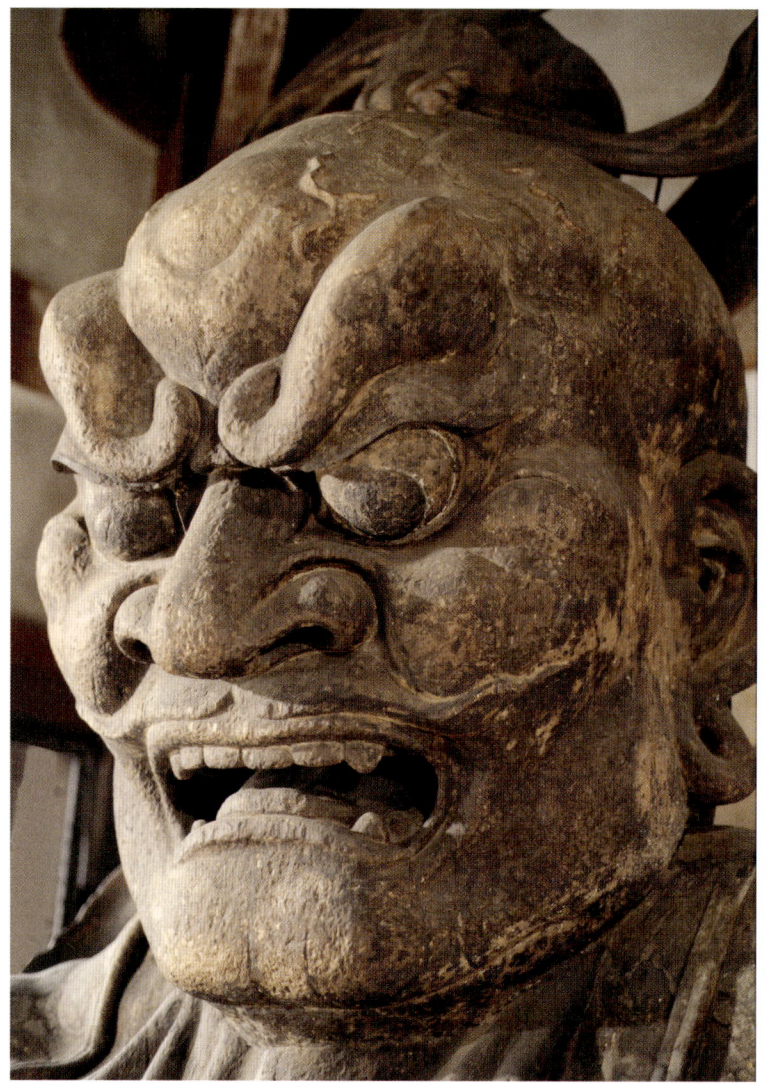

阿形
Agyō

斜めの角度から再度、顔の違いについて対比してみよう。

阿形は、かっと開いた口からパワーを外に発散させる。吽形は口を固く結び、鼻先に力感のベクトルが集まり、力を内に籠める。この違いは快慶と運慶の個性に基づくが、それぞれ同寺法華堂の◉塑造執金剛神立像と◉乾漆金剛力士立像（吽形）の古典彫刻を学んでいる。だが、阿形では目の見開きがもっと大きく、吽形では目尻がより吊り上がり、ともに非常に激しい気性の感情表現に高められている。

さらに阿形では顎の中央部が窪み、2分割の瘤が顎の肉どりを引きしめる。吽形ではひとつの塊の瘤が、への字に結んだ唇の力感を強調する。前者は快慶作の京都・金剛院の◎深沙大将立像、後者は運慶作の静岡・願成就院の制吒迦童子立像（◉不動明王および二童子立像のうち）のそれに酷似する。これも快慶と運慶の個性の違いを示すところである。

52

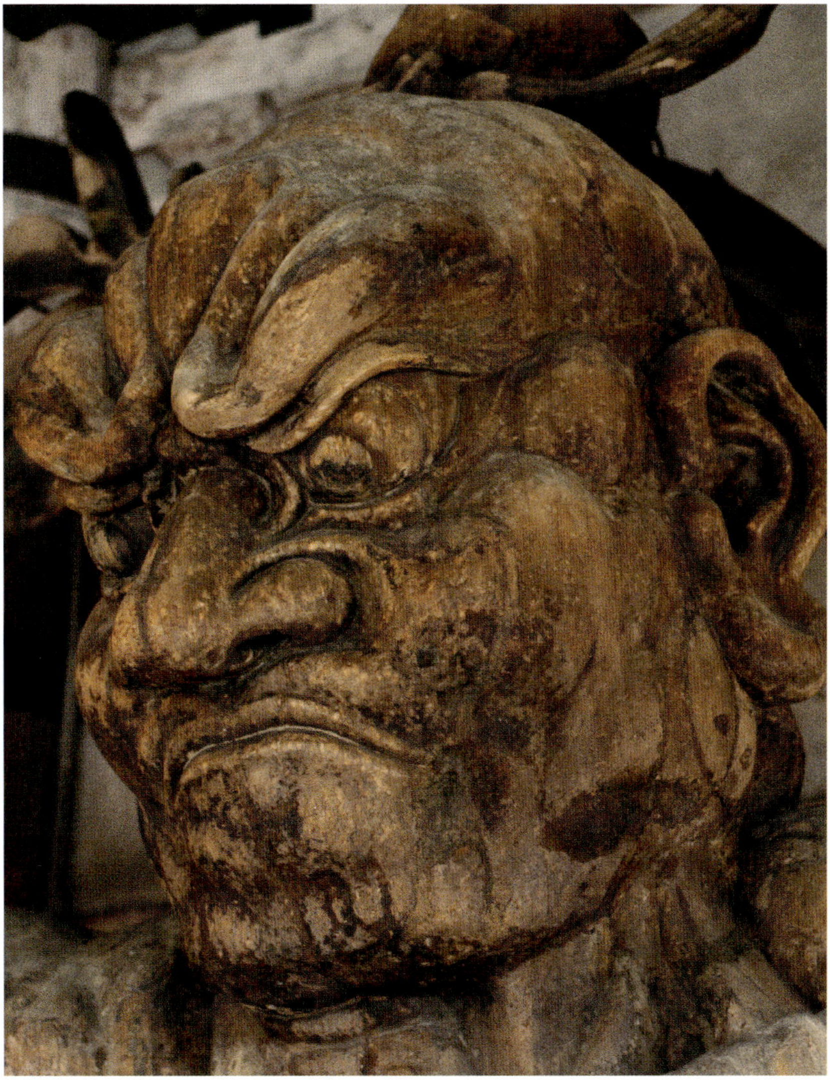

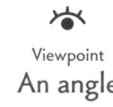

Viewpoint
An angle

吽形
Ungyō

Let's compare facial differences a second time from an angle.

The gaping mouth of Agyō radiates power. The firmly shut mouth of Ungyō concentrates its latent power internally. These differences are based on the individual personalities of Kaikei and Unkei, but each was influenced by classical sculpture from the Nara period found in the Hokkedō hall at Tōdaiji, specifically Agyō by the clay ◉*Standing Shukongōshin* and Ungyō by the dry-lacquer ◉*Standing Kongō Rikishi*. But they differ from the models with the eyes of Agyō opened more widely, and the eyes of Ungyō drawn up more highly to the sides, and both have a heightened emotional expressiveness projecting an extremely fierce air.

The center of Agyō's jaw is indented and divided into two lumps of flesh that pull the jaws tight. In the case of Ungyō, a single bulge of flesh emphasizes the power of the lips clenched tightly in an inverted v shape. The former work very closely resembles ◎*Jinja Daishō* by Kaikei at Kongō-in temple in Kyoto, and the latter statue, the *Seitaka Dōji* statue by Unkei at the Ganjōju-in temple in Shizuoka (which is part of ● *Standing Fudō Myōō and Two Attendant Youths*). These also indicate the differences in the individual characters of Kaikei and Unkei.

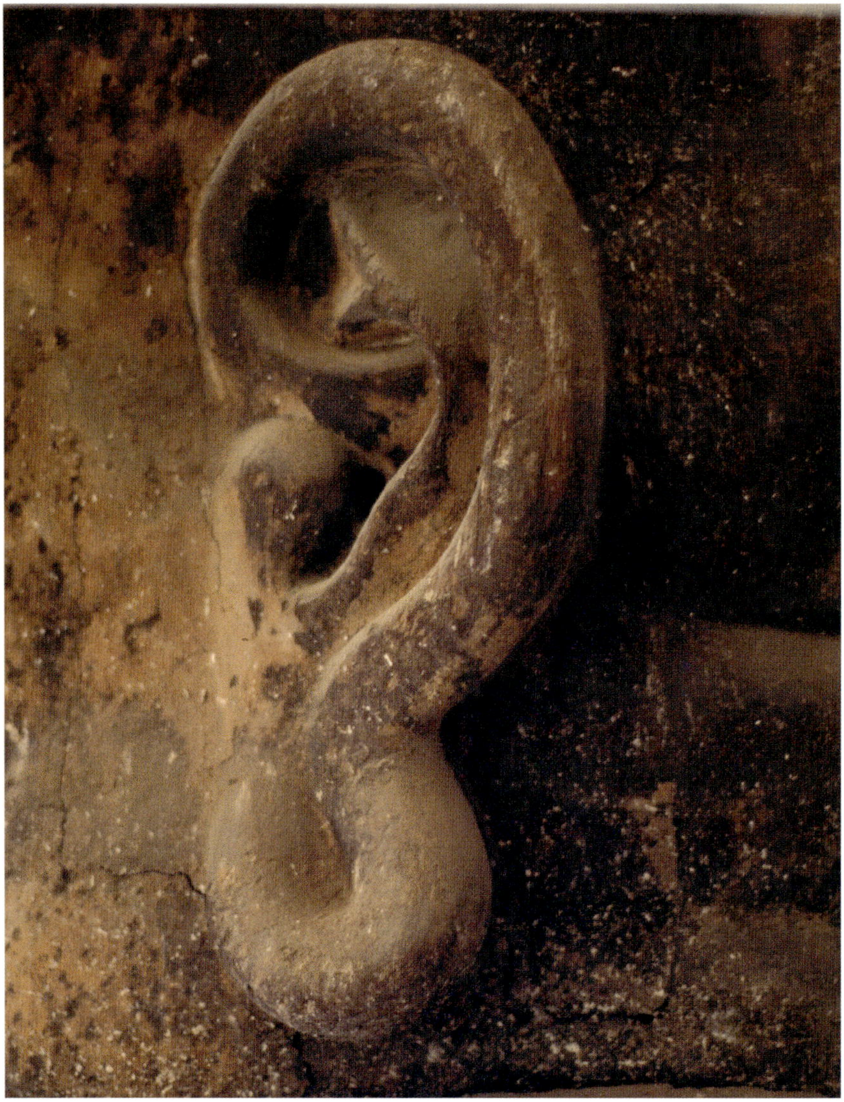

阿形
Agyō

次に細部を見てみよう。

耳を比べると、阿形の外耳輪(がいじりん)は癖のない表現だが、上方が大きく、耳朶(じだ)の小さいかたちは、快慶作の和歌山・金剛峯寺の広目天立像（◎ 四天王立像のうち）のそれに共通しており、快慶特有の表現である。

これに対して、運慶の外耳輪は上方の後寄りがくびれており、癖の強いかたちである。このような耳は運慶作の静岡・願成就院の◉ 毘沙門天立像に共通しており、運慶特有の表現である。

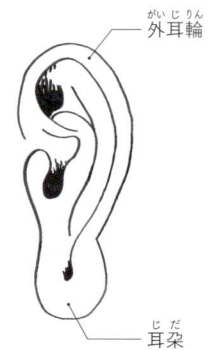

外耳輪(がいじりん)

耳朶(じだ)

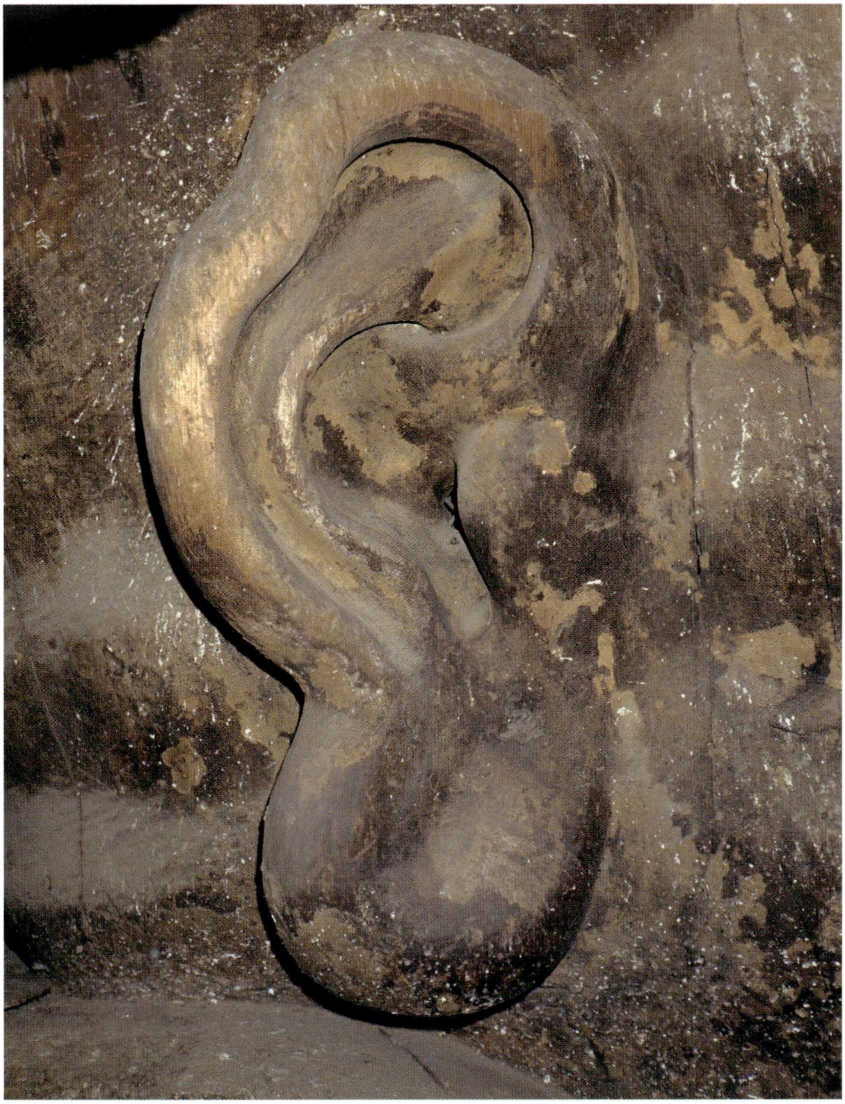

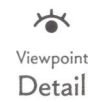

Viewpoint
Detail

吽形
Ungyō

Let's next look in more detail.

Comparing the ears, we see the representation of the outer shell of the ears of the Agyō statue shows no conspicuous mannerism, with the upper portion larger and the earlobes being smaller. These characteristics with the Kaikei's *Kōmokuten* at Kongōbuji (in Wakayama), which is one of the set of ◎*Shitennō*, demonstrating Kaikei's unique manner of expression.

In contrast, the ears of the Unkei statue are indented in the back upper portion in an idiosyncratic fashion. This ear shape is shared with Unkei's ◉*Standing Bishamonten* at Ganjōjuin temple in Shizuoka. This is a style of expression unique to Unkei.

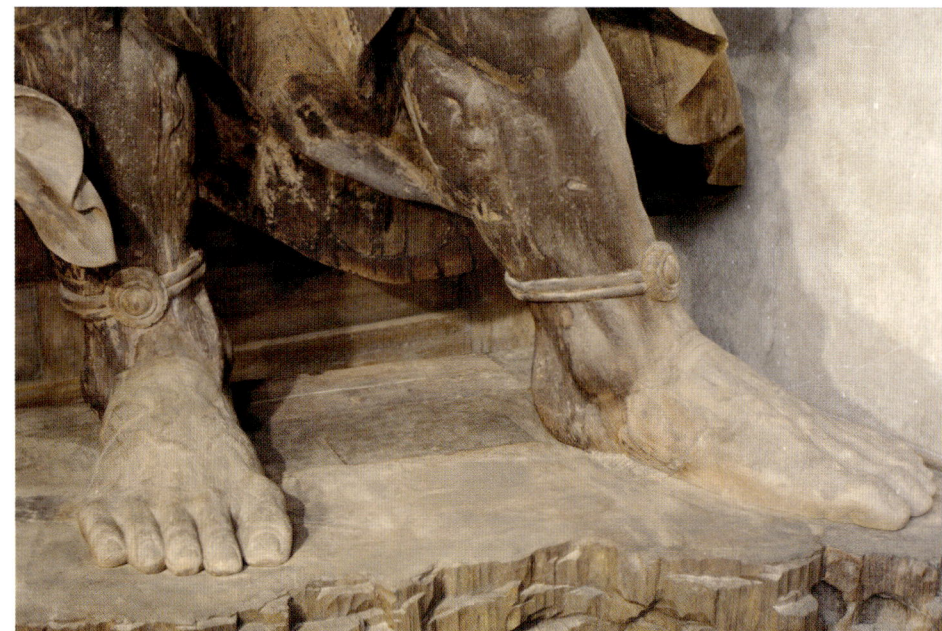

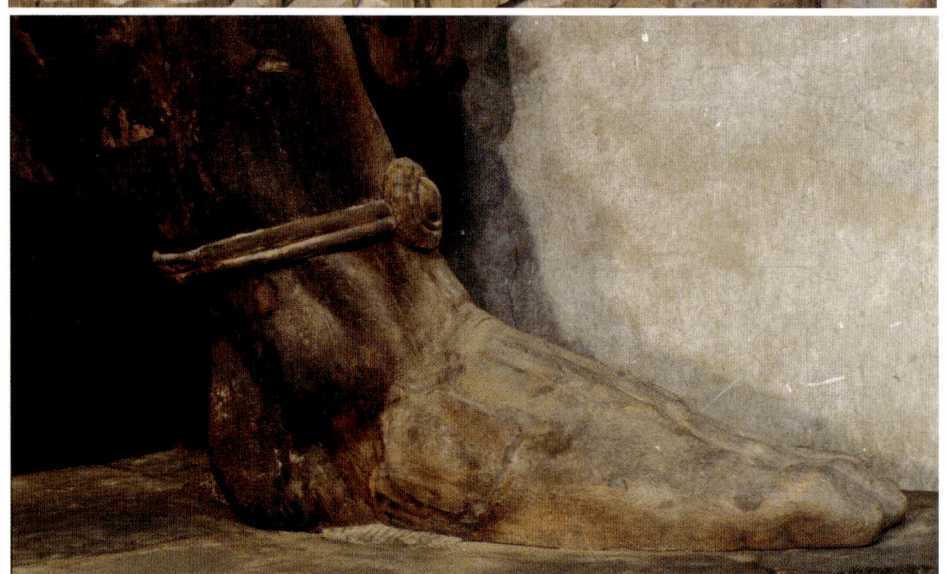

阿形
Agyō

次に足を比べてみよう。

これら2つの足のサイズの違いは明瞭だ。阿形の足は大きく、幅が広く、足の甲が低く、扁平である。吽形のそれは小さく、足の甲が高い。人の足にたとえるなら、靴のサイズが阿形は4E、吽形は3Eである。ここを認識すると面白いだろう。

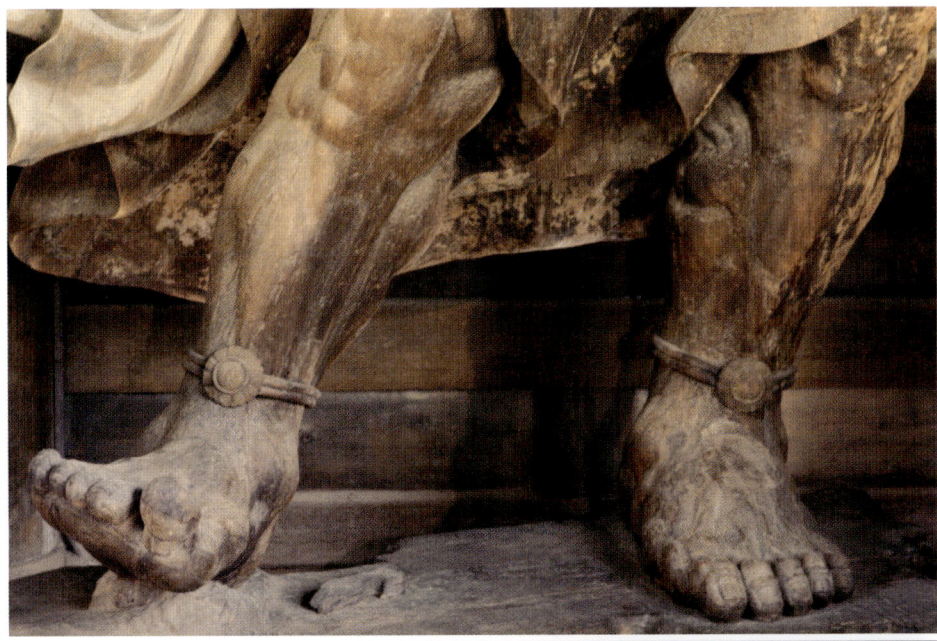

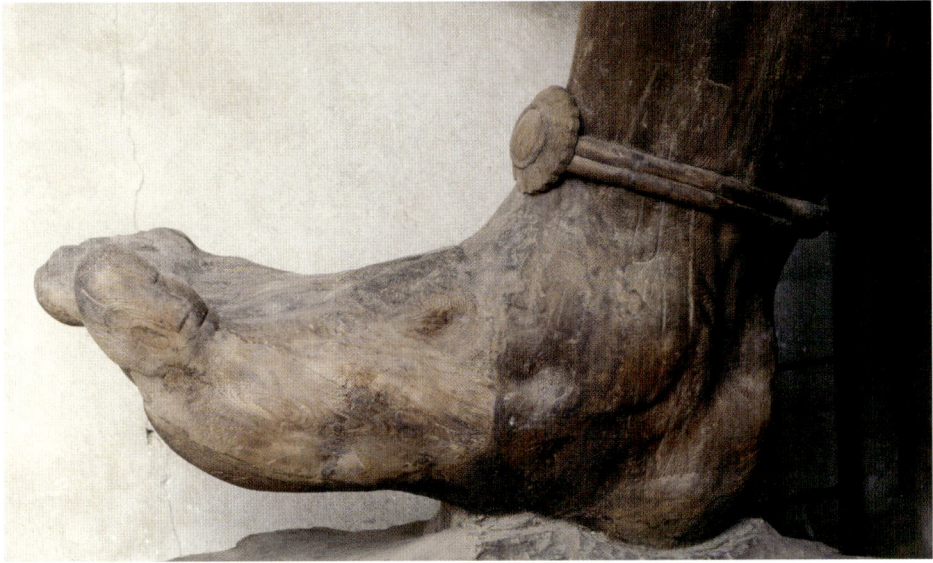

吽形
Ungyō

Let's compare the feet next.

The difference in the size of the feet is obvious. The feet of the open-mouthed Agyō statue are large and wide, and the top of the foot is low and flat. Those of the close-mouthed Ungyō statue are small, and the tops of feet are highly arched. If compared with human feet, the size of the shoes for Agyō statue would be 4Es and those of Ungyō statue 3Es. The sizes are clearly distinguishing features.

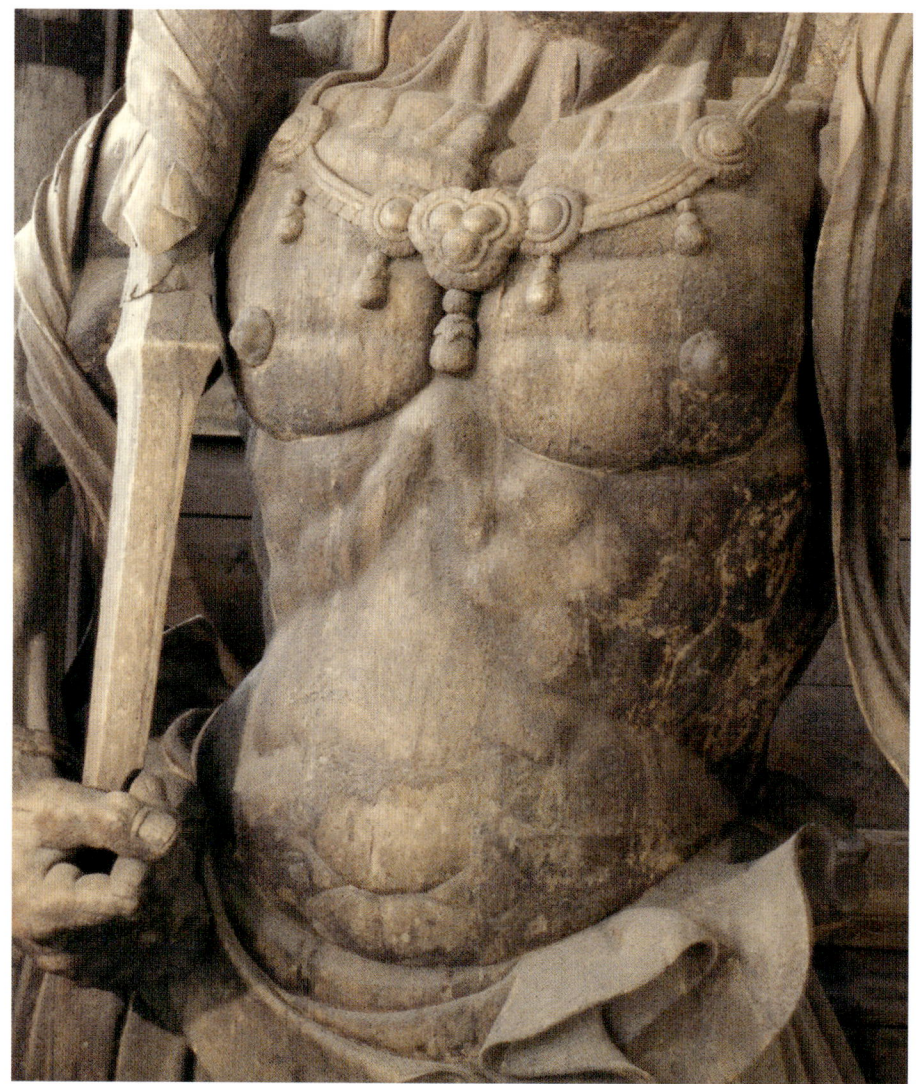

👁
細部
を見る

阿形
Agyō

筋肉表現も違う。

阿形の胸板はごつごつするものの、浅い彫り口で、肉どりの抑揚が小さい。あばら骨のくぼみが2筋、直線的にはっきりと刻まれるものの、平板である。吽形のそれは深い彫り口で胸の高まりが感じられ、肉どりが厚く隆起する。この筋肉表現の違いもまた快慶と運慶の作風の違いを示すものである。

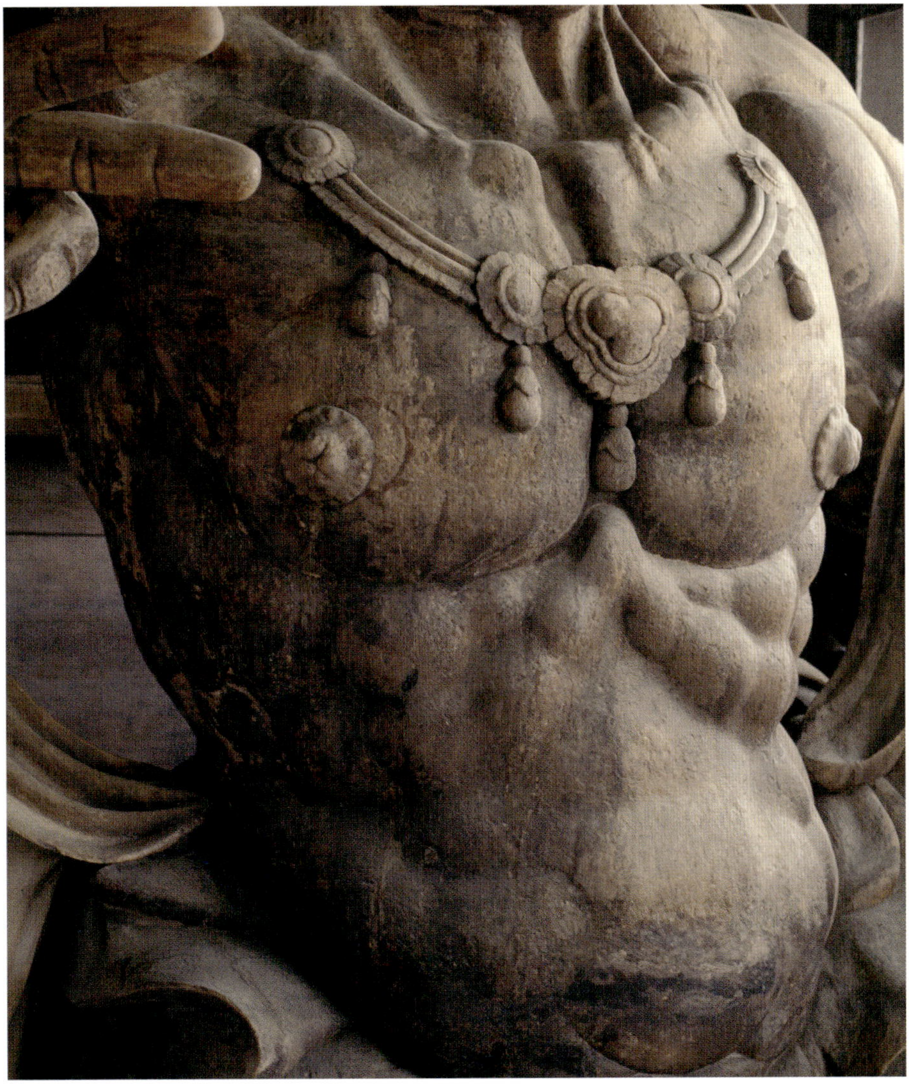

吽形
Ungyō

The representation of the musculature also differs.

The chest of the Agyō statue is rugged and rippled, but the carving is shallow and the modulation of the contours of the flesh is limited. There are two depressions across the rib cage, which are clearly incised and flat. Those of the Ungyō statue are deeply etched and the chest feels raised, and the flesh is thick and bulging. This difference in this expression of the musculature also indicates a difference in the styles of Kaikei and Unkei.

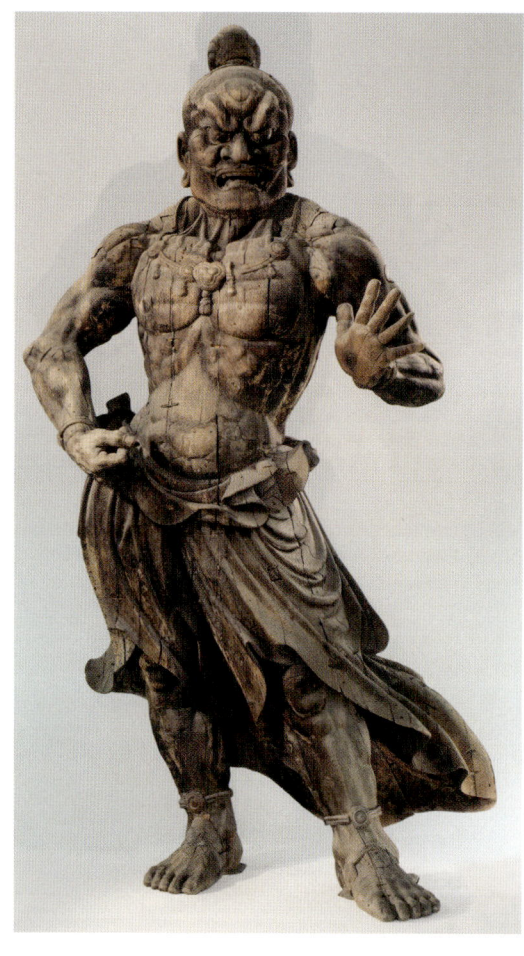

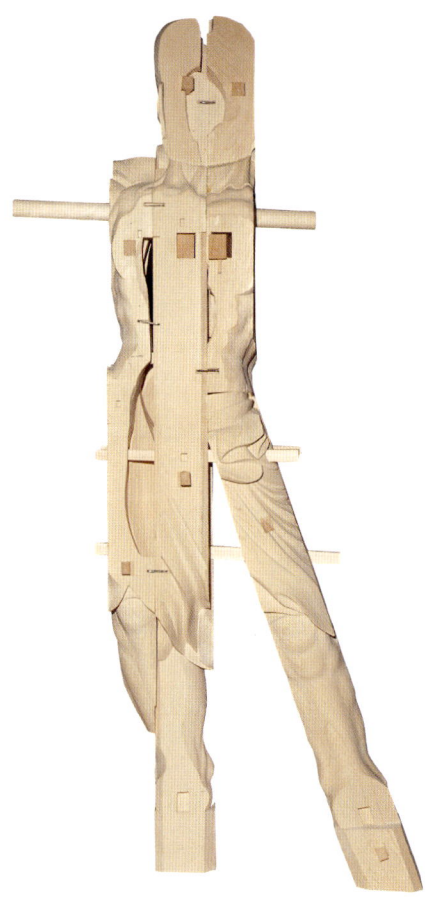

阿形
Agyō

雛型を作る。
^{ひながた}

8mを超える、この巨大な仁王像は、それぞれ大小約3000ピースの檜の木材からなり、基本構造をなすのは10本の根幹材である。これを南大門で組み立てるのだが、この作業には材木の調達も含めて仏師のほかに番匠（建築関係の工人）の参加があったことが分かっている。

この巨大な木彫の製作は、あらかじめ10分の1に縮尺した、80cm余りの彫刻が造られたと想像される。当時、これを「雛型」と呼んでいる。この雛型製作に阿形は快慶、吽形は運慶が担当したと仮定すれば、これら阿・吽の力士の作風がなぜ違うのか、その理由は分かりやすい。

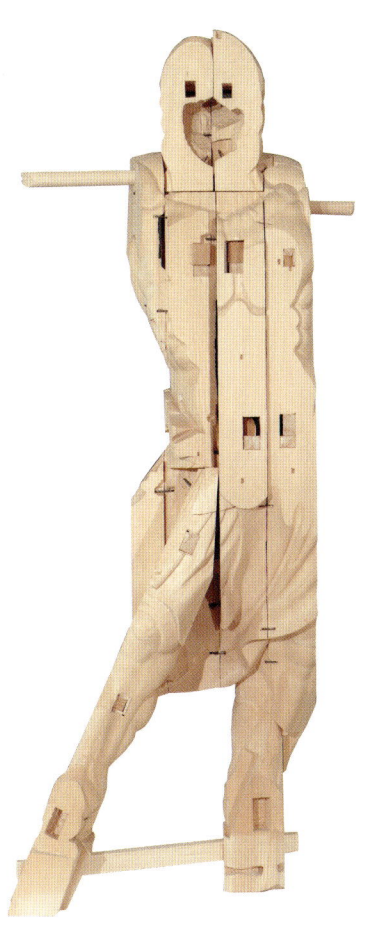

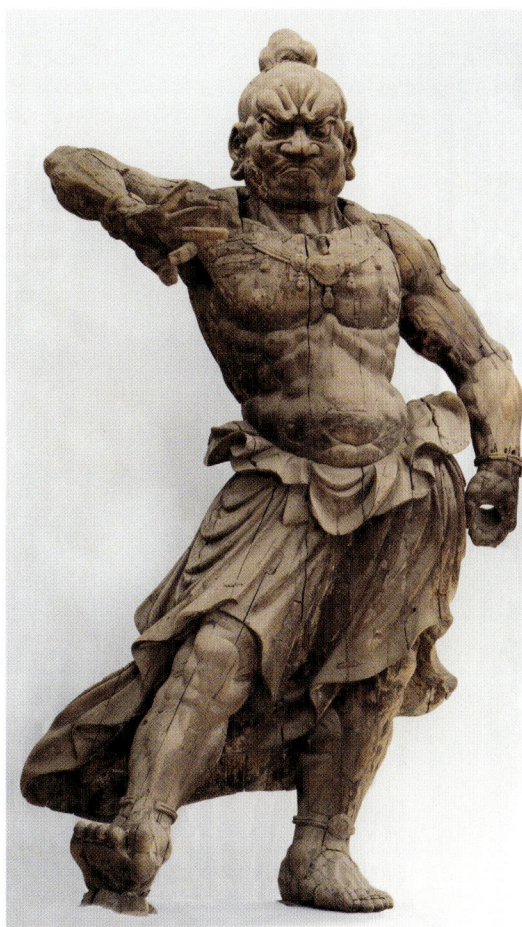

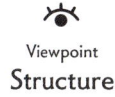
Viewpoint
Structure

吽形
Ungyō

Making a model.

The massive Niō statues, over 8 meters in height, are each composed of approximately 3,000 parts made from Japanese cypress (*hinoki*), and the basic structure is composed of ten main structural elements. These were assembled at the Nandaimon, and it is known that this operation required not only adjustments by the sculptors but also the participation of master carpenters (called *banshō* or *banjō* in Japanese).

It is estimated that a more than 80-centimeter tall model, or *hinagata*, on a scale of 1:10 was first created in order to produce these massive sculptures. If we assume that Unkei was in charge of producing the model for the Ungyō statue and that Kaikei was in charge of the Agyō model, it is eazy to understand why the styles of the Agyō and the Ungyō are so different.

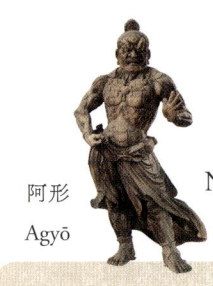

国宝 金剛力士立像
東大寺南大門所在

National Treasure *Two Standing Kongō Rikishi*
Nandaimon at Tōdaiji

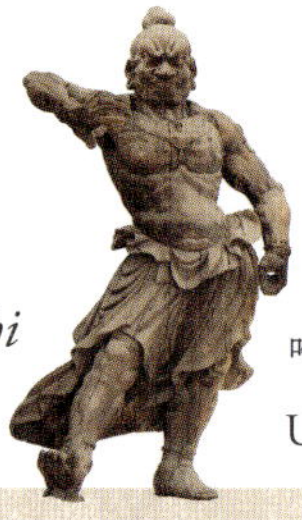

阿形
Agyō

吽形
Ungyō

大仏師運慶作
寄木造（檜） 彩色
鎌倉時代 (13c.)
建仁3年 (1203)
像内にそれぞれ「一切如来心秘密全身舎利宝篋印陀羅尼経」等を納める。

By Master Sculptor Unkei
Assembled-block construction (*hinoki*), painted
Kamakura period (13c.),
dated 1203 (Kennin 3)
Each statue contains a copy of the *Hōkyōin Daranikyō* and other items.

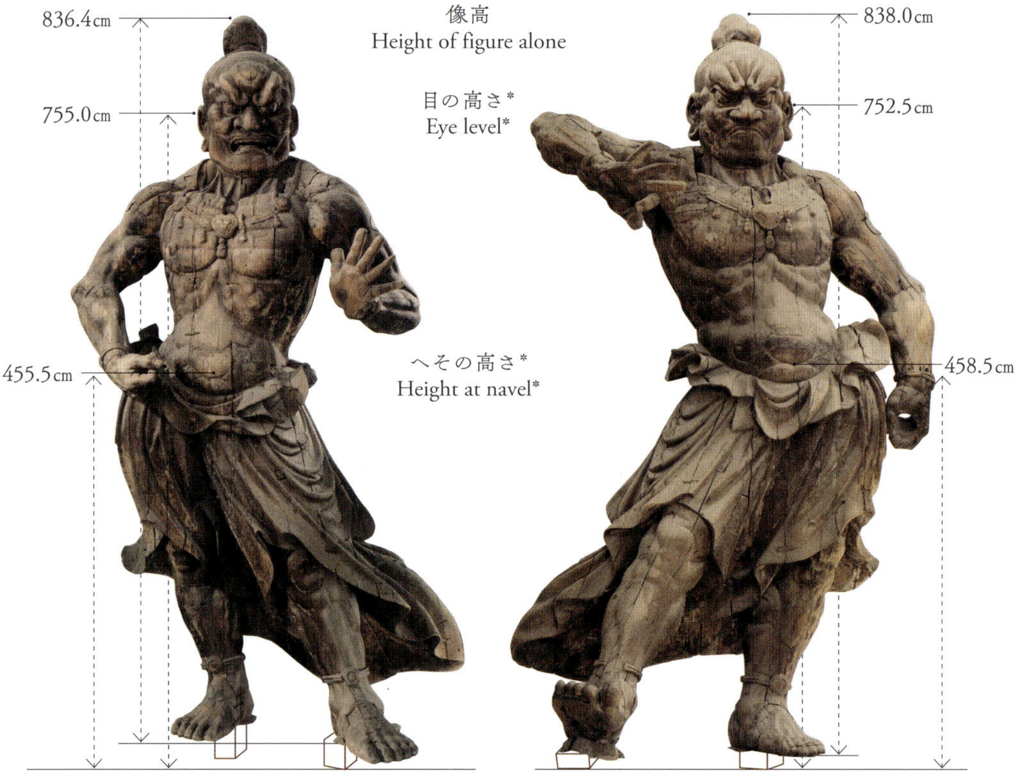

像高
Height of figure alone

836.4 cm

838.0 cm

目の高さ*
Eye level*

755.0 cm

752.5 cm

へその高さ*
Height at navel*

455.5 cm

458.5 cm

材の総数 (寄木造)
2987 箇 Total number of parts (assembled construction) 3115 箇

総重量
6675.2 kg Total weight 6868.5 kg

*台石柄 (はぞ) から 　　 (計測：美術院)
* Measured from the base of the tenons beneath the feet

2つの力士像はともに全身に力強さが目一杯にみなぎっているが、それぞれ個性がある。

The statues of these two guardians both exclude energetic force, but each has its own unique characteristics.

阿形 Agyō statue

頭と身体の均衡を保持しようとする意識が働く。
→**快慶の造形**

A conscious effort made to maintain the balance between the head and body
→ **therefore created by Kaikei**

×

吽形 Ungyō statue

頭と身体の均衡を積極的に破壊し、より強い力を示そうとする意欲的な感覚。
→**運慶の造形**

A deliberate effort to disturb the balance between the head and body and a conspicuous desire to depict fierce power
→ **therefore created by Unkei**

従来より上記のように結論付けられるが、両像の統一については、慶派仏師康慶の嫡子である運慶が指揮したとみてよいだろう。ところが、平成の大修理の新知見をもとに仁王像の仏師編制を考えた、次の大仏師の組合せの解釈が提示されている。ただし、総指揮官を運慶とみるのは両説同じである。

Similar conclusions have been drawn before, but given the unity of the two statues, we can conclude that Unkei, who led the Kei-ha school of sculptors founded by his father, Kōkei, supervised the overall project. However, when we consider the make up of the teams of sculptors involved in producing the Niō statues in light of the new knowledge obtained during the Heisei-era conservation, two interpretations of the make up of the teams of master sculptors become possible. Although there are two interpretations, both see Unkei as the head sculptor leading the whole project.

阿形：運慶と快慶　　　　　　　　①
吽形：定覚と湛慶
総指揮官でもあった運慶は阿形を快慶にまかせ、
吽形側の大仏師2人を直接指導した。

The Agyō statue was created by Unkei and Kaikei. The Ungyō statue was created by Jōkaku and Tankei. Unkei, the overall project leader, left the Agyō statue to Kaikei, and directed the other two master sculptors in producing the Ungyō statue.

阿形：快慶（のもとで定覚）　②
吽形：運慶（のもとで湛慶）

The Agyō statue was produced by Jōkaku under the direction of Kaikei.
The Ungyō statue was produced by Tankei under the direction of Unkei.

本書ではこれまで述べた「対比して見る視点」によって、やはり、②の見解の方が有力であるという立場にたつ。

As has been argued in this book up to this point, comparing works by viewing them from two or more viewpoints is critical and this supports view ②.

コラム　仁王像のかたちの修正
Column: Revisions made to the Appearance of the Niō Statues

建仁3年（1203）7月24日に着工した仁王像は、8月後半から9月頃、おそらく彫刻が終わり、彩色の仕事に入る前後、2躯ともに①眉と目、②腕、③へそなど、それぞれ同じ箇所で、かたちの修正が行われたことが分かっている。

Begun on the 24th day of the 7th month of Kennin 3 (1203), the carving of the Niō statues was probably completed in the latter half of the 8th month or by the 9th month at the latest. It is known that around the time of the start of the painting, revisions to the shape of 1) the brows and eyes, 2) the arms, 3) the navels and other parts were conducted in order that these elements would appear in the same locations on both statues.

① 眉と目　The eyes and brows
眉上面と上瞼に小材を矧ぎ足し、さらに下瞼を削ったとみられ（写真1）、阿形・吽形ともに視線をもっと下げる指示が出された（写真2）と推察される。

Small supplemental pieces of wood were added above the brows and on the upper eyelids, and the lower eyelids appear to have been recarved (photo. 1); it is presumed that orders were given to lower the sight lines of both statues (photo. 2).

1 阿形　平成の解体修理時に別材でできた上瞼を外したところ、修正前の元の眼の一部（白目）が現れた

When the upper eyelids of the Agyō statue were removed during the Heisei-period conservation, a part of the original eye became visible.

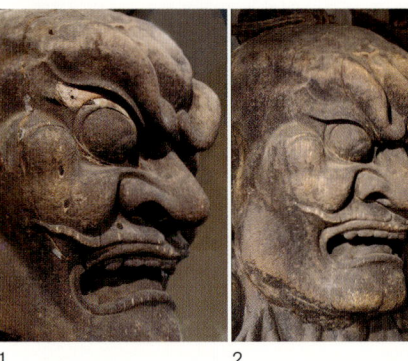

1 　　　　2

2 阿形　修正後の眼

The eyes of the Agyō statue after the revisions

3 吽形　修正時の眉や上瞼の小材を外したところ。阿形と同じように、元の白目や血走りの赤色が見える

When the wood for the brows and upper eyelids added during the revisions were removed, the original white of the eyes and red capillaries became visible.

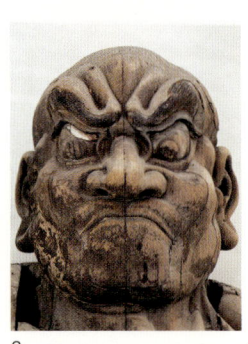

3 　　　　4

4 吽形　視線を下げるため、眉や瞼に小材をあてた図（美術院作成）

An illustration of the wood used for the brows and eyelids of the Ungyō statue to lower the line of sight (prepared by the Bijyutsuin)

② 腕　The arms

阿形では右腕の角度を開き、金剛杵を捧げ持つ手を脇腹まで下げた（写真5）。吽形では、右ひじを高くあげ、手首をより捻り、左腕は手首の角度を変えて、金剛杵をより斜めに下げるようにした。

The right arm of the Agyō statue is open at a wide angle and the hand that held up the vajra has been lowered to its side (photo. 5). The right arm of the Ungyō statue is held high and the wrist is twisted, while the left wrist is held at a different angle and the vajra is held downward at a greater angle.

それに応じて、おもに阿形では両肩、吽形では腋（わき）に細かい小材が補足され、より盛り上がった、あるいはより引きつった筋肉表現の効果が強調された。左右の乳首も外にずらしている（写真6）。このような修正は前に記したように、彩色施工の段階、下地塗りに前後する頃かと推察される。

The shoulders of the Agyō statue, and the side of the chest of the Ungyō statue were further molded with small supplemental pieces of wood with the result that a firmer musculature was emphasized. The left and right nipples were pulled to the sides (photo. 6). This type of revision, as noted before, was done around the time the base coat was painted and before the painters made their final application.

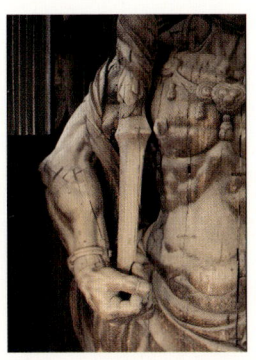

5 阿形　金剛杵を持つ右腕を下げた

The right hand of the Agyō statue grasping the vajra has been lowered

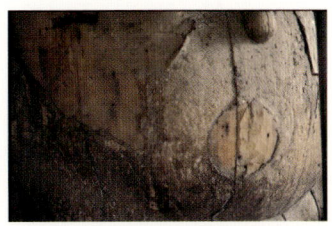

6 吽形　右の乳首が左にずれたことが分かる

It is clear the right nipple of the Ungyō statue has been displaced and moved to the left

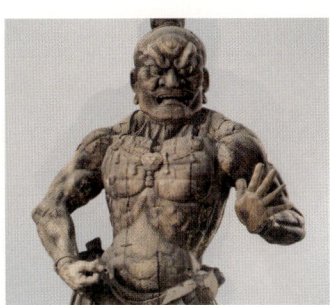

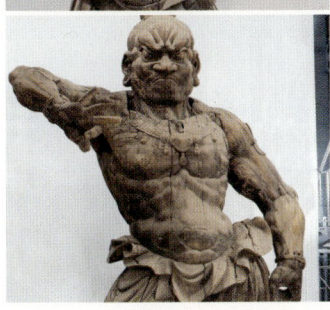

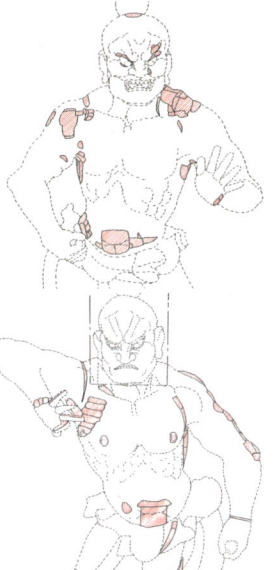

赤い斜線は修正部材の位置
（美術院作成）

The oblique red-shaded areas indicate the locations of the restored portions of the statues (photography by Bijyutsuin)

上　阿形、下　吽形

Upper images: The Agyō statue　Lower images: The Ungyō statue

③ へそ　The navels

阿形・吽形ともに15cmほど下げ、正面側だけ、裾を下にずらした（写真7・8）。

They have been lowered 15 centimeters on both statues and the skirts have been shifted lower only at the front (photos. 7 & 8).

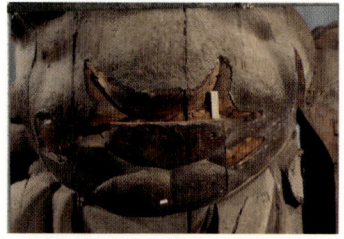
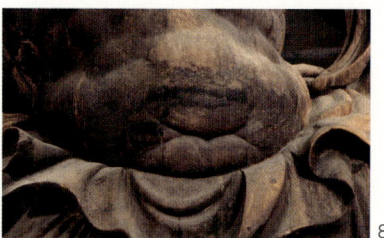

7 吽形　腹部の小材を解体していくと、元のへそが現れた。もとのへそは腹部の一番突き出たところ、修正されて動いたへそは下腹にあり、像の重心を下げるために修正が行われたことが分かる

In the process of removing the supplemental wood at the midsection, the original navel appeared on the Ungyō statue. The original navel was located where the stomach protruded most. After this revision, the altered navel was moved to the lower abdomen, so we know that the revision was carried out to lower its center of gravity.

8 吽形　修正後のへそは下腹にある

After the revision, the navel of the Ungyō statue was located in the lower abdomen.

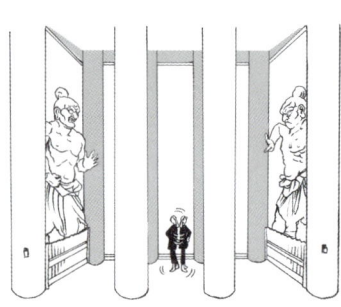

総指揮官による修正の指示

巨像彫刻は、工房の頭領が作った10分の1の雛型をもとに、巨大彫刻の設計や木寄せは現場で行われたと思われる。最終の修正は、南大門内に組まれた足場を取り払い、基壇に立ってそれぞれ像を下から見上げた時に行われたはずだ。その時、総指揮官は阿・吽2つの像の統一を図るために、かつ巨像の迫力がさらに増すように、像の視線を下に落し重心を低くするように、両像の担当仏師に命じたと考えられる。この時点での大きな修正は、巨像制作には通常含まれる工程のひとつであったと推測される。この時の修正は総指揮官の仕事であり、工房の頭領であった運慶であったことは疑いない。両雄並び立たずの言葉を引くまでもなく、阿形担当の責任者の快慶がもし総括する立場にあったとしたら、快慶の資質からすれば、いまとは違う修正がなされたのではないかと推量される。

It is thought that these massive sculptures were produced on site and assembled there according to plans based on 1:10-scale models that had been prepared by the head of the workshop. The final check must have been conducted after the scaffolding was removed and each statue standing on its pedestal was viewed from below. The official in charge of the whole project then ordered the sculptors in charge of the two statues to lower the line of sight, bringing down their centers of gravity in order to enhance their unity and increase their impact. It is estimated that this type of major revision was a regular step in the process of producing massive sculptures.

　　The revisions made were the work of the official in charge of the entire project, who was undoubtedly Unkei, the head of the workshop. There is an old Japanese adage roughly equivalent to "too many cooks spoil the broth," but if Kaikei, who was responsible for the Agyō statue, had been placed in charge of the entire project, one can easily imagine that the revisions would have been much different, particularly given what we know of Kaikei's character and temperament.

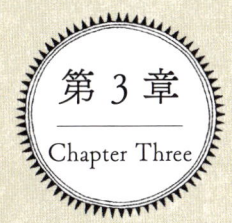

至宝の肖像彫刻
国宝 俊乗上人（重源）坐像　東大寺俊乗堂所在

これまで2つ以上の仏像を「対比」してみてきた。ここで肖像彫刻の傑作である東大寺俊乗堂の重源像1軀を、さまざまな角度から見てみよう。1軀でも「対比」の視点によって、皺数が多い着衣の表現をよく観察すれば、重源上人の感情表現が、そのような衣文表現に反映していることに気づくだろう。

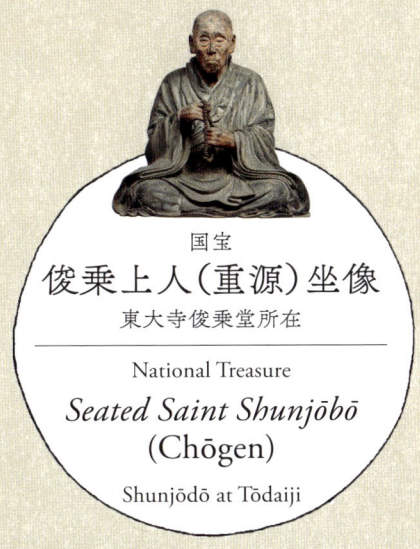

国宝
俊乗上人（重源）坐像
東大寺俊乗堂所在

National Treasure
Seated Saint Shunjōbō
(Chōgen)

Shunjōdō at Tōdaiji

The Ultimate Treasure of Portrait Sculpture
The National Treasure *Seated Saint Shunjō* (Chōgen), Shunjōdō, Tōdaiji

Previously, we compared two or more Buddhist statues. Now, let's view a single masterpiece of portrait sculpture from various angles. It is the satue of the saintly monk Chōgen, found in the Shunjōdō hall at Tōdaiji. Although it is just one statue, by comparing elements from different angles and carefully observing the representation of the robe with its many folds and creases, you will surely realize how the representation of the feelings of Chōgen Shōnin, as he is called in Japanese, is reflected in the expression of the drapery folds of his robes.

重源像を拝観する前に　俊乗房重源（1121～1206）について

　治承4年（1180）の平家の南都焼討後、東大寺の復興に尽力した僧侶。61歳で東大寺造営勧進職に就いた。仏師運慶と快慶の活躍もこの復興事業の時に大いに注目された。復興造営は足掛け20年余りを要した。彼が関わった主要な建物と仏像は次の通り。

▶　大仏殿や南大門をはじめとする巨大な木造建築
▶　銅造の大仏（盧舎那仏）、木造の両脇侍・四天王の巨像
▶　中門の二天、南大門の仁王像（巨大木彫像）

　建永元年（1206）、重源は86歳の生涯を終えたが、東大寺復興の偉大な功績をたたえて彼の肖像がつくられ、その遺徳を偲んだという。それが今日も同寺俊乗堂の本尊重源上人像である。従来、重源示寂後の制作と推定されてきたが、迫真性に富む表現は、当代の現実直視の写実精神に直に触れる感じであり、生前につくられた「寿像」とみる見解も捨てがたい。寿とは老人の長命を祝す意味である。

　前置きが長くなったが、さっそく次頁から見ていこう。ここでは重源像1軀をぐるっと一周し、さまざまな角度から見るわけだが、最終的には、本書のコンセプトである、対比でみる視点がこの像の造形にこめられていることに気づくだろう。

Before paying our respects to the Chōgen statue, let's make a brief overview of his life.

The monk Chōgen (1121-1206), also called Shunjōbō, devoted all his energy to the revival of Tōdaiji, which had burned down when the Taira clan attacked Nara in 1180 (Jishō 4). He was 61 years old when he was appointed to lead the campaign to solicit funds to rebuild Tōdaiji. Much attention has been given to the activities of the Buddhist sculptors Unkei and Kaikei during the rebuilding process. The rebuilding project took slightly more than twenty years to complete. The chief buildings and sculpture Chōgen was involved with are the following:

▶　the massive wooden structures such as the Daibutsuden (Great Buddha Hall) and the Nandaimon (Great Southern Gate)
▶　the bronze Great Buddha (Rushanabutsu / Vairocana), its two wooden attendant statues and the large-scale Four Guardian Kings (Shitennō)
▶　the two devas, or *ten*, in the middle gate, and the two massive wooden Niō in the Nandaimon

　Chōgen's life came to a close in his 86th year in 1206 (Kennei 1), but his achievements in the magnificent revival of Tōdaiji continued to be extolled, and a portrait sculpture of Chōgen was commissioned to remember his virtuous legacy. That statue is the *Seated Chōgen Shōnin*, which is still today the principal object of reverence at the temple's Shunjōdō hall. It was originally thought to have been created after Chōgen's death, but the powerful impact of the representation evokes a sense of being in direct touch with the spirit of realism based on first-hand observation that marked the age. It is thus difficult to abandon the idea that it is a *juzō*, a sculptural portrait produced when the model was alive. The word *ju* in the compound *juzō* signifies a celebration of longevity.

　As these prefatory remarks have been rather long-winded, let's now quickly move on to the facing page and begin our examination of this sculpture. In this chapter you will be able to circle around the statue of Chōgen and view it from various angles. This is ultimately the concept behind this book: comparative views of this statue will surely reveal to you the hidden essence of its sculptural form.

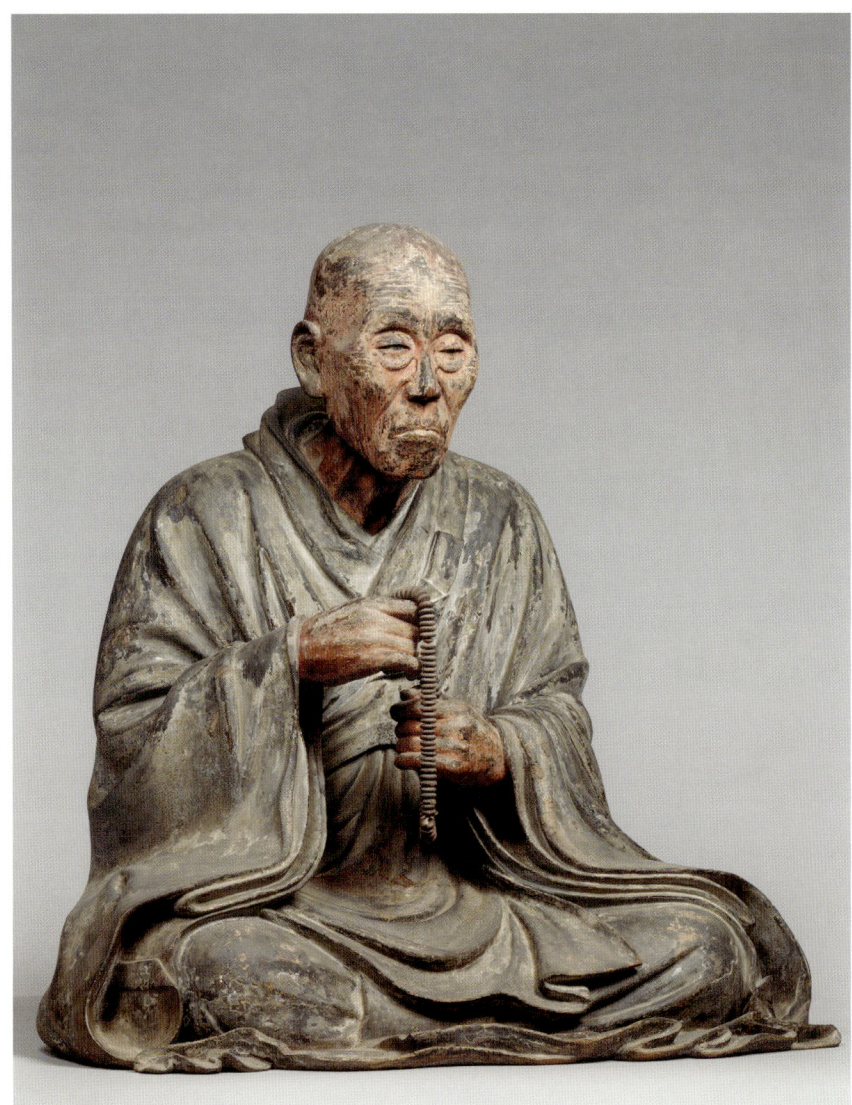

国宝 俊乗上人（重源）坐像 東大寺俊乗堂所在
National Treasure. *Seated Saint Shunjōbō* (Chōgen) Shunjōdō Hall, Tōdaiji

最初に重源像を正面右斜めの角度から見てみよう。

本像の姿勢や手のしぐさを図版で最初に理解するには、この角度がよいと思う。すなわち、顎を前に突き出し、背を丸め、数珠を爪繰る姿である。狭い肩幅や前のめりになった平らで小さな胸板などが、厚い布に覆われた感じで、法衣の下の痩せた老身が想像される。

Let's first view the Chōgen statue straight on, but from slightly to the statue's right.

This is the best angle to get an initial understanding of the pose and hand gestures from a photograph. We see the figure with the jutting jaw, slightly hunched back, and prayer beads in his fingertips. The narrow shoulders and the small, flat chest are bent forward. We get a sense of the thick fabric of the robes that clothe him, allowing us to imagine the emaciated body beneath the priestly robes.

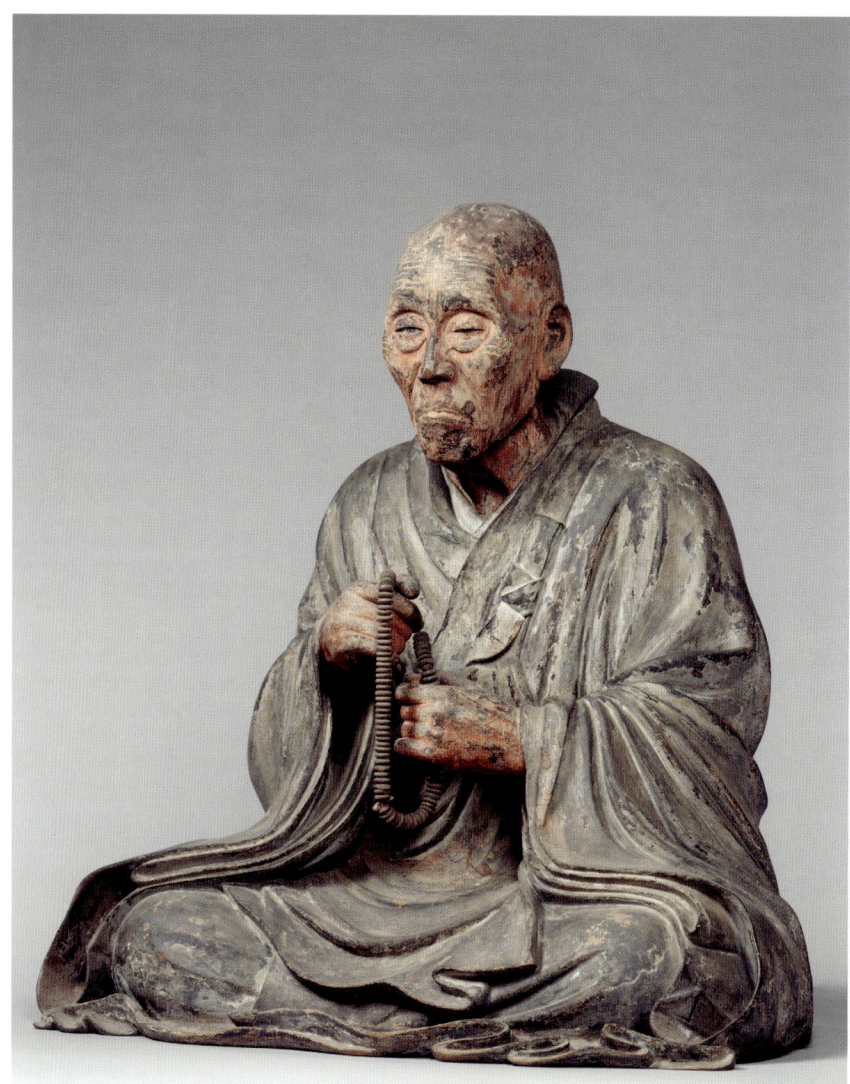

重源上人坐像
Seated Saint Chōgen

正面左斜めの角度から見てみよう。

襟際や袖口をみると、白い色の内衣が見え、法衣2枚を重ね着していることがわかる。さらにその上に袈裟をつけており、左胸前で袈裟の吊り紐を結んでいる。その着こなしは、痩せた老体には、だぶついた感じである。

Let's now look at the statue from an angle slightly to the statue's left.

Examining the edge of the collar and the sleeve, we can see the white of an inner robe so it is clear that Chōgen wears two robes. Over these he wears a surplice (*kesa*), and the hanging sash of the surplice is tied in front of the left side of his chest. These robes gives us a sense of how baggy and ill fitting they are and how emaciated his aged body is.

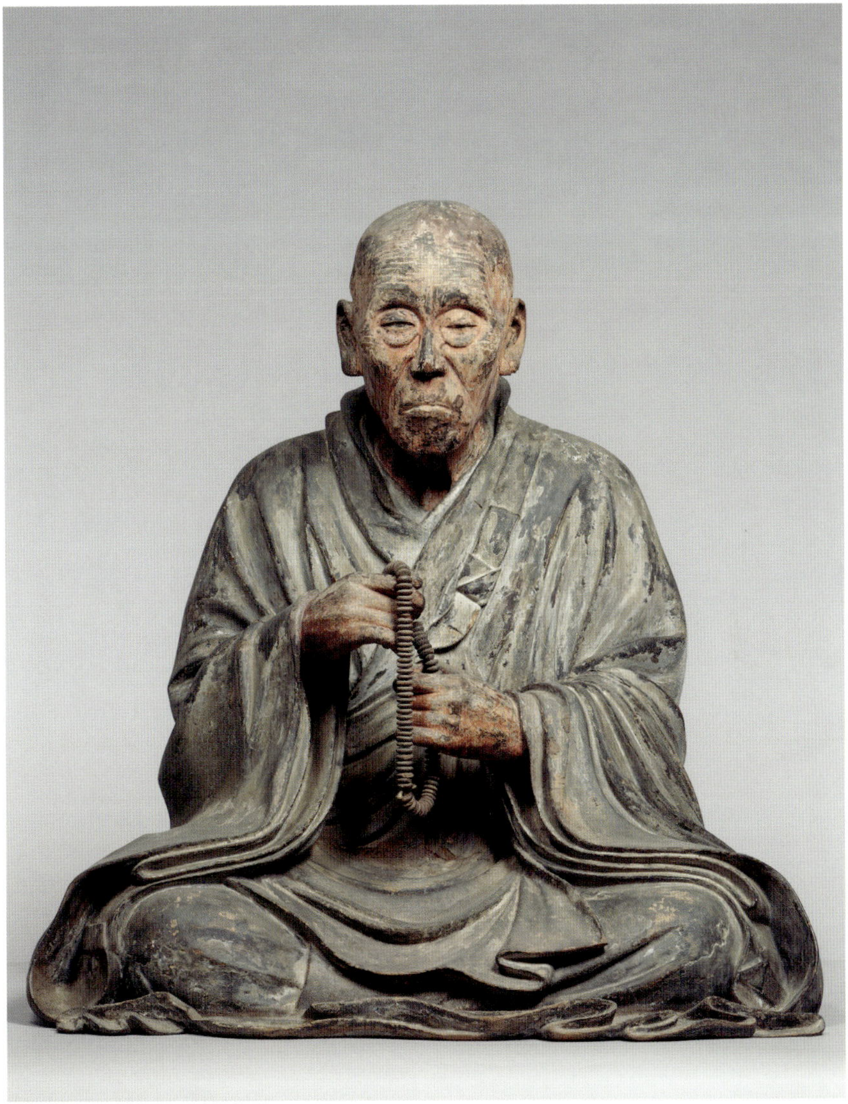

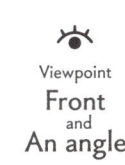

Viewpoint
Front
and
An angle

重源上人坐像
Seated Saint Chōgen

次に正面から見てみよう。

正面では安定した、正三角形に近い構図が見えてくる
だろう。空気をはらんだ袖口のふくらみが、短い膝張り
に広い幅を与えて、より安定感のある容姿の効果をも
たらしているのがわかる。

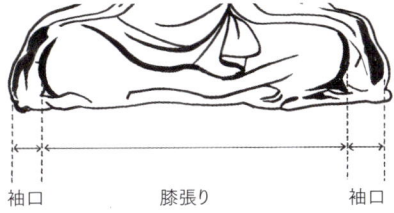

袖口　　　　　膝張り　　　　袖口

Let's next compare how the entire statue is seen head-on and how it looks from an angle.

Stable when seen straight-on from the front, you probably feel that its composition resembles a nearly perfect equilateral triangle. The puffy sleeves apparently inflated with air give a broader feel to the shortened thighs, producing an effect that enhances the feeling of stability.

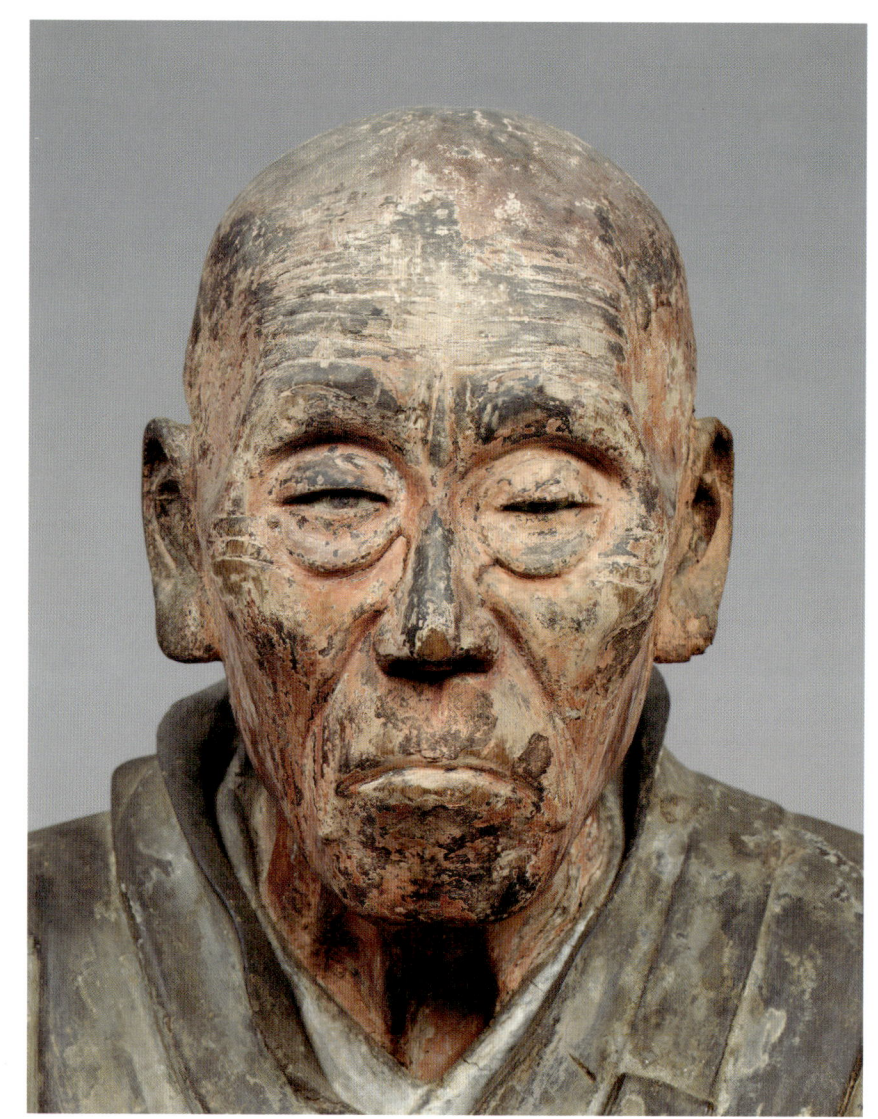

重源上人坐像
Seated Saint Chōgen

顔のアップを正面と斜めから対比してみよう。

眼窩が深くくぼみ、左右の眼の見開きが異なるのは正面からわかる。左眼の方が上瞼がかぶさり細い目であるが、眼光の鋭さは左右とも同じである。右眼の黒目は一点を見つめるようなまなざしである。

頬がこけ、顎の尖った骨格は、斜めの角度から見た方が印象的である。

筋ばった首筋と同様に、への字に固く結んだ口元は力が入る。このような顔つきは、彼の強靭な精神と不屈の意思が反映していると考えられよう。ここにみえる写実精神の高まりは、第4章で紹介する無著・世親像のそれに並ぶものである。

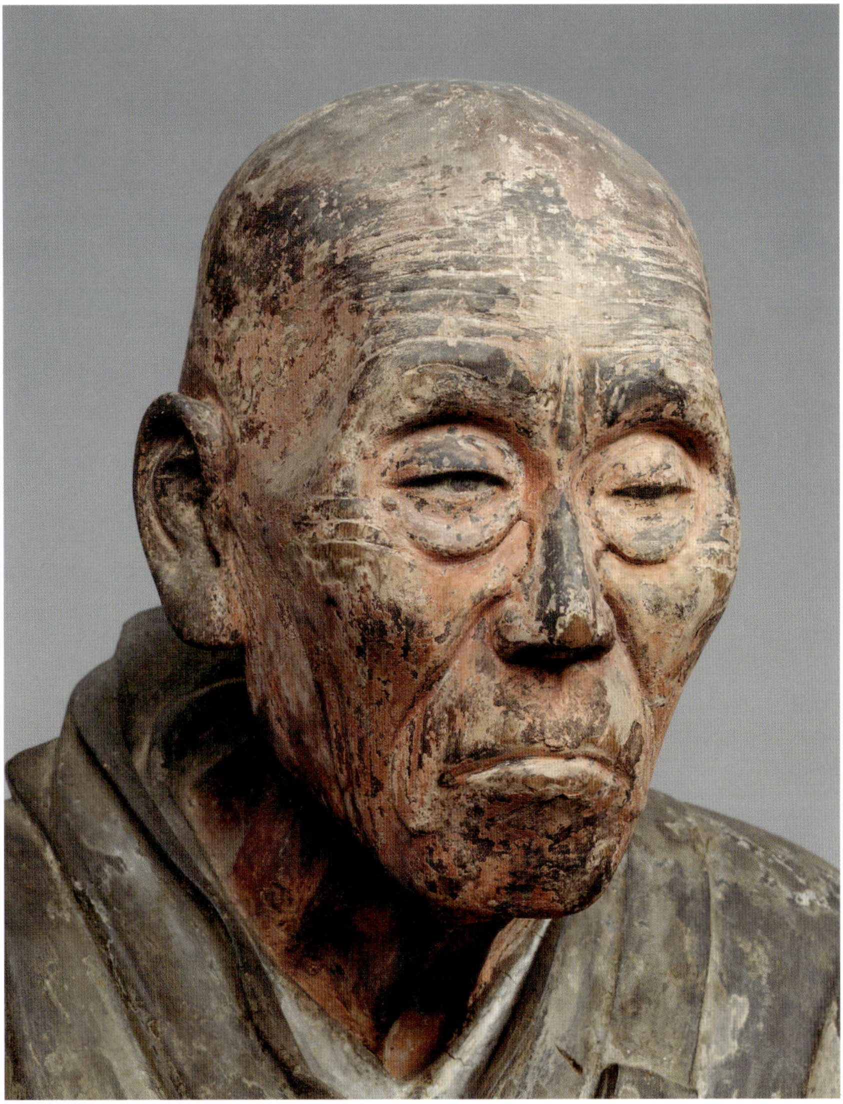

重源上人坐像
Seated Saint Chōgen

Let's compare close-ups of the face from head-on and from an angle.

It is clear from the front view that the eye sockets are deeply sunken and the degree to which the left and right eyes are open differs. The left squints and the upper lid droops, but the sharp glint is the same in both eyes. The gaze of the pupil of the right eye appears to be staring out at a point directly in front of him.

The hollow cheeks and the pointed bones of the jaw are striking when seen from an angle. As with the strained sinews of the neck, the inverted v-shape of the firmly closed mouth evoke his power. This kind of facial expression can be understood as reflecting Chōgen's tenacious spirit and indomitable will. The prominence of the spirit of realism seen here is equal to that seen in the Muchaku and Seshin statues addressed in chapter four.

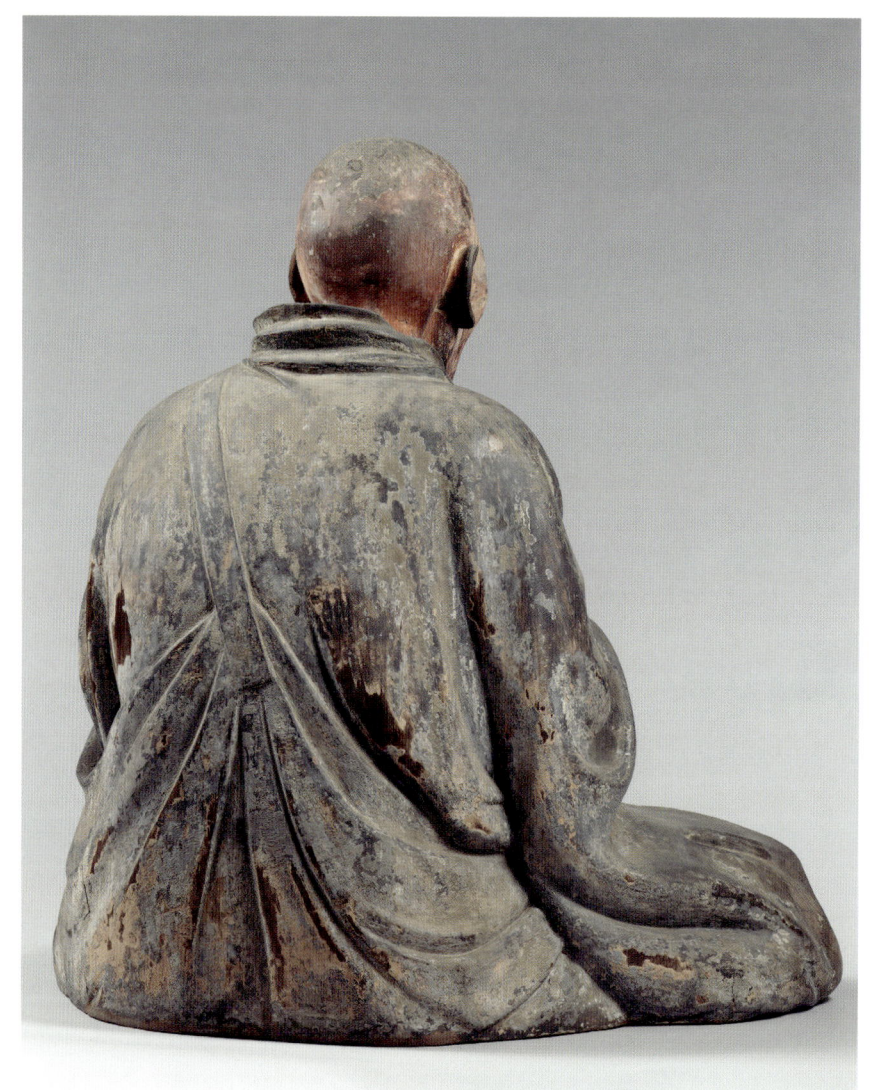

重源上人坐像
Seated Saint Chōgen

斜め後ろからの姿と背面とを対比してみよう。

正面から見ていた印象よりも意外に身体が大きく見えるのではないだろうか。晩年の重源上人として、法衣の下の痩せた老身の姿をこれまで想像してきた。一体、この深い体奥にみる豊かな量感と、痩せた老体のイメージとのあいだには、どのような関係性が考えられるだろうか。

この背中の豊かな張りを見るとき、彫刻としての充実感を失わないようにした観念的な造形と捉えることができるかもしれない。深読みするなら、彼の気丈夫な性格、すなわち彼の存在感を高める理想化した表現といえようか。

なお袈裟は、背中の中央あたりで通常よりも吊り紐が長く伸びて、ずり下がっている。観念的な造形のなかにあらわされたこの「現実感」が、重源像本来の表現である。

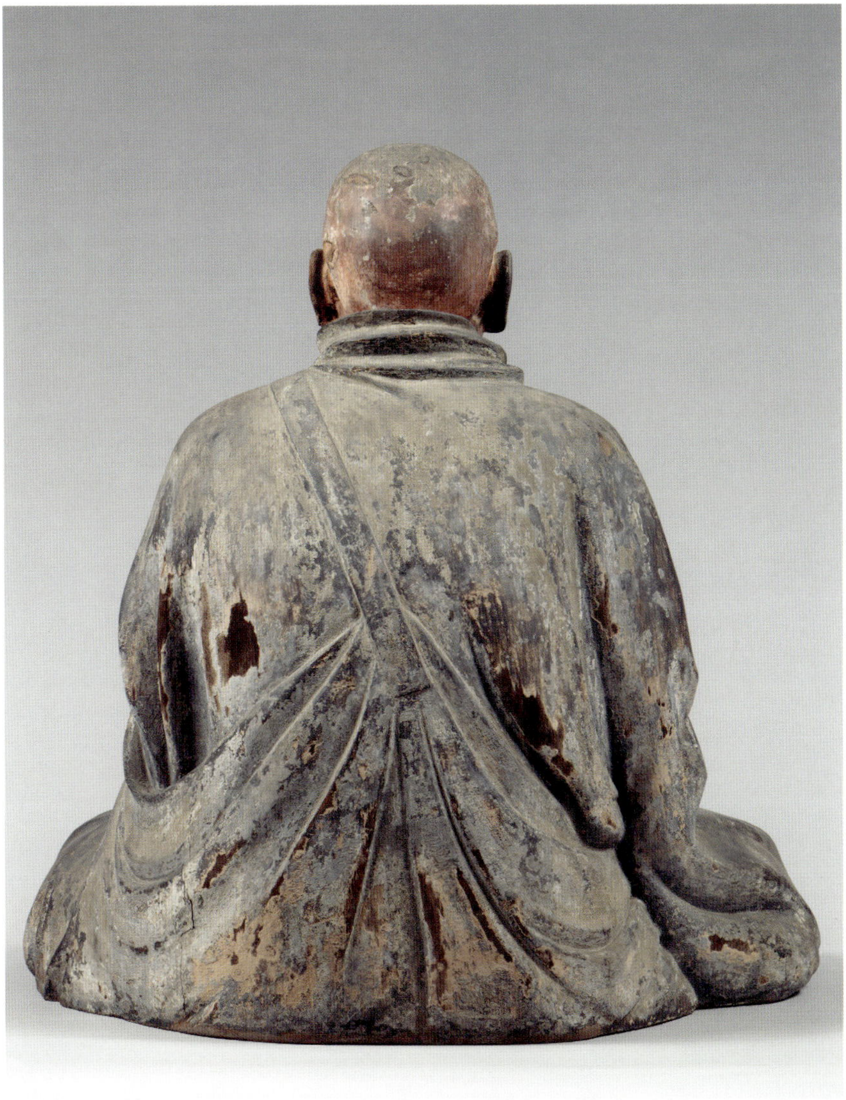

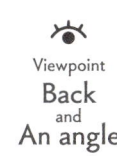

Viewpoint
Back
and
An angle

重源上人坐像
Seated Saint Chōgen

Let's compare views of the statue from the back and at an angle.

Why are we surprised to find that the body appears larger than when view from the front? Up to this point, we have pictured the emaciated, aged figure of Chōgen Shōnin under his priestly robes in the last years of his life. What is the relationship between the sense of volume seen here with its profound depth and the body of the emaciated old man that we have imagined?

When you see the strong tension in the back, you may be able to grasp a feel for a conception of sculptural form that attempts to preclude any loss of the sense of the work as a fully realized sculpture. If we delve more deeply, we surely see Chōgen's firm character, or in other words, an idealized representation that enhances his presence.

As for his surplice, the strap that would normally hang from the center of the back and extend downward, has sagged. The sense of realism inherent in conceptual sculptural form is the authentic expression of the Chōgen statue.

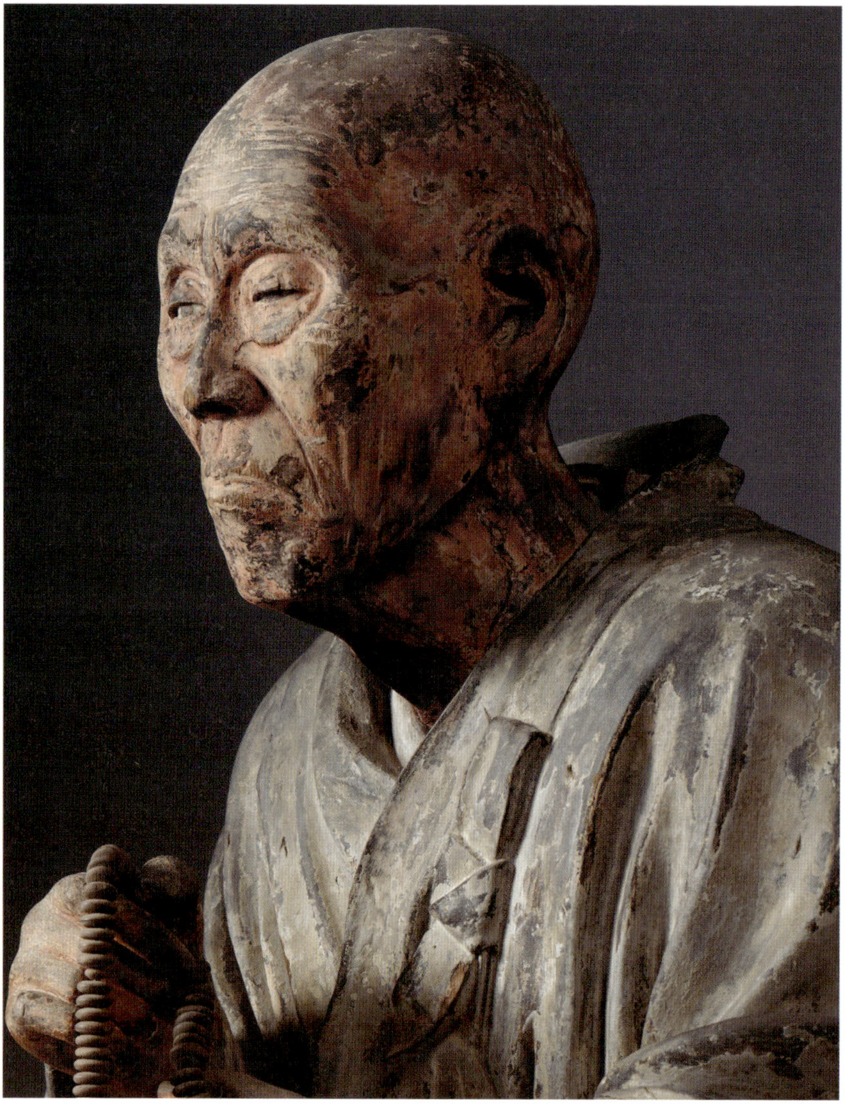

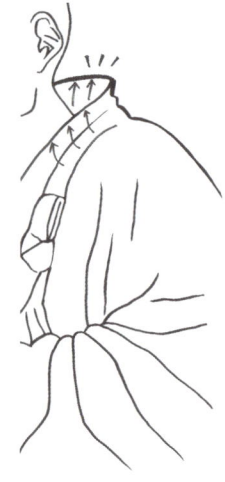

重源上人坐像
Seated Saint Chōgen

上半身を左右斜めの角度から比べてみる。

頸まわりの襟の表現が違っていることに気づく。法衣の襟は、
頸まわりを広く開け、左側は大きくたわみ、張りがある。
一方で、右側の襟は撚れて潰れている。この対照は、彼の複
雑な性格を示す象徴表現のように見える。

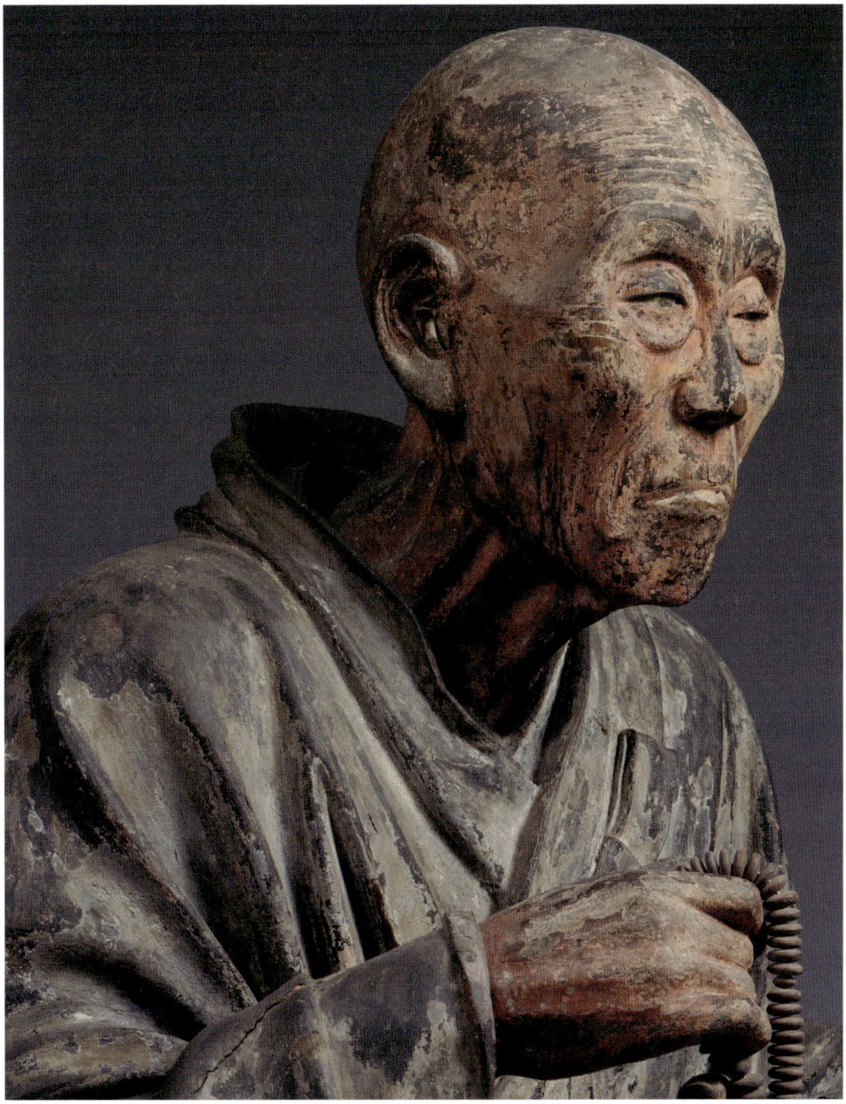

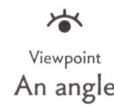

重源上人坐像
Seated Saint Chōgen

Comparing the upper body from left and right angles.

You'll notice that there is a difference in the way the collar is represented. The collar of his monk's robe is opened loosely around his neck, but on the left side it curves widely though it is still stiff.

On the other hand, the collar on the right side is twisted and limp. This contrast can be seen as a symbolic representation of Chōgen's complex character.

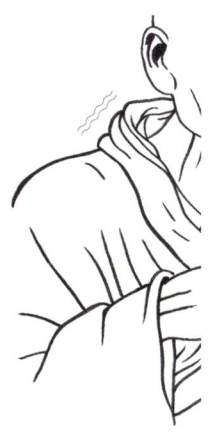

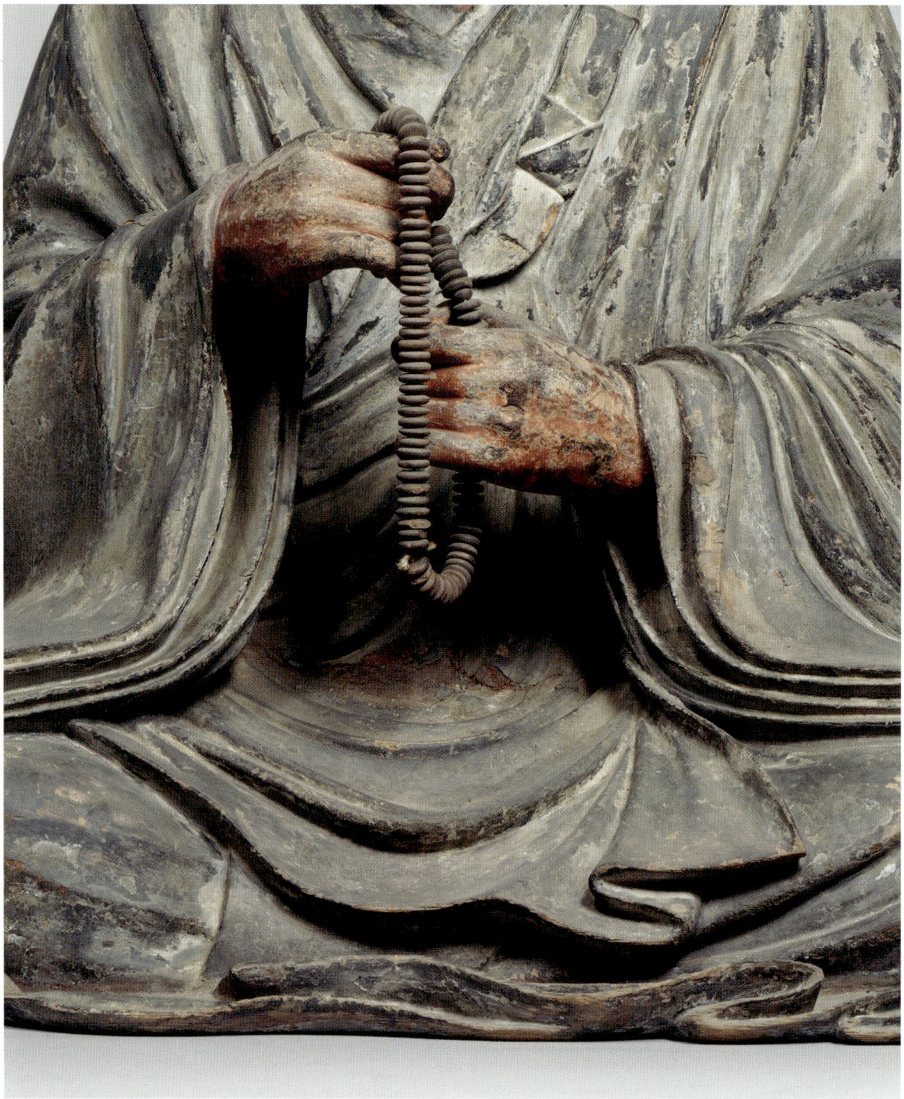

重源上人坐像
Seated Saint Chōgen

袈裟と吊り紐の質感の違いに注目しよう。

膝前にかかる袈裟の皺は凹面をつくって、大きくたるむ。
その布の縁が、右手の袖口と同じように厚い布地かと錯
覚するほど分厚くなっている。
吊り紐の帯は、左右に２筋のくぼみがあり、縁がめくれ、
くたくたになった古裂の感じである。まさに現実直視の写
実精神によって、袈裟と吊り紐の質感の違いが対比される。

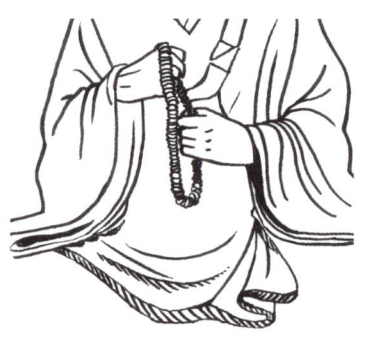

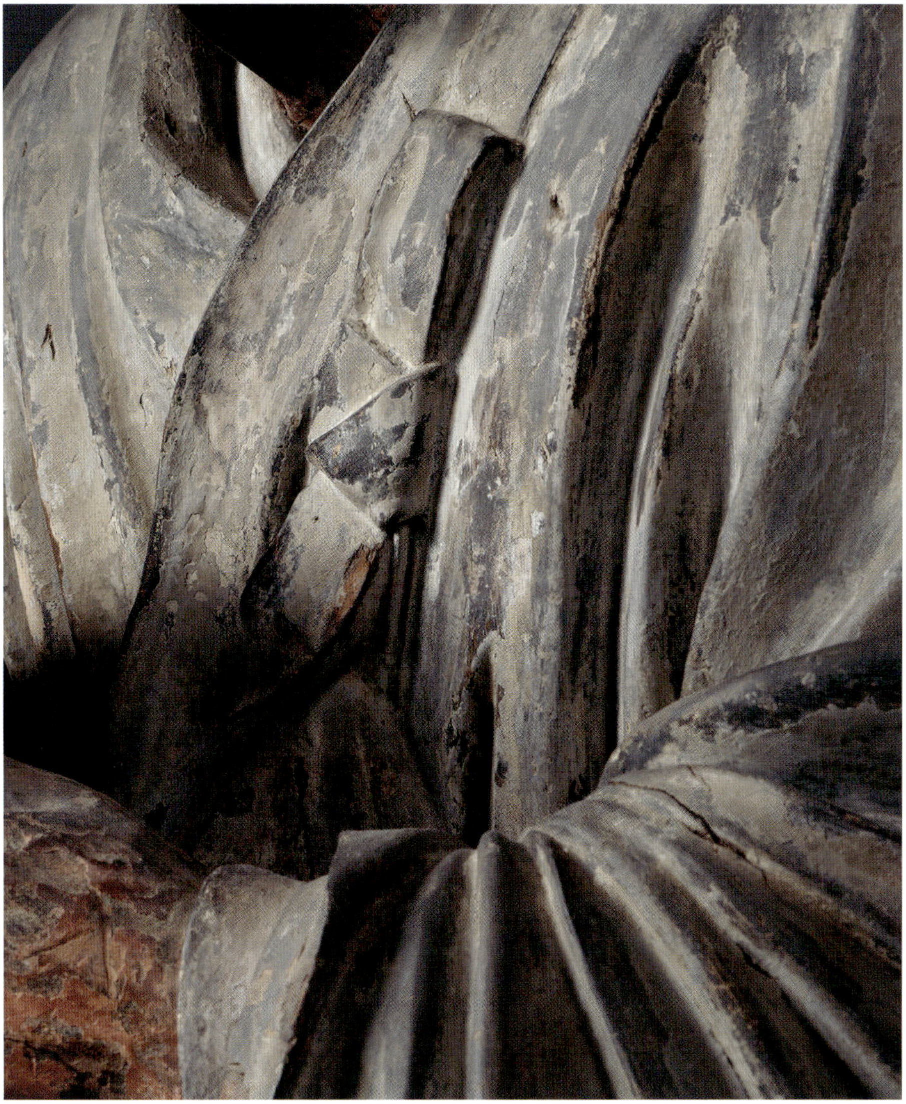

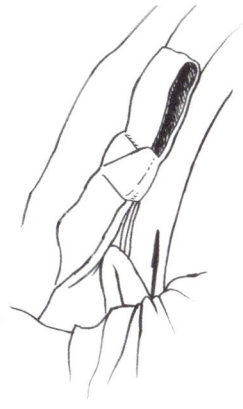

重源上人坐像
Seated Saint Chōgen

Let's view the differences in the feel of surplice and hanging sash.

The folds and creases of the surplice draped over the knees are concave and quite slack. The hems of the cloth are thick enough to give the mistaken impression that they are thick fabric just as is the case with the opening of the right sleeve.

The hanging sash has the feel of an old worn rag with turned up edges and two indented lines on right and left. The contrast seen in the difference between the feel of the surplice and of the hanging sash is a result of the spirit of realism based on actual observation.

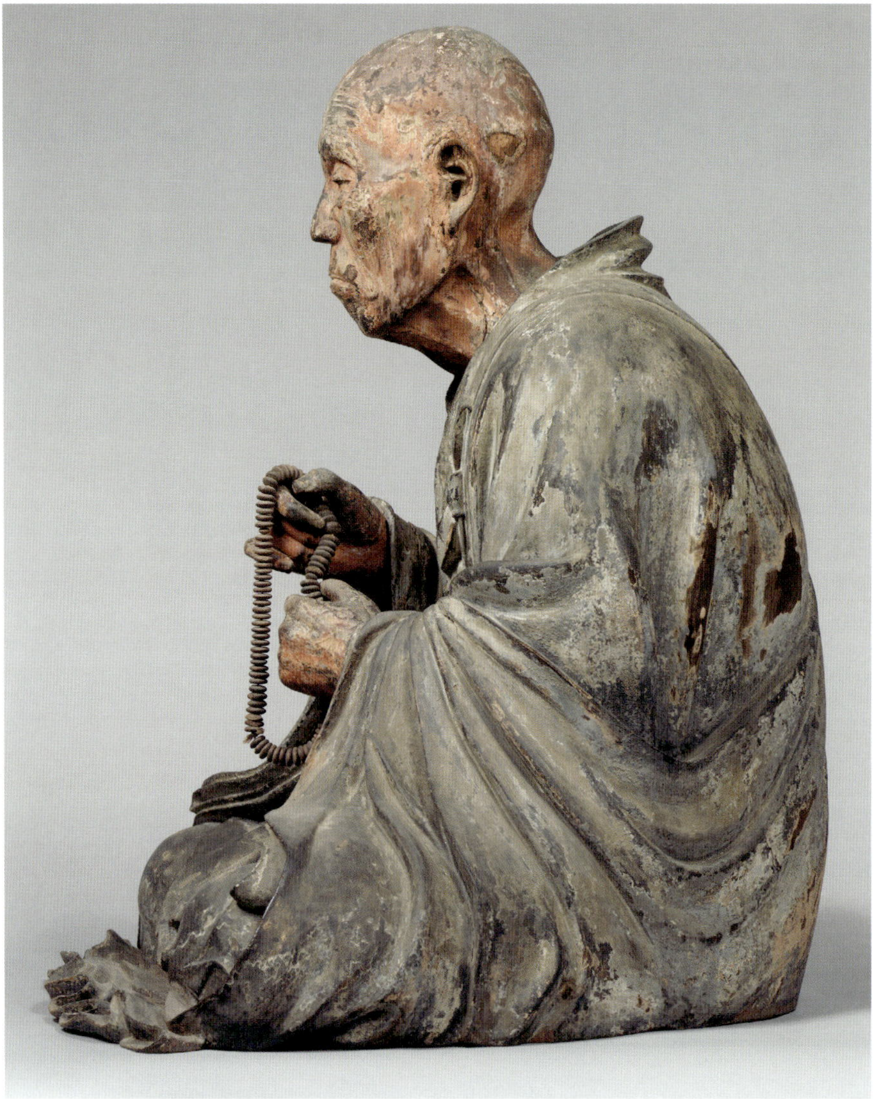

重源上人坐像
Seated Saint Chōgen

左右の側面を比べてみると、
衣文線の扱いに違いが見えてくる。

左側面では、衣のだぶつきが目立つ。肩から下に走る2つの
折れ皺は、肘の上で角度を変え、強いたるみと折れをつくる。
右側面では皺が深く大ぶりで、強ばった感じにたわむ。皺の
陰影が、毛筆の筆腹で引いた強い筆線に似た勢いがある。

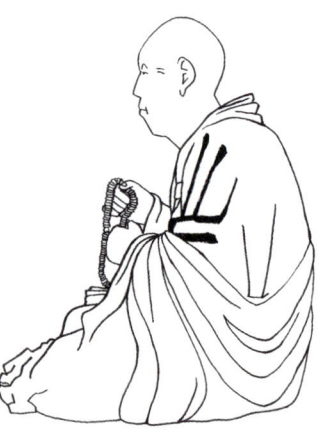

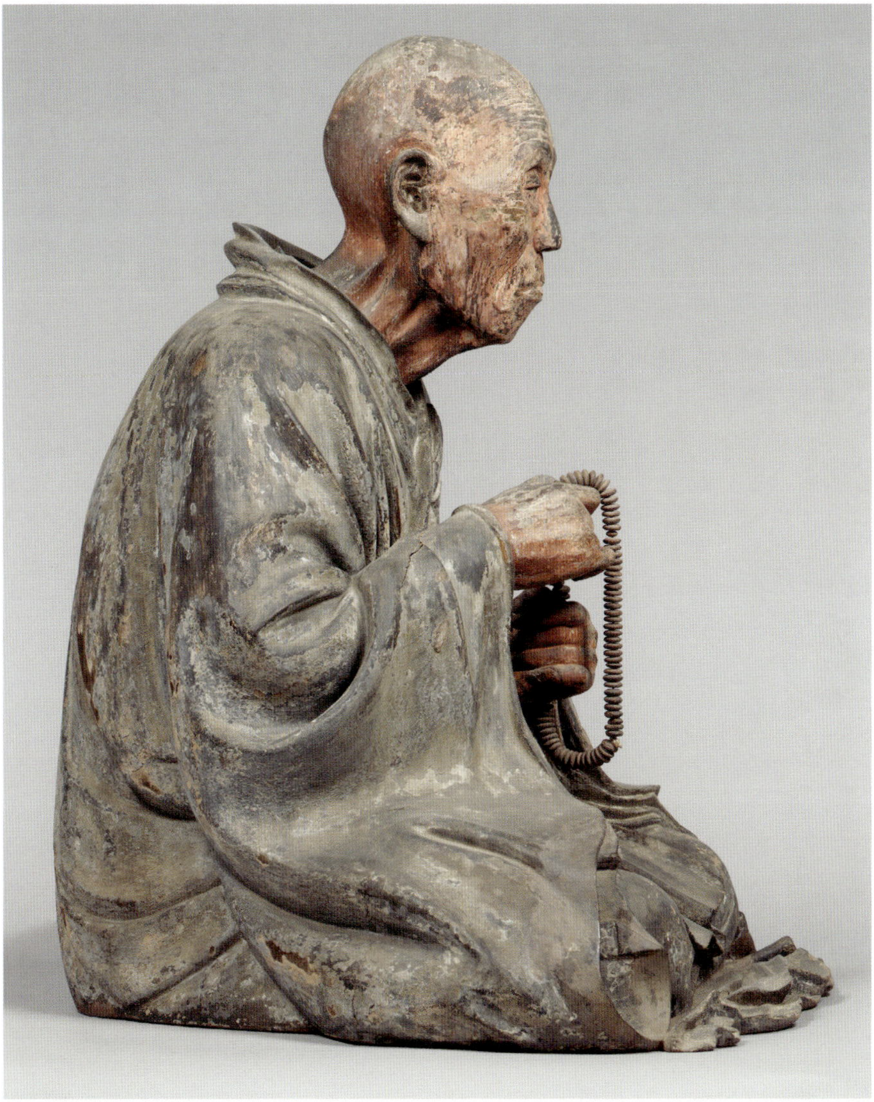

Viewpoint
Detail

重源上人坐像
Seated Saint Chōgen

When we compare the left and right sides, we see a difference in the treatment in the patterns of the drapery folds.

On the left, the bagginess of the robe is conspicuous. The two creases that run downward from the shoulder change direction above the elbow, increasing the slack and creating more creases.

On the right, the creases are deep and wide and bend with a stiff feel. The shadows of the creases have dynamism similar to powerful brush strokes created using the side of a writing brush rather than the tip.

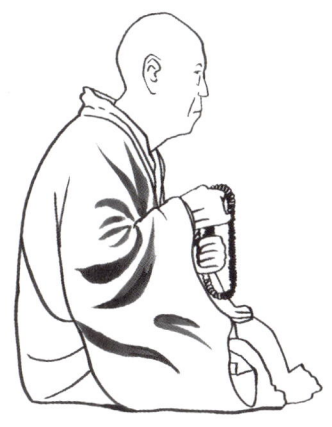

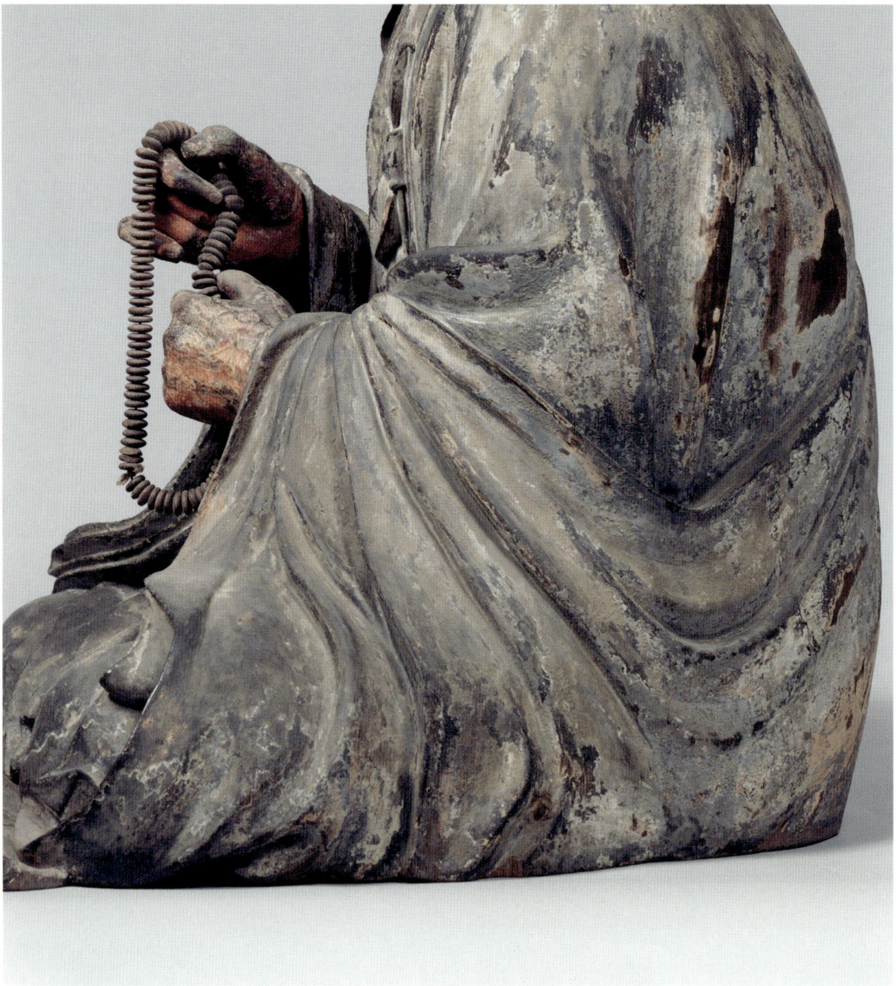

重源上人坐像
Seated Saint Chōgen

もっと寄ってみよう。

左腕にかかる袈裟は、ひじ下でV字形の皺をつくる。ずり落ちた袈裟を腕に引き寄せ、だぶついた法衣を上から締める所作のように見える。この動きを、彼の気力のいまだ衰えぬ精神の緊張の持続と見れば、そのような性格の持ち主は、周囲の人々にも細やかな心づかいをする人であったかと推測する。

右袖は厚地の布という感じで、随所に空気をはらみ、皺のうねりが強い。右腕で袖先をはらう所作のように見える。この皺のうねりが復興事業の重圧を象徴し、その所作が重圧に押し潰されぬ気性からなされたと見れば、それは意志の強い心根を象徴するかのようでもある。重源像にこめられた複雑な心理を、法衣の皺の対比から読みとくのは、まさに作者の創造力に触れるところだろう。

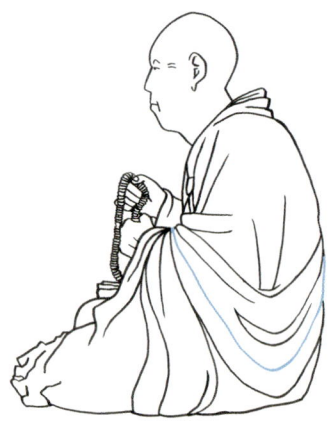

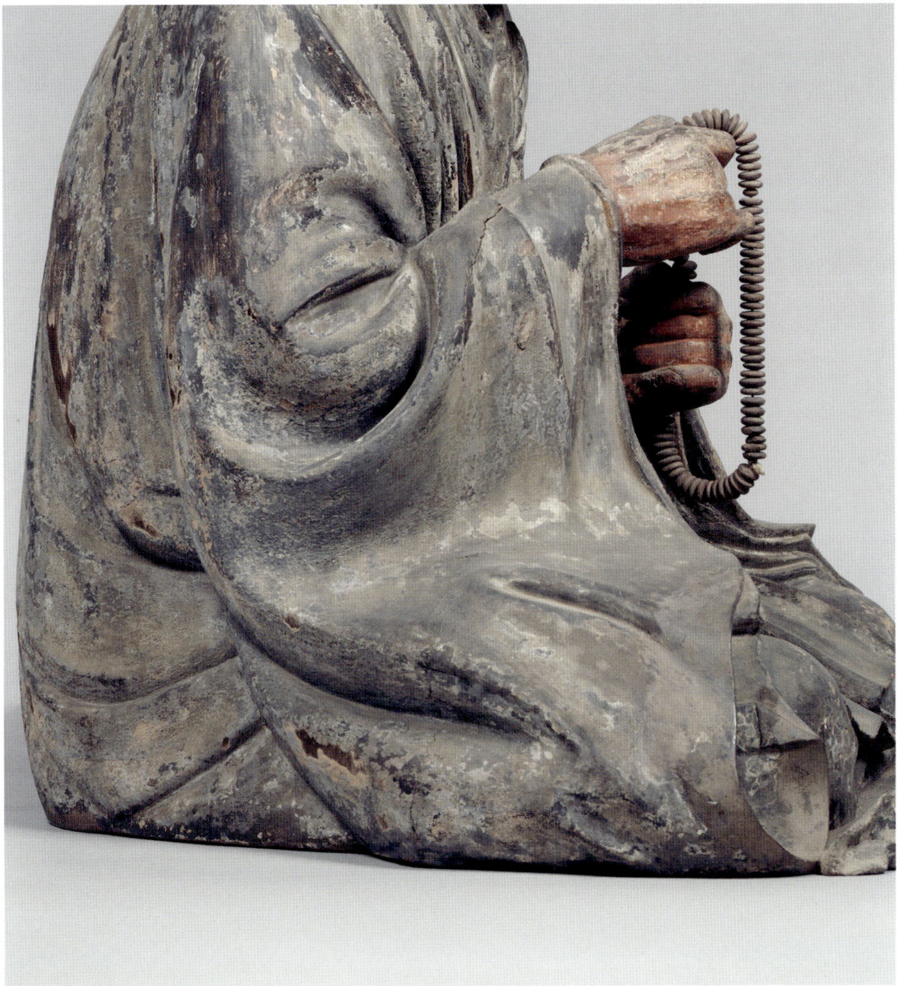

重源上人坐像
Seated Saint Chōgen

Let's take a closer look.

The surplice draped over the left arm forms a v-shaped creases below the left elbow. The sagging cloth is being pulled tight by the arm that appears to be making a gesture to lessen the slack of the inner robe. If we see this movement as the persistence of the spiritual tension inherent in Chōgen's unflagging vitality, and consider his character, we can imagine someone sensitive to the feelings of those around him.

The right sleeve has the feel of thick fabric, puffy with powerfully undulating creases. The right arm appears to be gesturing to shake free of the sleeve. The undulations in the folds of the robe symbolize the stresses of the reconstruction project. If we see the act of flicking back the hem of the sleeve as stemming from the great vitality that refused to be crushed by such pressures, this seems symbolic of the strong will of his basic character.

Interpreting the complex psychology of the Chōgen statue by comparing the creases in the monk's robe surely means coming in touch with the creativity of the sculptor.

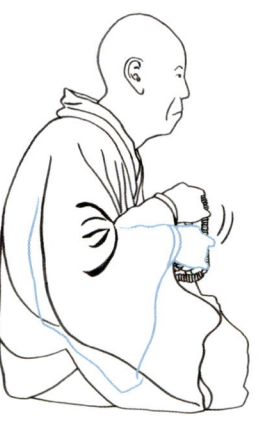

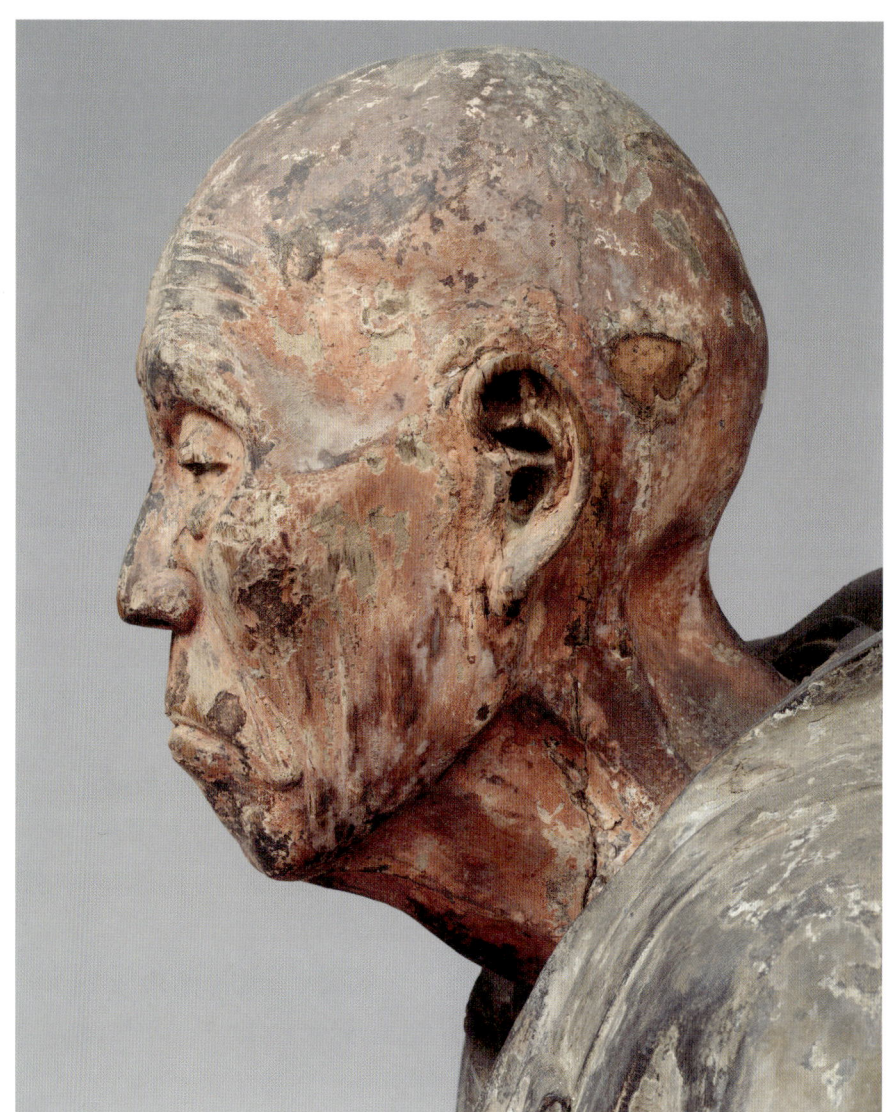

重源上人坐像
Seated Saint Chōgen

心情を対比の視点から読みとく

重源上人は年老いたとはいえ、20年余りにわたる東大寺復興の目標達成のために払われた強靭なエネルギーと不屈の精神力に対して、周囲の人々は畏敬の念を抱いて本像の造立を願ったのは疑いないだろう。

頑固一徹の老人の強い意志をあらわす感情表現と、周囲の人々に対する細やかな心づかいが働いた心情表現とのあいだで、重源像の作者はどちらに心惹かれたのだろうか。ここでも作者の創造力の琴線に触れる思いがする。

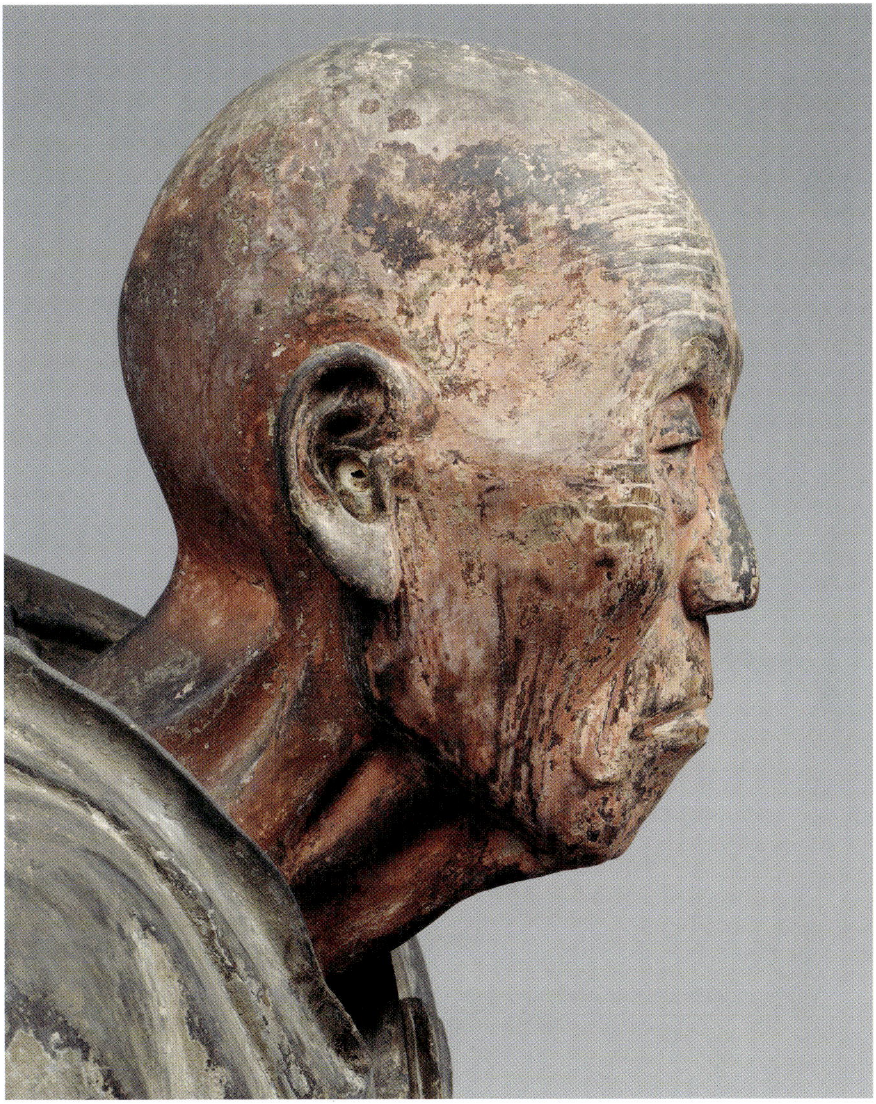

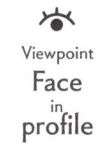

重源上人坐像
Seated Saint Chōgen

Let's interpret the statue from the standpoint of contrasting emotions

Although we have described Chōgen Shōnin as aged, it is undoubtedly the case that his associates who sponsored this statue held him in awe, admiring the boundless energy and indomitable spirit that he exercised for more than twenty years in attaining his goal of reviving Tōdaiji.

Which side of his personality was the sculptor who created the Chōgen statue drawn to? Did he wish to represent the will of a stubborn old man or express the feelings of a sensitive man considerate of those around him? I feel that with this question we come in touch with the wellsprings of the sculptor's creativity.

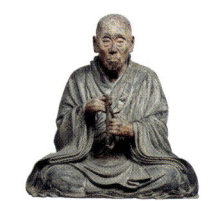

寄木造（檜）	Assembled-block construction (*hinoki*)
彩色	Colors
像高81.8cm	Height 81.8 cm
鎌倉時代13c.	Kamakura period 13th century
東大寺	Tōdaiji

国宝 重源上人像
東大寺俊乗堂所在

National Treasure *Seated Shōnin Chōgen*
Shunjōdō at Tōdaiji

重源像にみる作者の鋭い観察眼
The sharp, discerning eye of the sculptor as seen in the Chōgen statue

1. 現実直視の写実的表現
眼窩が窪み頬のこけた、痩せた老貌。背を丸め、顎を前に出した老身の姿勢。
だぶついた法衣の着こなし。古裂を思わす袈裟の吊り紐。

2. 存在感を増す観念的表現
袖口を膨らませて膝の張りを広くみせる正面観。
痩せた老体のイメージを覆う、厚みのある体奥。

3. 強い精神性の表現
鋭いまなざしや固く結んだ口元などの表情。
東大寺復興の意志を貫いた強靭な精神と不屈の意思の反映。

対比の表現
- 張りのある左襟とよじれた右襟の対比の妙。
- だぶついた法衣の左側を、左腕にかかる袈裟で引きしめる所作と、うねりの強い大きな皺が集まる法衣の右袖先を右腕ではらうかのような所作。

1. The realistic expression of direct observation of the physical world
The sunken eyes and hollow cheeks of an emaciated, aged man / the posture of an elderly person with a slightly hunched back and protruding jaw / wearing ill-fitting, baggy robes / the hanging sash of the surplice reminiscent of a scrap of old clothing.

2. The conceptual expression that enhances the presence of the statue
The frontal view that shows puffy sleeves and widely spread knees / the depth of the figure that conceals the image of the emaciated and aged body.

3. The strong spiritual expression
The facial expression featuring a sharp gaze and firmly clenched mouth / a reflection of the indomitable will in carrying out the revival of Tōdaiji.

Contrasting Representations
- The taut stiffness of the left collar vs. the twisted right collar.
- The action of pulling the surplice tightly over the left arm on left side of the baggy monk's robe vs. the act of flicking away the hem of the right sleeve on the right side of the monk's robe where strongly undulating creases are concentrated.

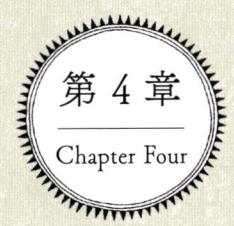

対比で気づく運慶の構想力

国宝 無著菩薩立像 世親菩薩立像 興福寺北円堂所在

次に対比してみる仏像のコンセプトの典型として、興福寺北円堂の無著・世親像を見てみよう。これら2つの像が細部の表現にいたるまで、それぞれ「対比の関係」で構想されていることに気づくだろう。

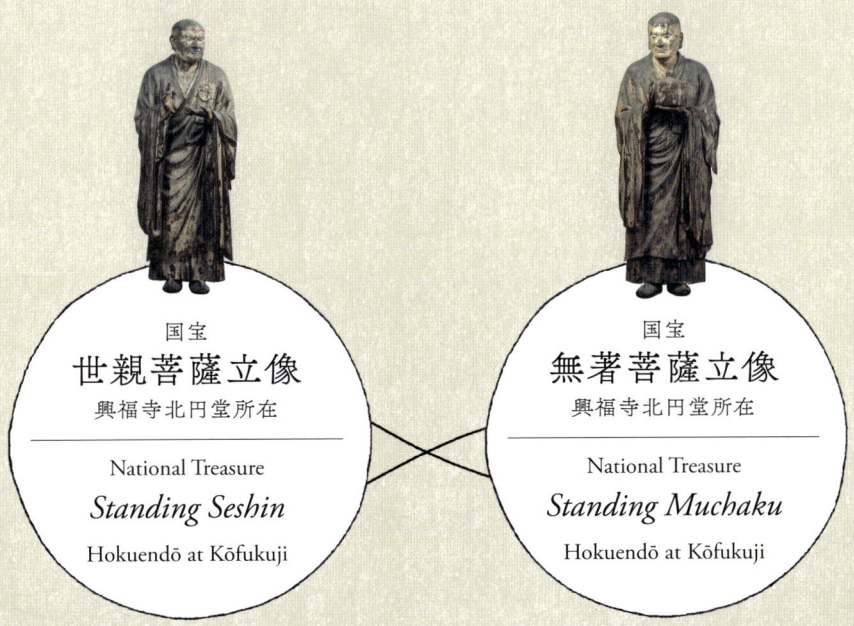

国宝
世親菩薩立像
興福寺北円堂所在

National Treasure
Standing Seshin
Hokuendō at Kōfukuji

国宝
無著菩薩立像
興福寺北円堂所在

National Treasure
Standing Muchaku
Hokuendō at Kōfukuji

The conceptual power of the Buddhist sculptor Unkei as seen through visual comparison

The National Treasures *Standing Muchaku* and *Standing Seshin* statues, Hokuendō at Kōfukuji

Next, let's make a visual comparison of the statues of Muchaku (or Mujaku) and Seshin in the Hokuendō hall at Kōfukuji. These statues serve as classic examples embodying the conception of Buddhist sculpture. This will help you realize that these two statues were conceived to be contrasting down to the smallest detail of their sculptural representation.

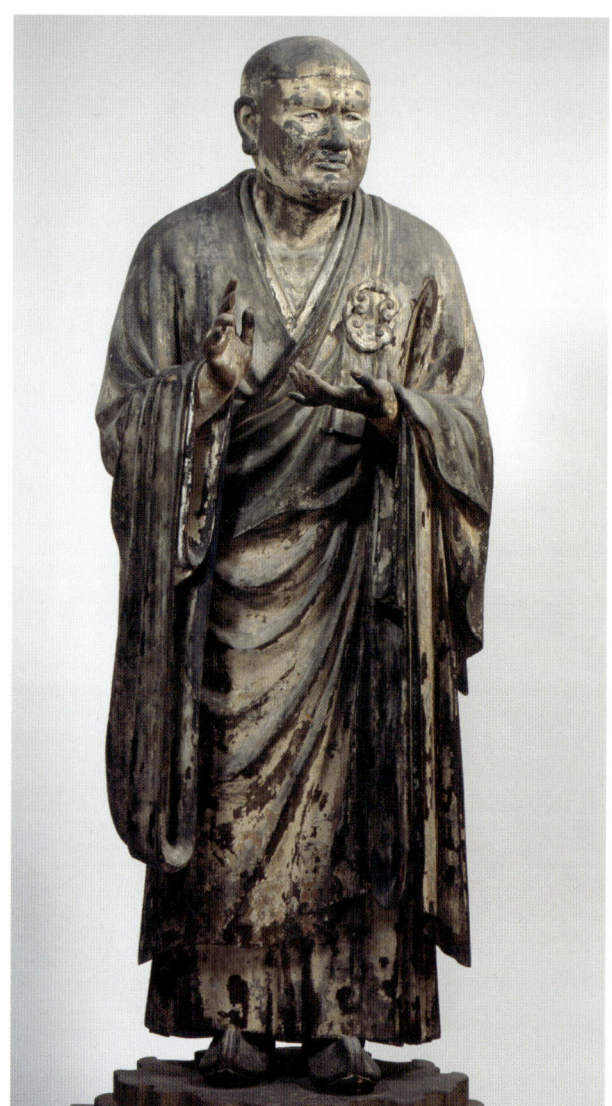

正面
から見る

国宝 世親菩薩立像（興福寺北円堂所在）
National Treasure *Standing Seshin* (Hokuendō at Kōfukuji)

無著と世親

無著（右）と世親（左）は古代インド（4〜5c.）の仏教哲学者で、弥勒如来の説いたとされる
唯識思想について兄の無著は教理的な基礎を築き、弟の世親が組織大成したといわれる。

世親像は、顔を左に向けて遠く前の方を見つめる。肩や胸の肉取りが充実し、がっちりとした身体
つきである。

無著像は右に顔を向け、顎を引いて視線を下に落とす。肩の肉が落ちて、胸板は平板で、法衣
の下には痩せた老体が想像される。

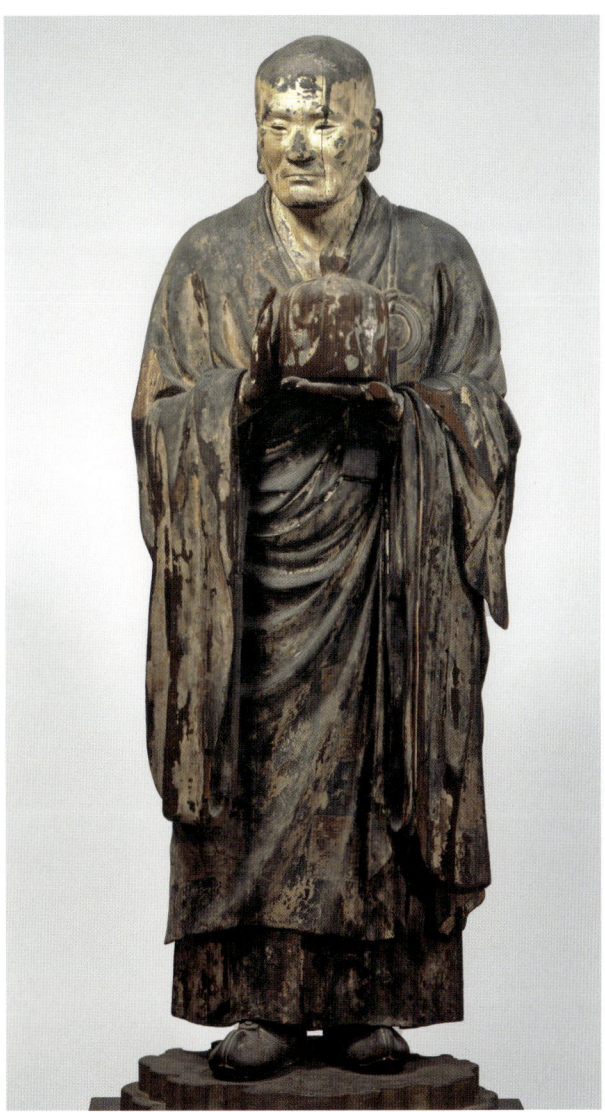

Viewpoint
Front

国宝 無著菩薩立像（興福寺北円堂所在）
National Treasure *Standing Muchaku* (Hokuendō at Kōfukuji)

Muchaku and Seshin

Muchaku (on the right), whose name is Asaṅga in Sanskrit, and Seshin (on the left), who was called Vasubandu, were ancient Indian philosophers who lived during the 4th-5th centuries. Muchaku, who was Seshin's elder brother, established the doctrinal foundation of the faith, and Seshin perfected Consciousness–only thought which is said to have been propounded by Miroku nyorai (the Buddha Maitreya). Seshin turns his face to the left and stares off into the distance before him. The flesh of his shoulders and chest are full and his body is hard and solid.

Muchaku turns his head to the right, draws in his chin and casts his eyes downward. The flesh of his shoulders slumps and his chest is flat. One can imagine the aged, emaciated body beneath the monk's robe.

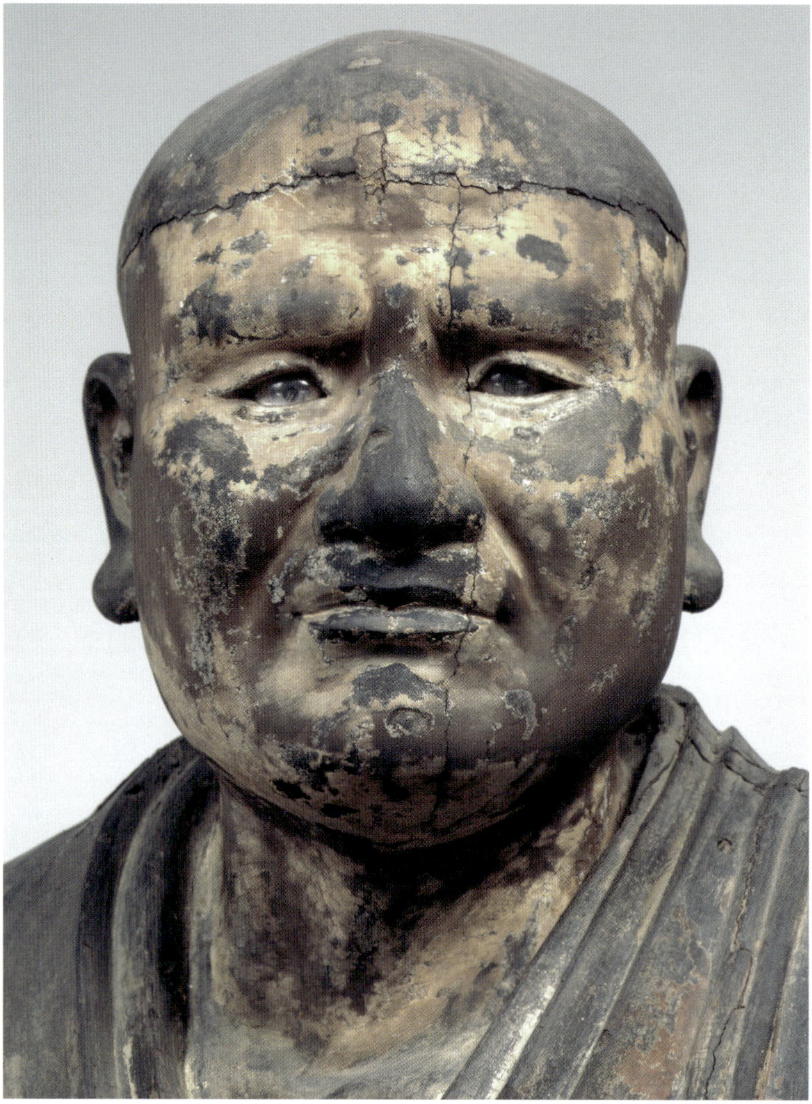

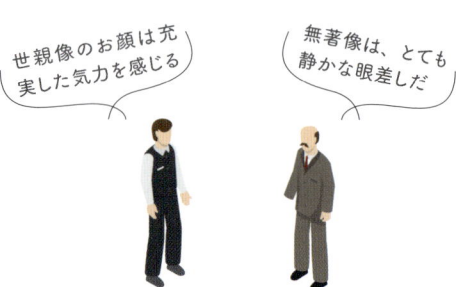

世親菩薩立像
Standing Seshin

老と壮の顔つき

無著は老貌、世親はより若い顔つきで、
世親は額の上方が特に突き出ている。と
もに頬骨が出て、落ち込んだ瞼の奥に、
玉眼製のうるんだ眼があり、眼光が鋭い。

世親像のお顔は充
実した気力を感じる

無著像は、とても
静かな眼差しだ

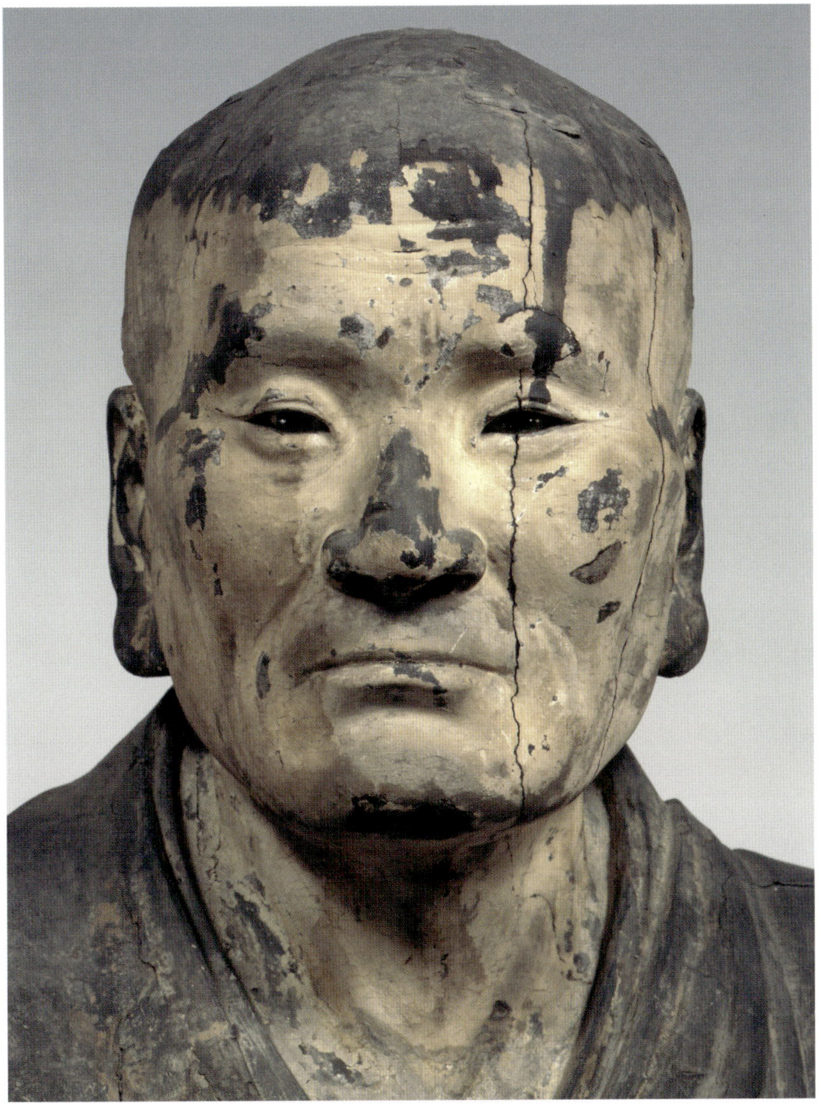

無著菩薩立像
Standing Muchaku

Aged and youthful faces

Muchaku has an aged face while Seshin has a younger-looking countenance and his forehead protrudes conspicuously. Both have prominent cheekbones and project a penetrating light from the depths of their gleaming sunken eyes, which are made of crystal.

無著菩薩立像
Standing Muchaku

無著の表情

無著は頰がこけ、鼻先が尖り気味で、小鼻や上唇の肉厚が薄い。口元の深い皺、顎の薄い肉取りの引き締まりなど、年齢を積み重ねた思慮深さと慎ましさが感じられ、気概を内に込めた表情である。

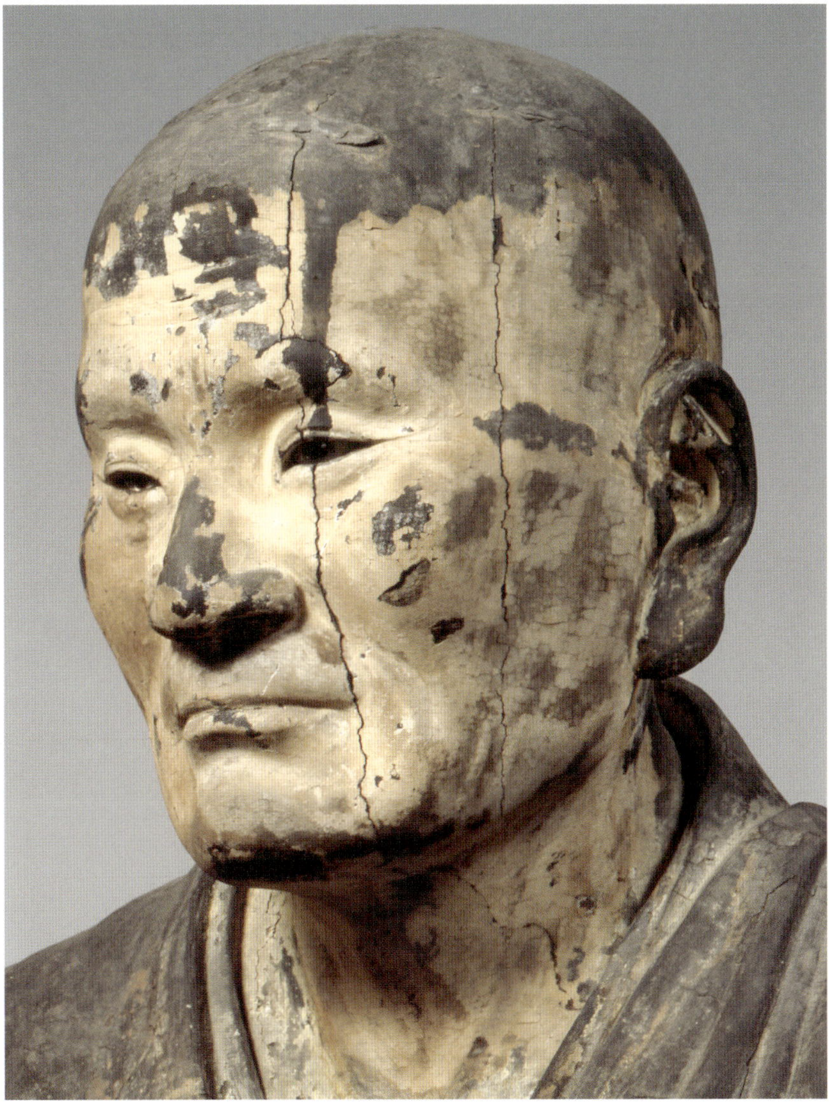

無著菩薩立像
Standing Muchaku

Muchaku's facial expression

Muchaku's cheeks are hollow, the tip of his nose is drawn to a point and the flesh of the nostrils and upper lip are thin. The deep wrinkles around the mouth and the strained thin flesh of the jaw evoke a sense of the depth of his thought as well as his humble reserve mirrored in a facial expression that embodies his strong spirit.

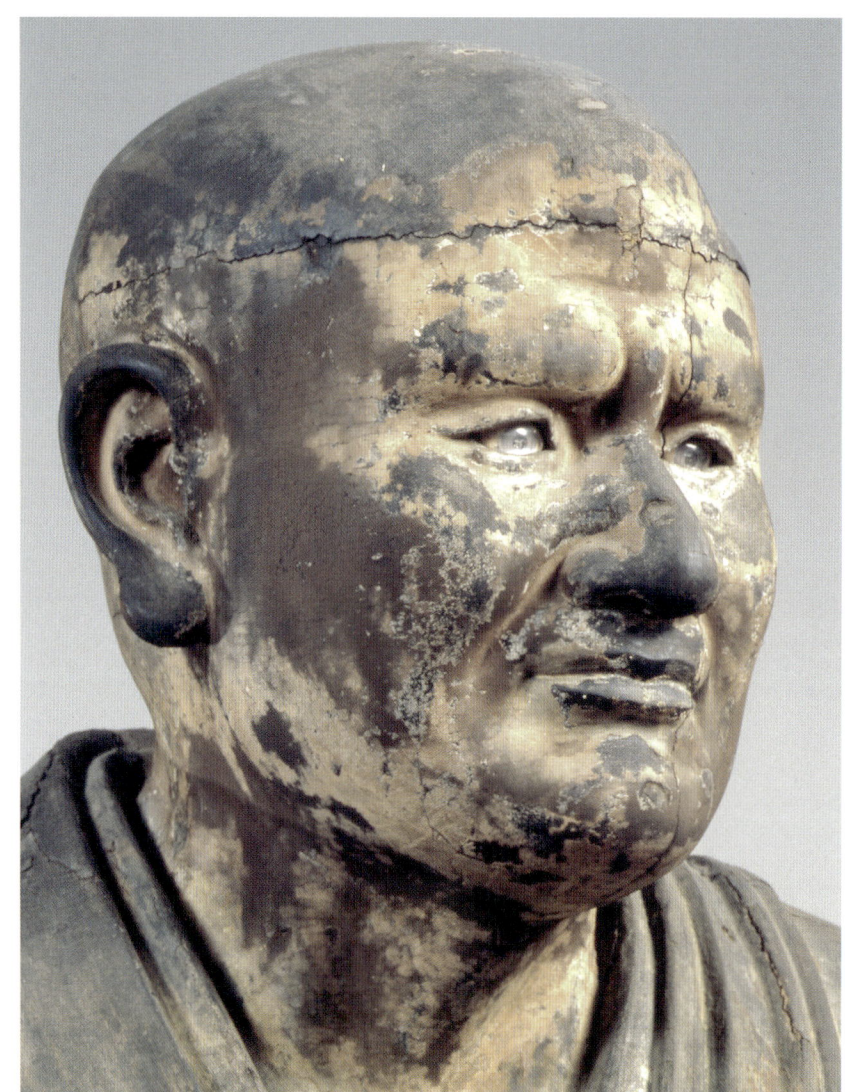

世親菩薩立像
Standing Seshin

世親の表情

世親は、頬の肉取りが充実し、太い眉をひそめ、鼻りょうが太く鼻先が丸くて大きい。唇の縁どり
が明瞭で、力がこもった口の結び方である。壮年期の健康的で、充足感に満ちた、活力ある気
丈夫な顔つきである。

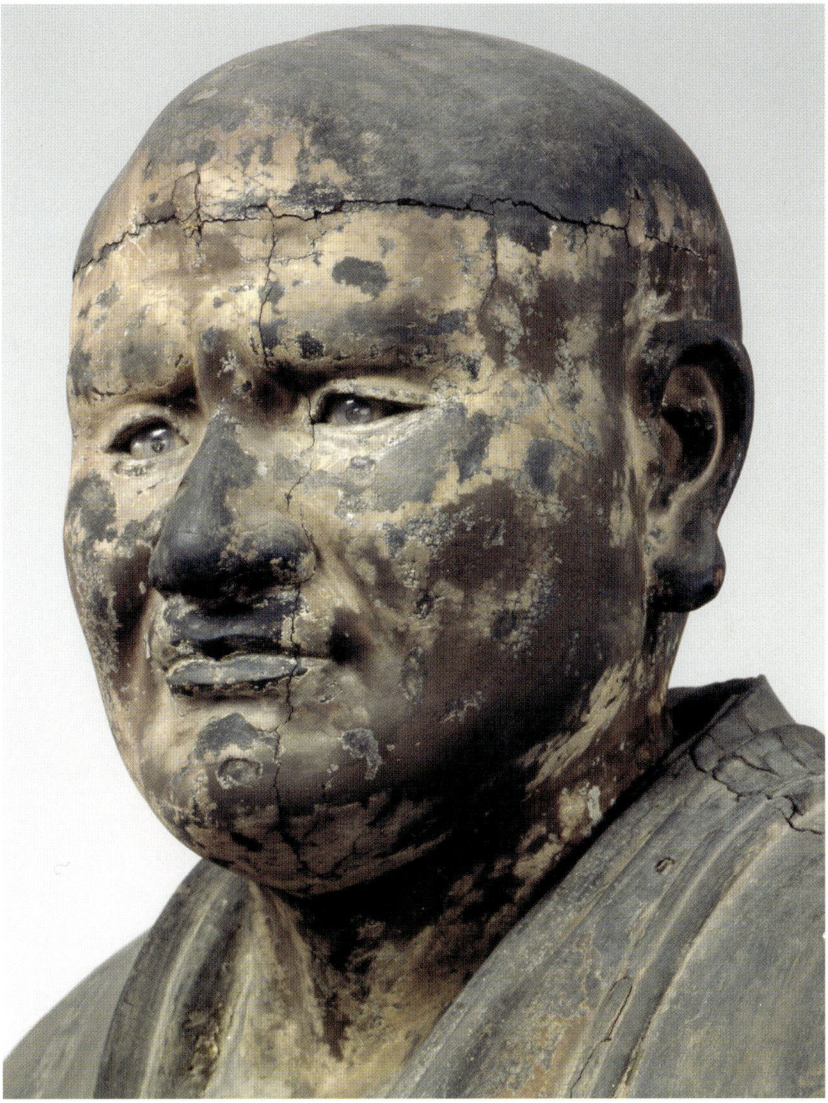

世親菩薩立像
Standing Seshin

Seshin's facial expression

Seshin has full, fleshy cheeks, his thick brows are knitted, and the bridge of his nose is thick and the tip is rounded. The edges of his lips are crisply delineated and the mouth firmly sealed. The face radiates youthful vigor, demonstrating a lively strong-spirited character.

Viewpoint
Face

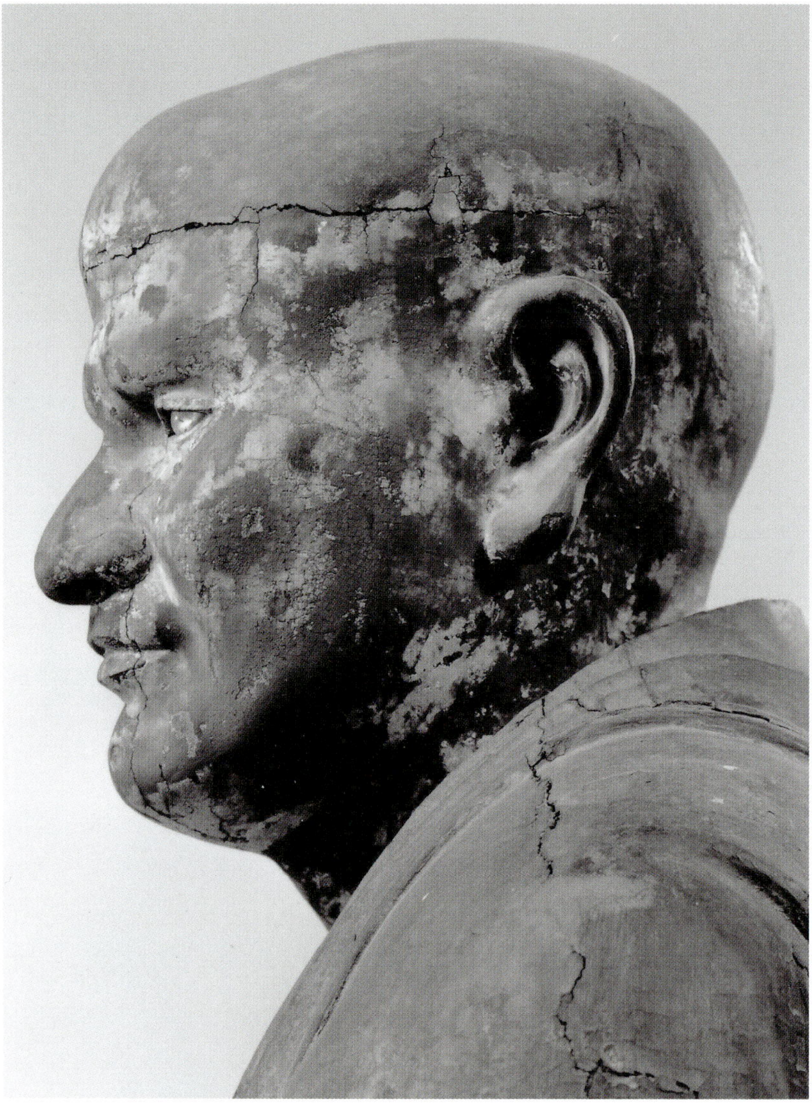

世親菩薩立像
Standing Seshin

耳のちがい

耳のかたちは年齢差を示す表現ではないが、無著の
耳輪や耳朶は薄く、世親のそれは厚い肉取りであり、
相互に対比される関係にある。

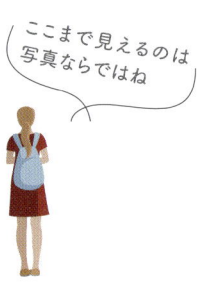

ここまで見えるのは
写真ならではね

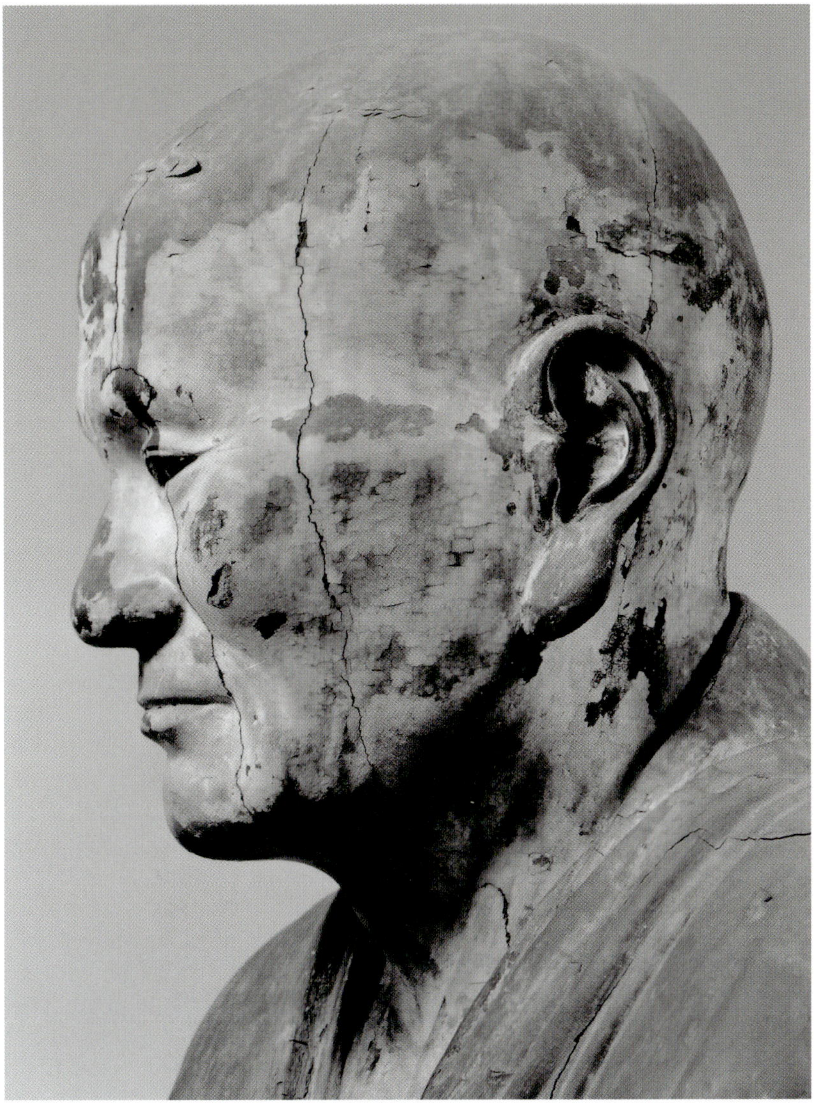

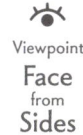

無著菩薩立像
Standing Muchaku

Differences in the ears

The shape of their ears does not give any indication of the gap in their ages, but as the helix and lobe of Muchaku's ears are thin and those of Seshin are thick and fleshy, they are contrasting.

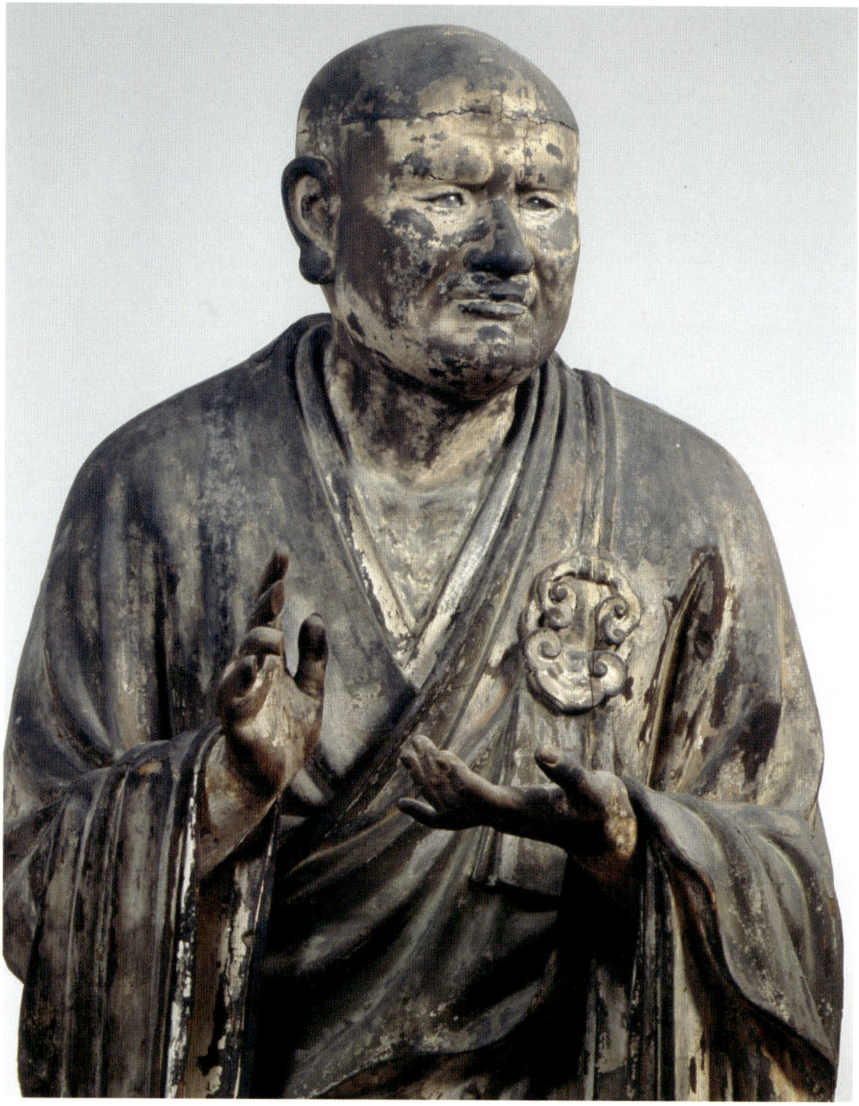

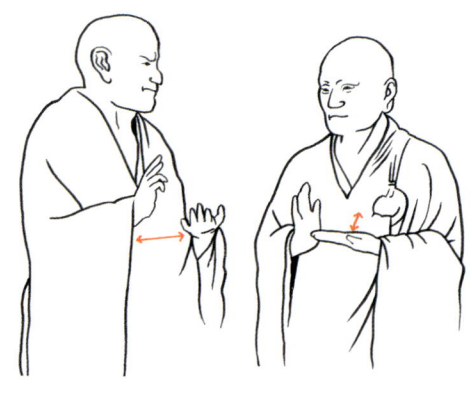

世親菩薩立像
Standing Seshin

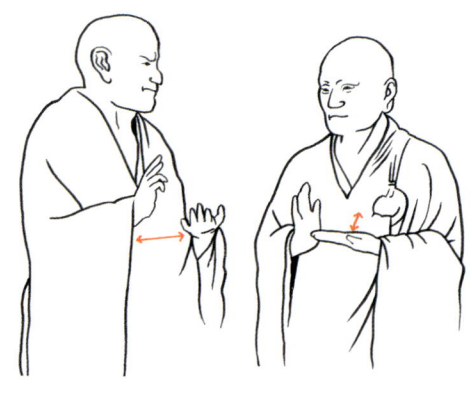

手を見る

持物のささげ方

気力が充実した世親は、小さな持物（現状欠失）を、軽く指をまげた掌の上に載せる。軽そうな持物を前に突き出して余裕で持つといった感じである。老齢の無著は、指をまっすぐ伸ばして大きな包みを掌に載せる。重そうな包みを胸に引き寄せて一所懸命、大切に持つといった感じである。

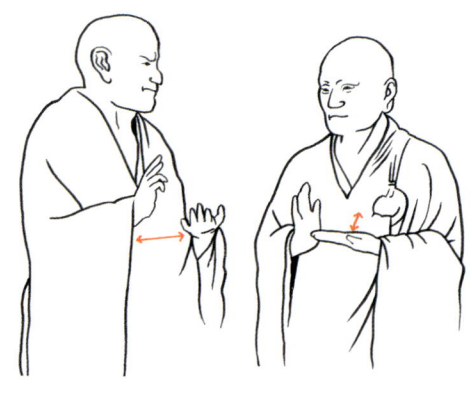

98

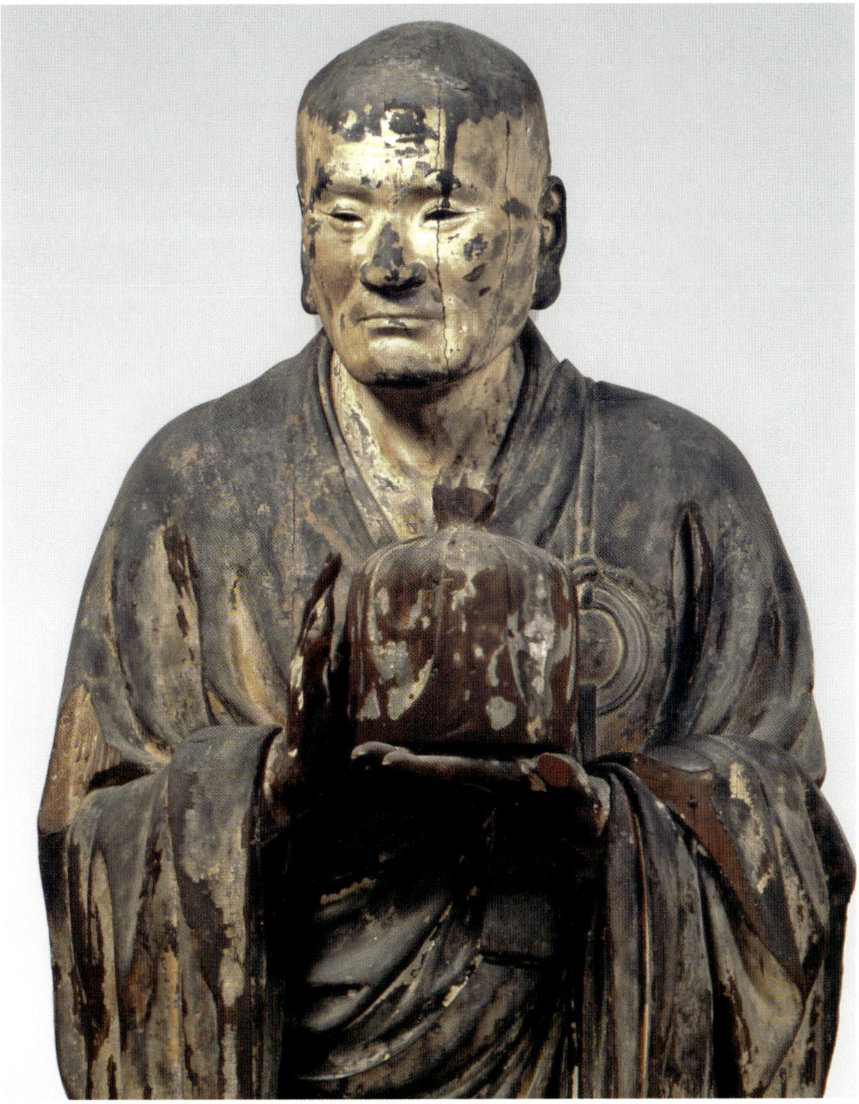

Viewpoint
Hands

無著菩薩立像
Standing Muchaku

How the offerings are made

The vigorous Seshin once held a small object (now lost) lightly on the palm of his hand with upturned fingers. One senses that he is presenting this light object forward with great ease.

The aged Muchaku stretches his fingers outward holding a wrapped object on the palm of one hand. He strains mightily to draw the bundle to his chest, giving us the feeling that he is holding something precious.

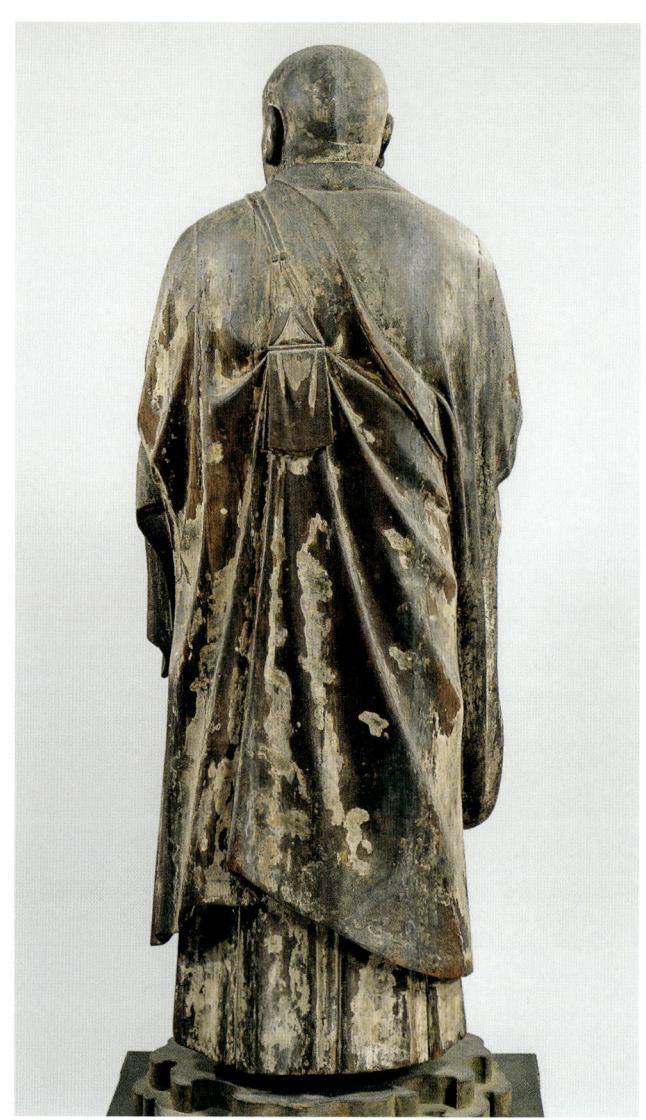

世親菩薩立像
Standing Seshin

背中の表情

背面では無著の袈裟は皺数が多く、複雑に乱れている。痩せた小柄な身体に対して、だぶつき気味の布皺である。世親のそれは皺数が少なく、間隔も開いて整いがある。大柄な身体に対して、布がピンと張った布皺である。

背面
から見る

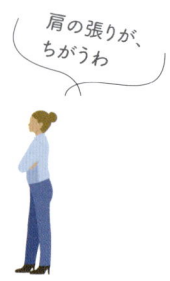

肩の張りが、ちがうわ

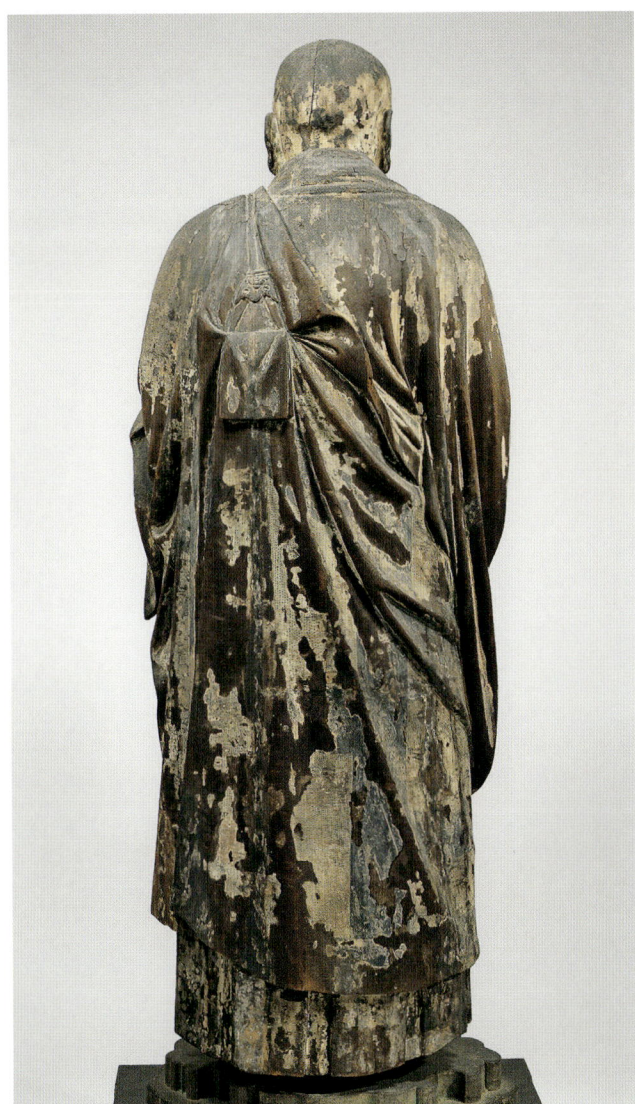

無著菩薩立像
Standing Muchaku

The representation of the back

Muchaku's surplice (*kesa*) has many wrinkles and creases that are complex and disordered. The baggy, loose-fitting and heavily creased cloth contrasts with his emaciated small frame. The number of creases in Seshin's surplice is fewer, and the distance between them is wider and more orderly. In contrast to his large frame, the creases in the fabric are pulled taut.

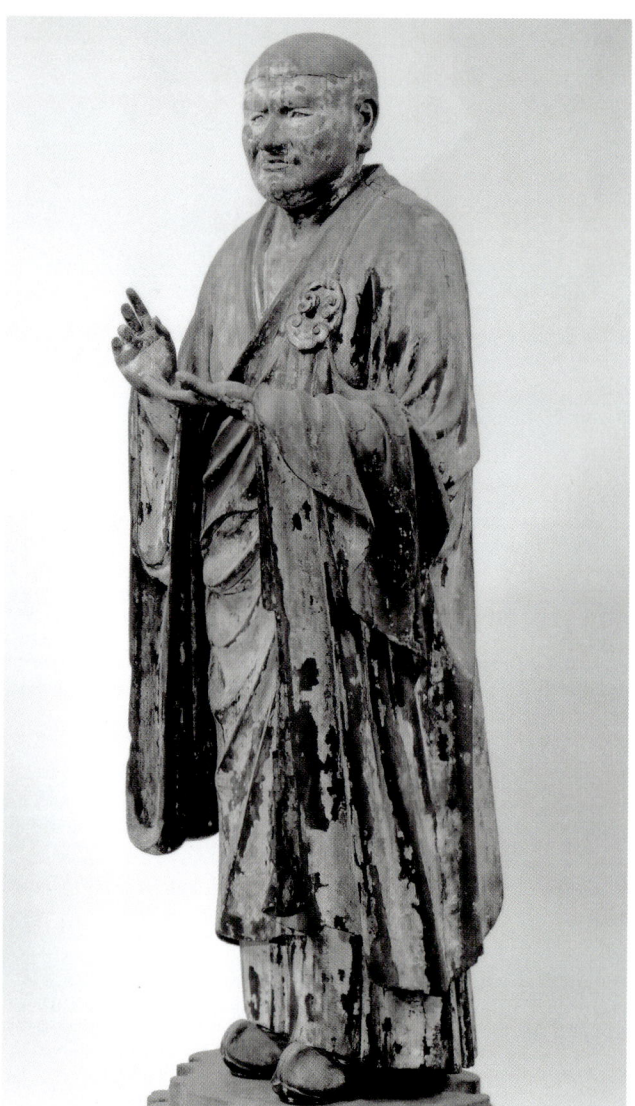

世親菩薩立像
Standing Seshin

袖口のちがい

無著の袖口は、開きが小さく萎んだ風に見え、よじれて力なく垂れる。世親のそれは開きが大きく、力強くまっすぐに垂れる。まさに対照的な袖口の表現である。

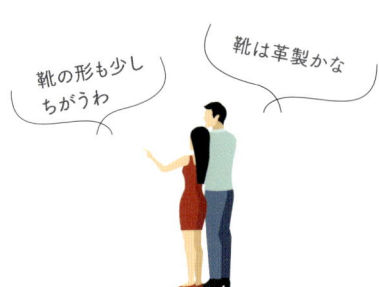

靴の形も少しちがうわ

靴は革製かな

102

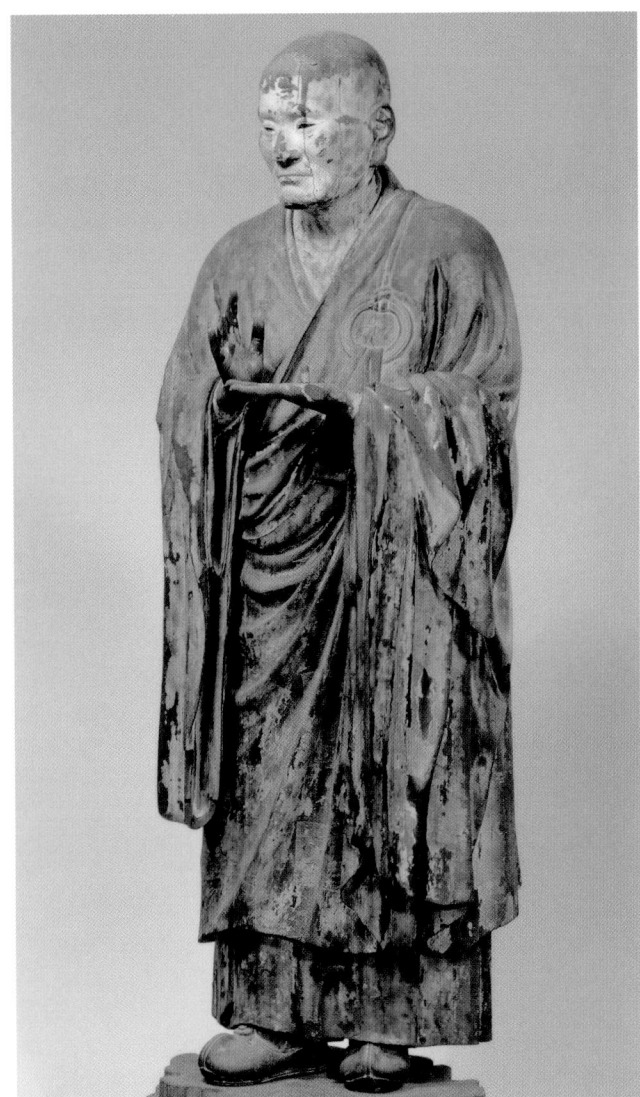

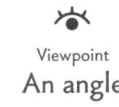

Viewpoint
An angle

無著菩薩立像
Standing Muchaku

Differences in the openings of the sleeves

The openings of Muchaku's sleeves are narrow and seem wilted, twisted and drooping listlessly. Seshin's are opened wide and hang straight down powerfully. The representations of the sleeve openings is truly contrasting.

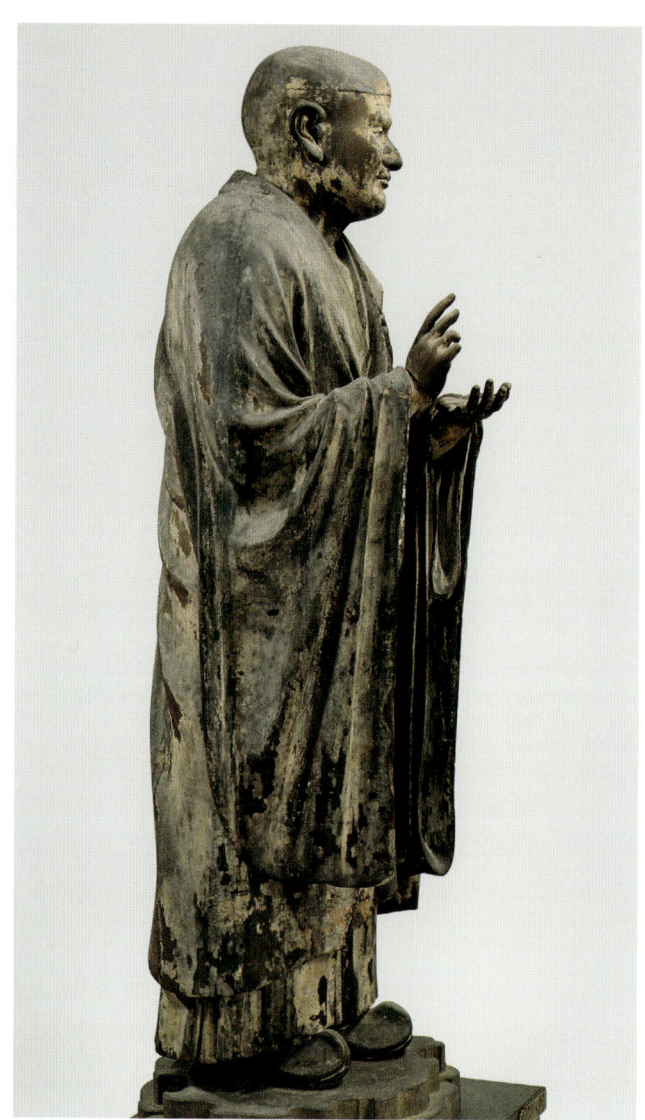

側面
から見る

世親菩薩立像
Standing Seshin

袖の質感

右側面から見ると、衣文のちがいもよくわかる。
無著の袖は、くたくたに萎えて着古したような質感の布であり、
皺もよじれた曲線をつくる。世親のそれはパリッとした厚地風の新
品の布に似ており、衣文が太く、かつストレートに流れ、彫り口
も深く大振りである。

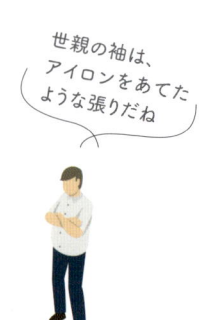

世親の袖は、
アイロンをあてた
ような張りだね

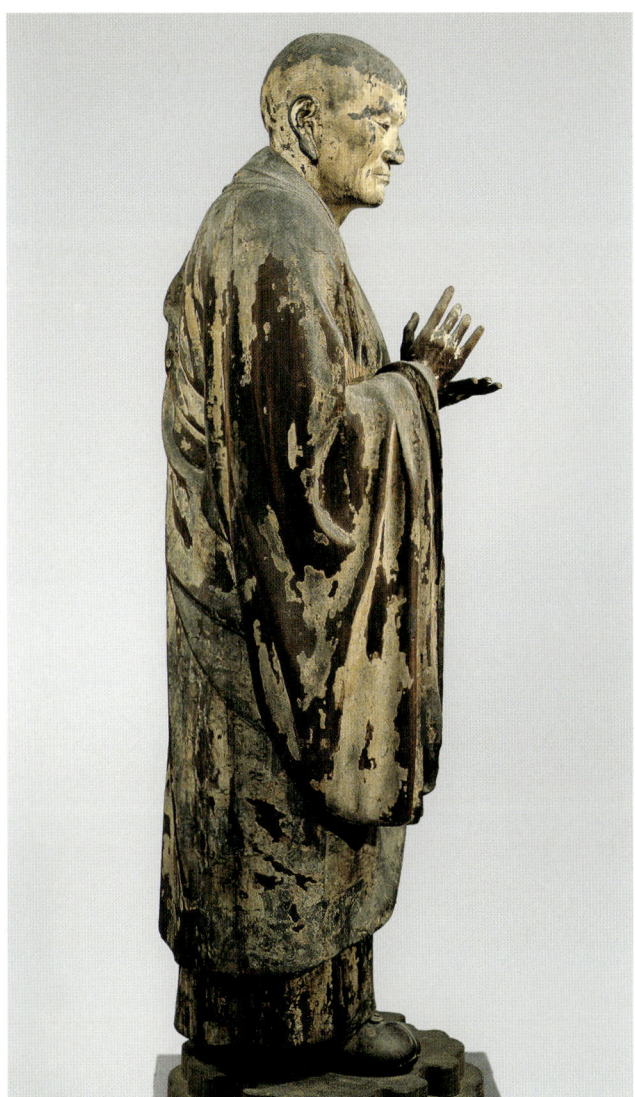

Viewpoint
Side

無著菩薩立像
Standing Muchaku

The different feel of the sleeves

Viewing the right side of both statues, we see obvious differences in the patterns of the creases and folds in the robes.

Muchaku's sleeve droops limply, the fabric is worn, and the creases are twisted and curved. Seshin's resembles new fabric that is thick and crisp. The wide folds of the drapery flow straight, and the carving is deep.

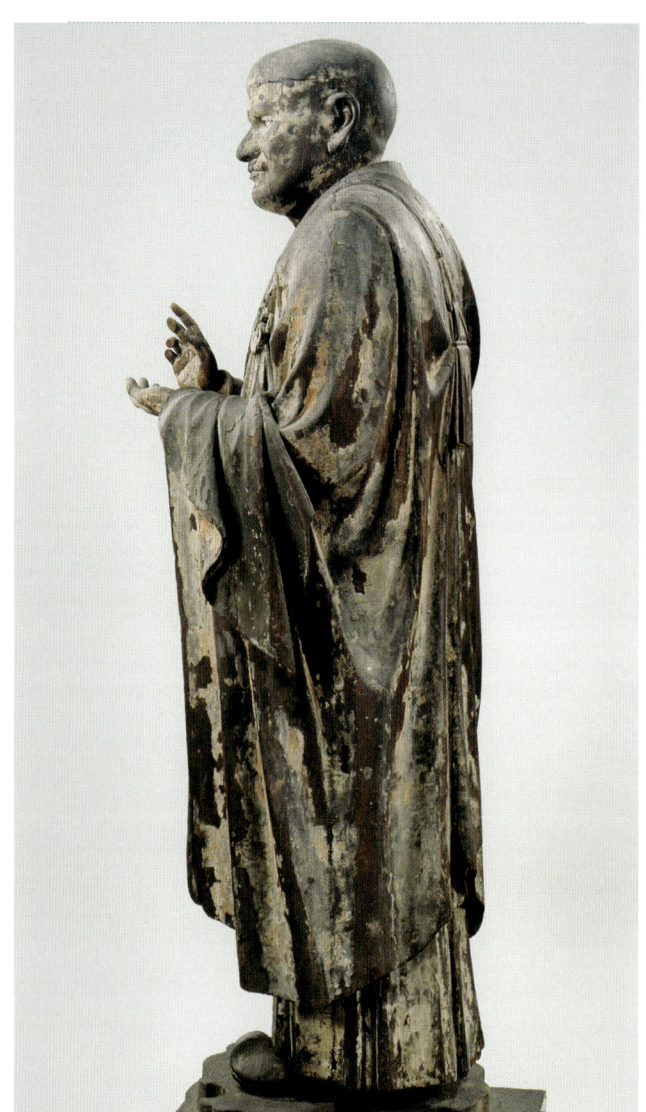

世親菩薩立像
Standing Seshin

袖の表情

老境に入った無著の心理は、張りが萎えた袖の布地に投影されている。壮健の世親では、彼の意欲的な心情が張りのある袖の表現に反映されている。
これは、第3章の重源像の衣文表現に、2つの感情表現を読みといた視点と同じである。

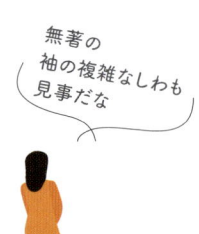

無著の
袖の複雑なしわも
見事だな

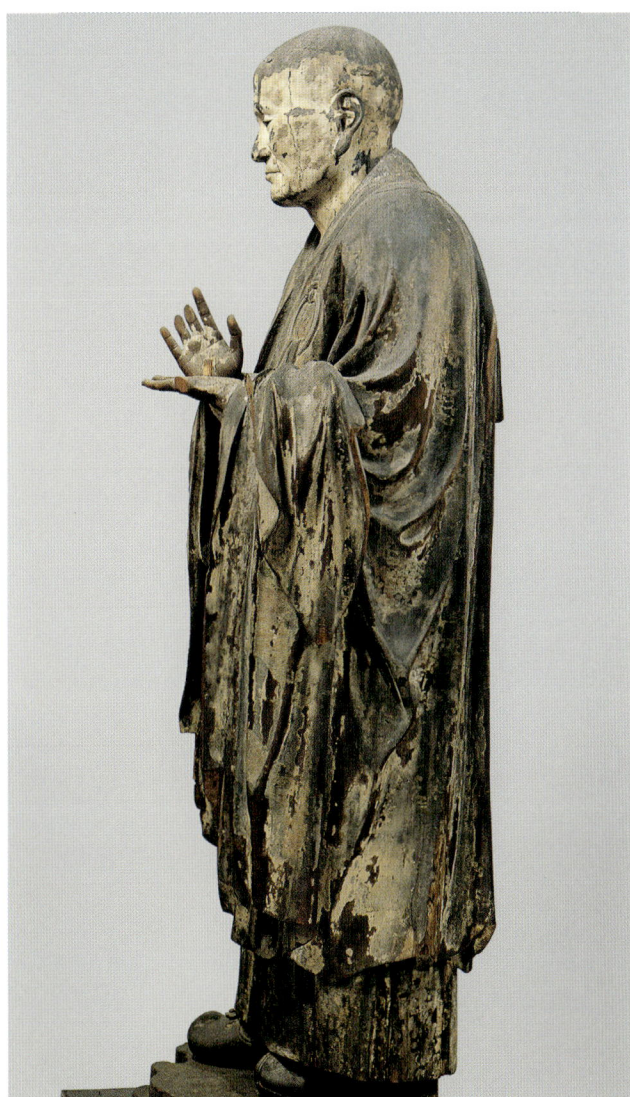

無著菩薩立像
Standing Muchaku

Representation of the sleeves

The psychological state of the aged Muchaku is projected on the fabric of the drooping sleeves that completely lack tension. As for Seshin with his youthful vigor, his highly motivated personality is reflected in the representation of the taut sleeves. This is same viewpoint that allows for two interpretations of the expression of emotions in the representation of Chōgen's robes seen in chapter three.

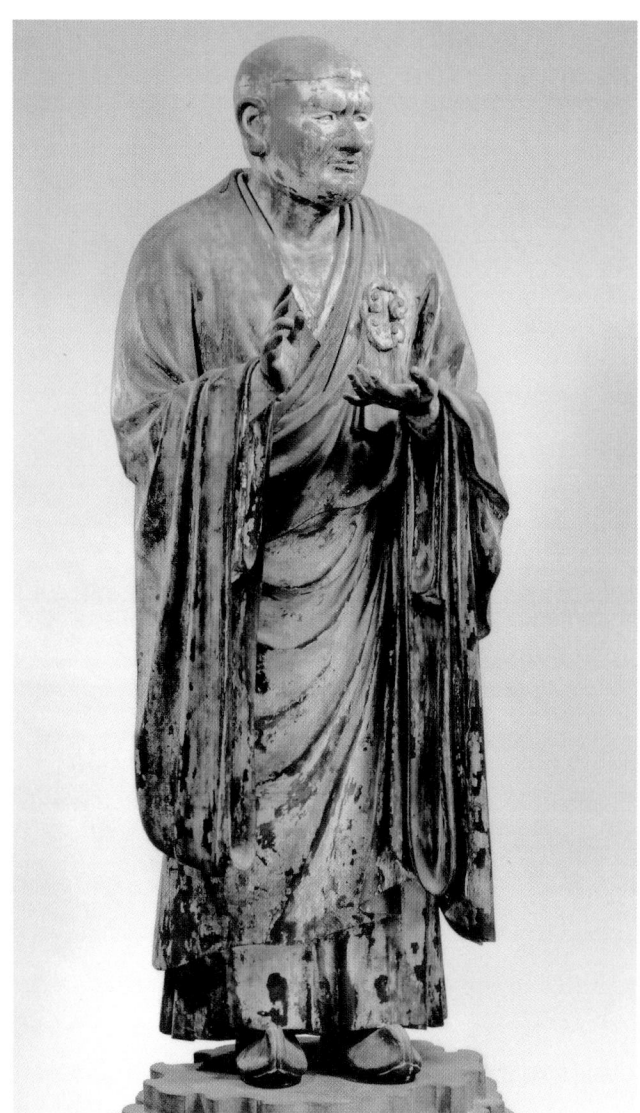

斜め
から見る

世親菩薩立像
Standing Seshin

気力のちがい

世親を脂の乗った壮年期の哲学者にたとえるなら、袖に刻まれた簡潔で強い調子の衣文表現は、今後の仏教研究への気概を象徴するかのようにも見える。

無著を老哲学者にたとえるなら、織物としての張りがなくなった衣の皺の表現は、仏教哲学を究めて来た彼の老境の心理を暗示するようでもあり、体力の衰えを示唆するようにも見える。

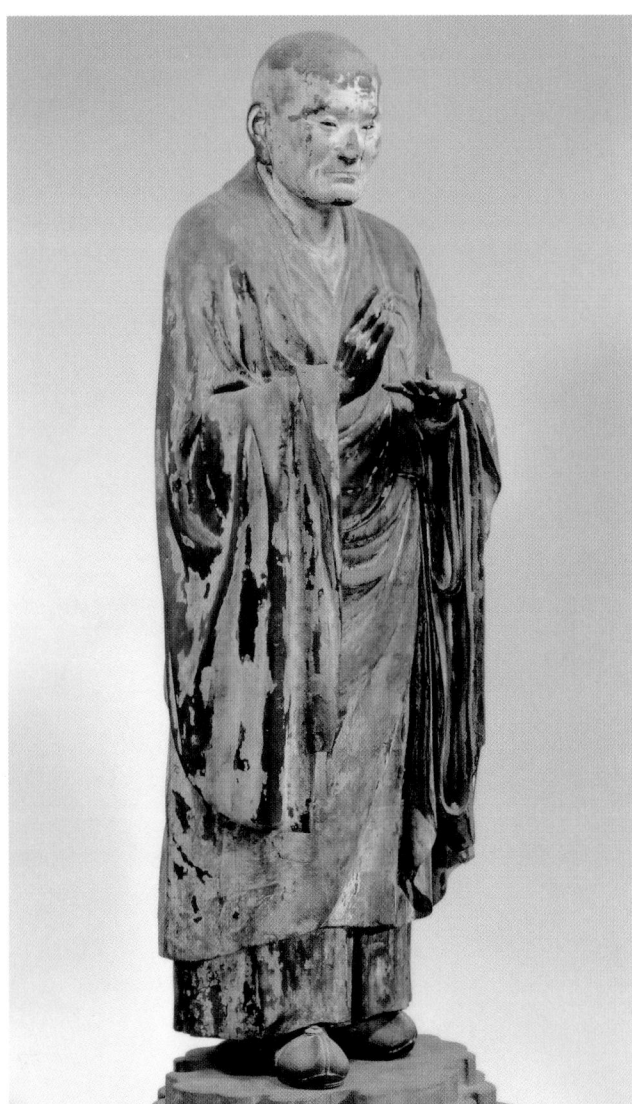

無著菩薩立像
Standing Muchaku

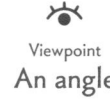

Viewpoint
An angle

Differences in the level of vitality

Seshin is an example of a youthful philosopher in his prime. The simplicity and power of the carving of the sleeves appear to be symbolic of the strong spirit he will need in his study of Buddhism.

Muchaku is an example of an aged philosopher. The movement of the limp sleeves hints at the psychology of an aged man who has already plumbed the depths of Buddhist philosophy, and appears to indicate the deterioration of physical strength.

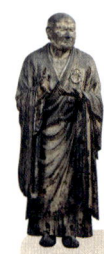
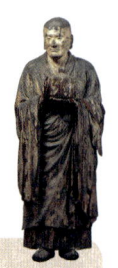

国宝 無著菩薩立像・世親菩薩立像
興福寺北円堂所在

National-Treasure Statues of *Standing Muchaku* and *Standing Seshin*
Hokuendō at Kōfukuji

大仏師運慶作	By Master Buddhist sculptor Unkei
寄木造（桂）	Assembled-block construction (*katsura*)
玉眼　彩色	Inserted crystal eyes, pigments
像高　無著194.7cm世親191.6cm	Heights: Muchaku 194.7 cm., Seshin 191.6 cm.
鎌倉時代13c.　建暦2年（1212）	Kamakura period, 13th century, 1212 (Kenryaku 2)

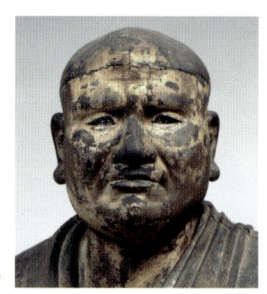
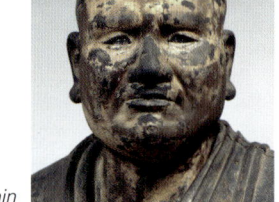

世親菩薩立像
Standing Seshin

無著菩薩立像
Standing Muchaku

　無著・世親像の表現を比べて見ると、顔や体形のみならず、身体を覆う衣の質感において、無著では枯れた感じに、世親では張り切った力強い感じにあらわされているのに気づく。両者を対比して見ることを促す造形思考が、確かに働いているのである。

　特に記すべきは、この造形思考が人間観察に基づく感情の表出にまで及んでいることだろう。「人間主義」の造形精神がしっかりと貫かれていることに深い感動を覚える。

　西洋のイタリア・ルネサンス美術（人間賛歌）は15〜16世紀だが、それよりおよそ300年も前に東洋・日本の仏教美術の世界では、人間観察に基づく透徹した眼の働きが、この無著・世親像を通して語られていたとは、ほんとうに大きな驚きである。建暦2年（1212）大仏師運慶の工房によってつくられた名作である。

When we visually compare the statues of Muchaku and Seshin, we realize it is not only in the form of the face and body, but also in the feel of the texture of their clothing that Muchaku evokes a feeling of withered old age, and Seshin a sense of robust vigor. A conception of sculptural form promoting the visual contrast of the two is operating here.

It should be noted in particular that this conception of sculptural form is a product of a sensibility that emerged from an emphasis on human observation. This profound sentiment is firmly linked to the spirit of sculptural form grounded in Humanism.

The "hymn to humanity" inherent in the Italian Renaissance Art was in the 15-16th centruies, but it is truly astounding that some 300 years earlier in the East, within the realm of Japanese Buddhist art, it was already in operation in the skilled eyes of a master thoroughly trained in the observation of living human beings. Moreover, it is still being conveyed to us today in the statues of Muchaku and Seshin. These famed works were produced in the workshop led by the master Buddhist sculptor Unkei.

コラム　運慶の眼と対比の造形思考
Column: Unkei's eye and contrasting concepts of sculptural form

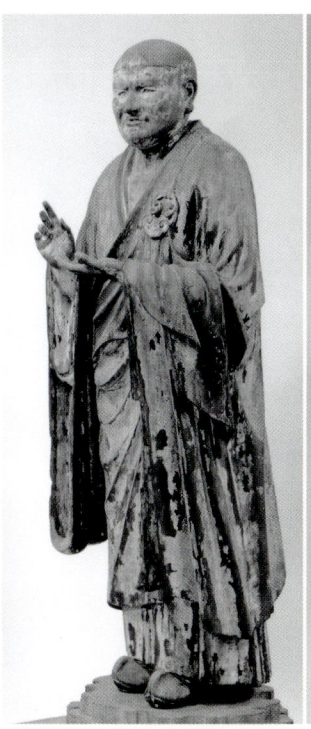 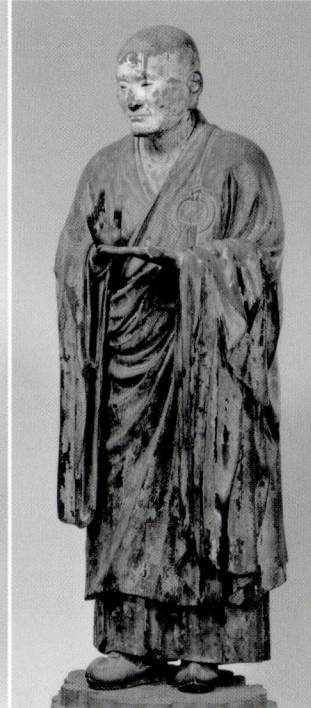 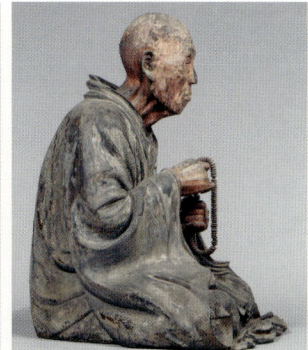 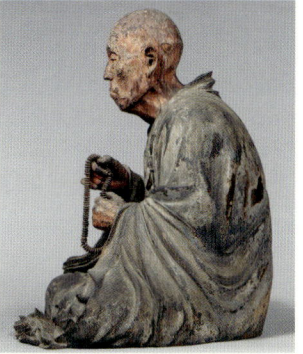

左・中央
世親・無著像　袖口の開きの対比
Left and center
Statues of Muchaku and Seshin: Comparing the
openings of the sleeves

右上・右下
重源像　両袖にみる対比
Left on top, right below
The Chōgen statue: Comparing
the sleeves

　無著・世親像のそれぞれの特色を、対比の関係でとらえるならば、このような造形思考は、重源上人像にみた、両袖の衣文表現の扱いにもいえるだろう。重源像の右側は深い皺が生じた袖をはらう所作、左側はだぶついた法衣を袈裟で締める所作であることに気づくと、そのような対比によって、重源上人の複雑な心理を読みとることができるだろう。それは重源像の作者の創造力に触れるところでもある。

If we see the chief characteristic of the statues of Muchaku and Seshin as a contrasting relationship, we realize the same concept of sculptural form is also seen in the statue of Chōgen Shōnin and can be demonstrated in the treatment of the pattern of drapery folds of the sleeves. In the right sleeve of the statue of Chōgen one feels the strong will that was part of his fundamental nature, but in the left side one senses his sensitive concern for others. This is also related to the creativity of the sculptor of the Chōgen statue.

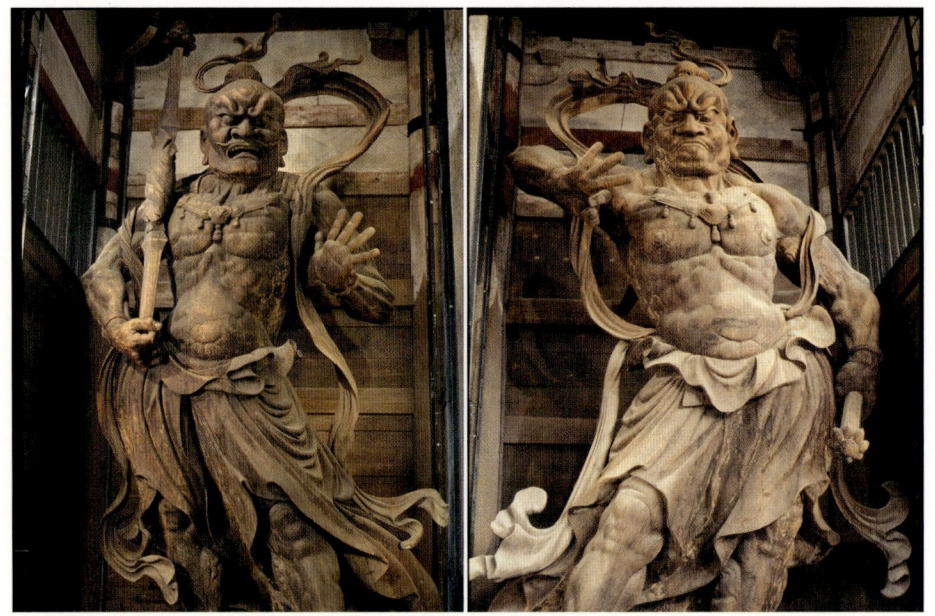

東大寺南大門仁王像　顔、胸板、裳の折り返しなど随所に作風の違いがあらわれている。

Different styles are evident in various parts of the Niō statues in the Nandaimon at Tōdaiji, including the faces, chests, and the way the skirts are blown by the wind.

　南大門仁王像の阿形像・吽形像の2軀の関係においても、対比の造形思考が徹底されているとみるべきだろう。すなわち、快慶と運慶の個性のちがいがそれぞれ阿形・吽形の作風に反映しているがゆえに、両像を対比して見ることができるのである。さらに制作の途中で造形上の修正が行われたとき、あらためて2軀一具としての統一が再度確認されたのである。

　無著・世親像では、実際に鑿と彫刻刀をふるったのは、それぞれ現場担当仏師の運助（六男）と運賀（五男）である。しかし、両像制作の構想段階で「対比の造形」を思考したのは、指揮官運慶であることは疑いない。無著・世親像を含めた北円堂諸仏の造立を主宰したのが大仏師運慶だからである。

　このことは、先に見た重源上人像の制作の構想にも共通しており、むしろ重源像の方が、無著・世親像にみた造形思考の先例といえる。要するに、重源像にみた対比の造形も、大仏師運慶の構想による可能性が高いと私は考えている。

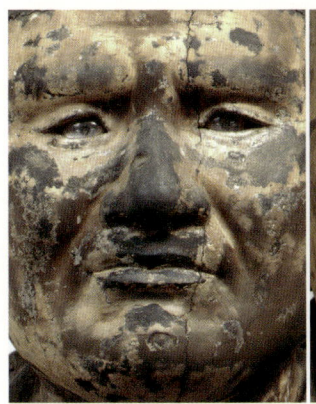
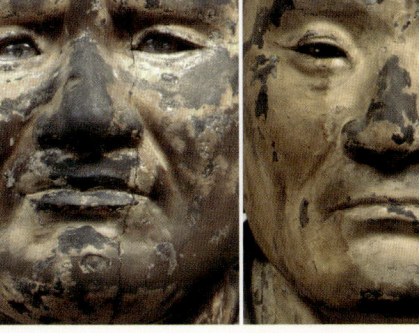
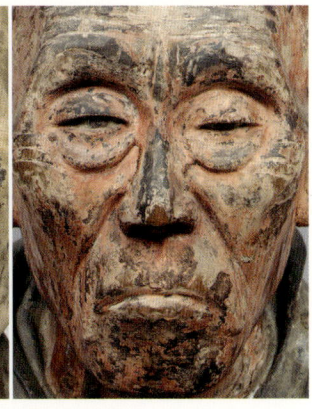

世親菩薩立像
Standing Seshin

無著菩薩立像
Standing Muchaku

重源上人坐像
Seated Saint Chōgen

In the relationship between the Niō, the Ungyō and Agyō statues in the Nandaimon at Tōdaiji, we can surely see a conception of contrasting sculptural form at work throughout. In other words, because the differences in the individual personalities of the sculptors Unkei and Kaikei are reflected in the styles of the Agyō and Ungyō statues, it is possible to view them in terms of visual contrast. Moreover, because revisions were made to the sculptural form in the midst of the project, we can again reconfirm that the unity of the two figures marked them as a single set.

In the case of the Muchaku and Seshin statues, the chisels and blades that were actually wielded by the Buddhist sculptors in charge of the site were in the hands of Unjo (Unkei's sixth son) and Unga (his fifth son) respectively. However, at the conceptual stage of both statues, the concept of "contrasting sculptural forms" had already been hit upon, and the director behind the scenes was undoubtedly Unkei. This is due to the fact that the Master Buddhist Sculptor Unkei led the project to produce all the Buddhist statues for the Hokuendō, including those of Muchaku and Seshin.

This is a shared conceptual element behind the production of the Chōgen statue that we examined earlier. The Chōgen statue is instead the forerunner of the sculptural form seen in the *Muchaku* and *Seshin* statues. In short, I believe it highly likely that the contrasting sculptural form seen in the Chōgen statue was based on the conceptualization of the Master Buddhist Sculptor Unkei.

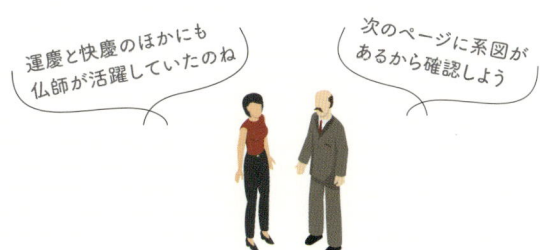

運慶と快慶のほかにも
仏師が活躍していたのね

次のページに系図が
あるから確認しよう

国宝 無著・世親像の豆知識
Knowledge in a Nutshel: Muchaku and Seshin Statues

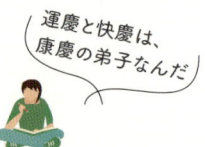

運慶と快慶は、康慶の弟子なんだ

慶派仏師系図　The Lineage of the Kei school of Buddhist sculptors

康慶　Kōkei
運慶　Unkei
湛慶　Tankei　←国宝 仁王像　関係者
Assistant sculptor, National Treasure Niō statue
康運　Kōun
康弁　Kōben　←国宝 天燈鬼・龍燈鬼像　作者
Main sculptor, National Treasure Tentōki and Ryūtōki statues
康勝　Kōshō
運賀　Unga
運助　Unjo　←国宝 無著・世親像　担当者
Supervising sculptor, National Treasure Muchaku and Seshin statues
定覚　Jōkaku　←国宝 仁王像　関係者
Assistant sculptor, National Treasure Niō statue
快慶　Kaikei

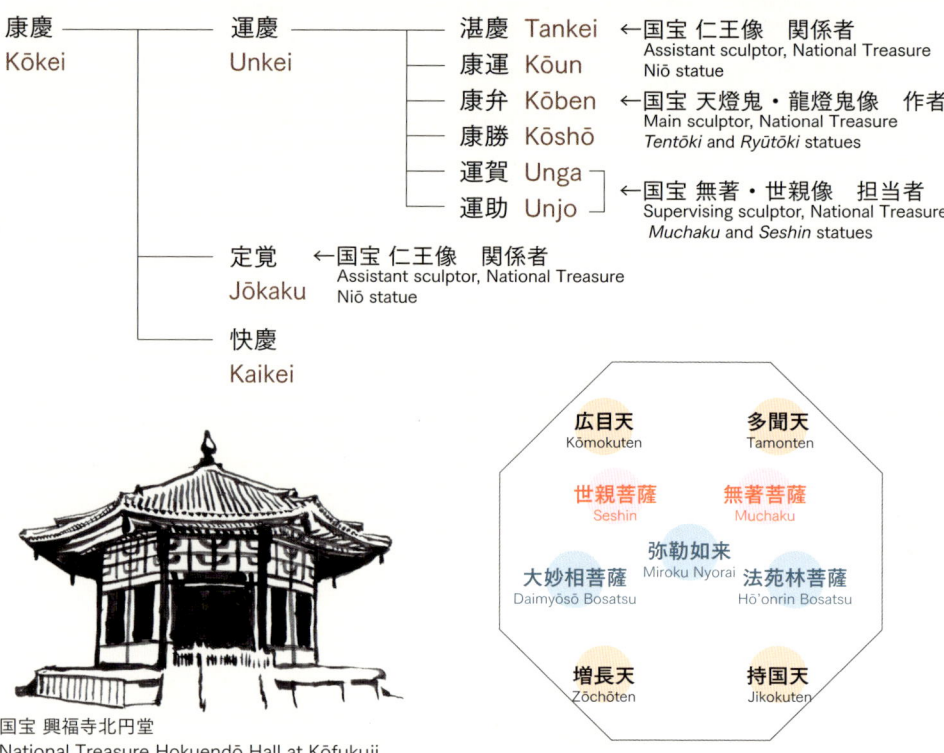

広目天　Kōmokuten
多聞天　Tamonten
世親菩薩　Seshin
無著菩薩　Muchaku
弥勒如来　Miroku Nyorai
大妙相菩薩　Daimyōsō Bosatsu
法苑林菩薩　Hō'onrin Bosatsu
増長天　Zōchōten
持国天　Jikokuten

国宝 興福寺北円堂
National Treasure Hokuendō Hall at Kōfukuji

国宝 興福寺北円堂 諸尊配置図
Diagram of the placement of icons, National Treasure Hokuendō at Kōfukuji

平氏の南都焼討後の鎌倉復興期、北円堂には弥勒三尊のやや後方、左右に無著・世親像、周囲に四天王像が祀られた。現在、両脇侍（法苑林菩薩像・大妙相菩薩像）は室町時代の作に変わり、四天王像は奈良 大安寺伝来の像が安置される。当初の四天王像は長く南円堂に伝わり、今日、平成30年落慶の中金堂に安置される。

After the restoration of the Nara temples, which had been burned by the warriors of the Taira clan, a Miroku Triad was enshrined in the rebuilt Hokuendō hall. Shortly thereafter, the three icons were flanked by the statues of Muchaku and Seshin and surrounded by the Four Guardian Kings (Shitennō). Today the two attendant deities (the bodhisattvas Hōonrin and Daimyōsō) from the Miroku Triad have been replaced by later works in Muromachi period (1336-1573), and the current Guardian Kings are those that were brought from Daianji, another Nara temple. The original Guardian Kings were preserved for many years in the Nan'endō hall, but as of 2018 they have been enshrined in the newly dedicated Chūkondō hall at Kōfukuji.

仁王像に学んだ筋肉表現

国宝 天燈鬼立像（てんとうきりゅうぞう） 龍燈鬼立像（りゅうとうきりゅうぞう） 興福寺国宝館所在

ここでは応用編として、鎌倉彫刻の天燈鬼・龍燈鬼の像をとりあげ、第2章で紹介した東大寺南大門仁王像と比べて見てみよう。両者共通の造形感覚に気づくとき、それは作者の系譜を考えるヒントにつながるだろう。

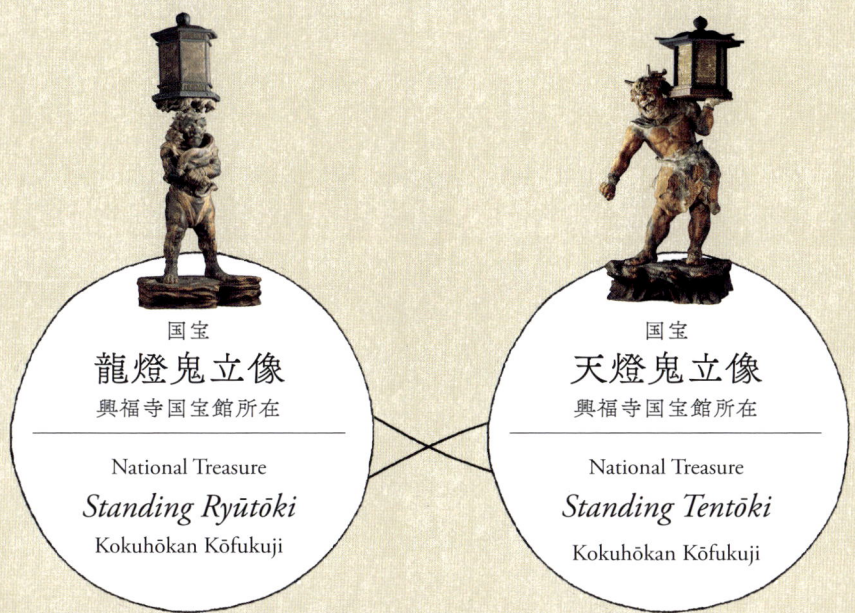

国宝
龍燈鬼立像
興福寺国宝館所在

National Treasure
Standing Ryūtōki
Kokuhōkan Kōfukuji

国宝
天燈鬼立像
興福寺国宝館所在

National Treasure
Standing Tentōki
Kokuhōkan Kōfukuji

The Artistic Representation of Musculature Based on the Niō Statues

The National Treasure *Standing Tentōki* and *Ryūtōki* statues in Kokuhōkan at Kōfukuji

In this section on how to apply the principles explained in this book, we'll take up the Kamakura-period statues of the *Standing Tentōki* (Demon of the Heavenly Lantern) *and Standing Ryūtōki* (Demon of the Dragon Lantern), and compare them to the Niō statues in the Nandaimon of Tōdaiji discussed in chapter 2. When you realize that there is a shared sense of sculptural form in the two pairs of statues, it will surely help you to think about the background and lineage of the sculptors.

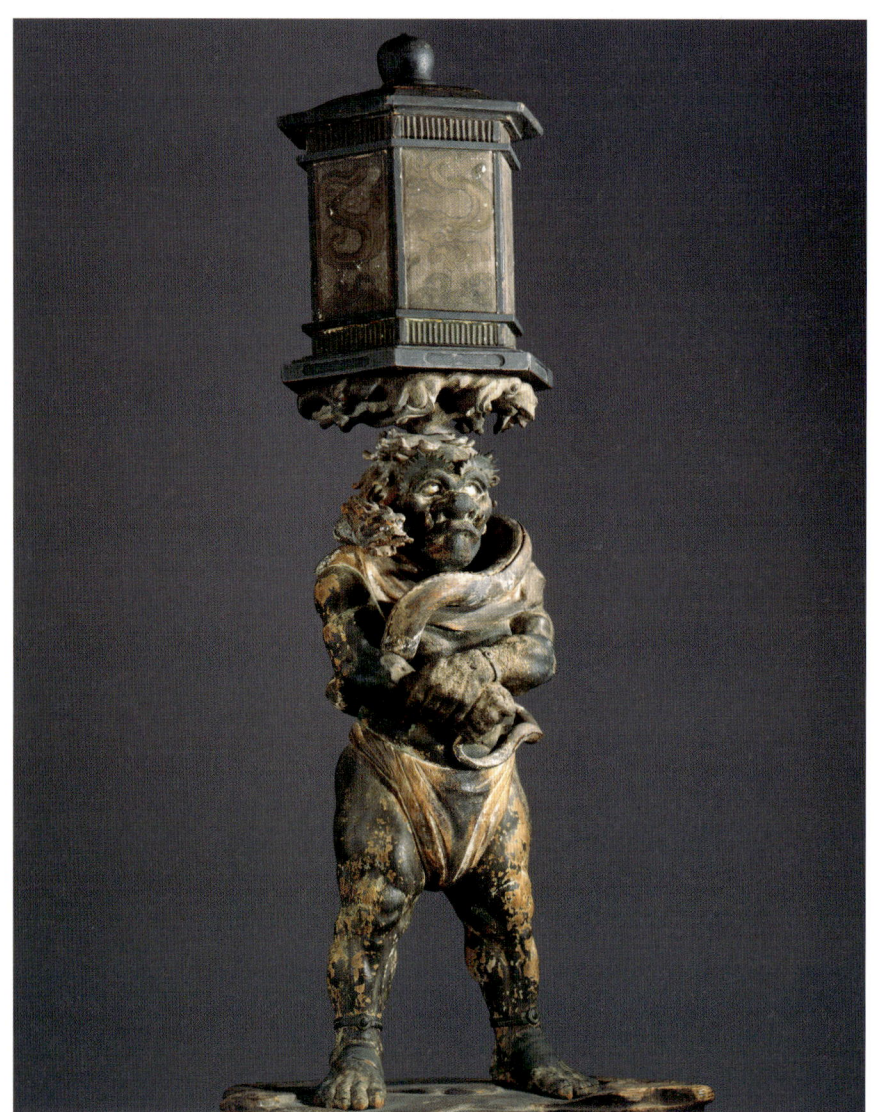

国宝 龍燈鬼立像 興福寺国宝館所在
National Treasure. *Standing Ryūtōki*, Kokuhōkan at Kōfukuji

全身をみてみよう。

一対の鬼形が燈籠を捧げている。口の開閉の違いで仁王像のように阿・吽に区別される（燈籠は明治時代の補作）。

左の龍燈鬼は、頭に燈籠をのせ、左手は腹前で、拳を握る右手の手首をつかみ、両足を開いて立つ。上目づかいのおどけた表情が特徴的で、龍を襟巻き風に首に巻く。

右の天燈鬼は、左肩に燈籠をのせて左手を添え、右腕を右下方に伸ばし、右足を一歩前に踏み出して立つ。頭に２角があり、目は眉間にあるものと合わせて３目である。眉を寄せ、目を見開いて睨みつけ、口を開けて怒号する激しい気性が特徴的である。両像ともに全身に力がみなぎった静・動の対比のポーズである。

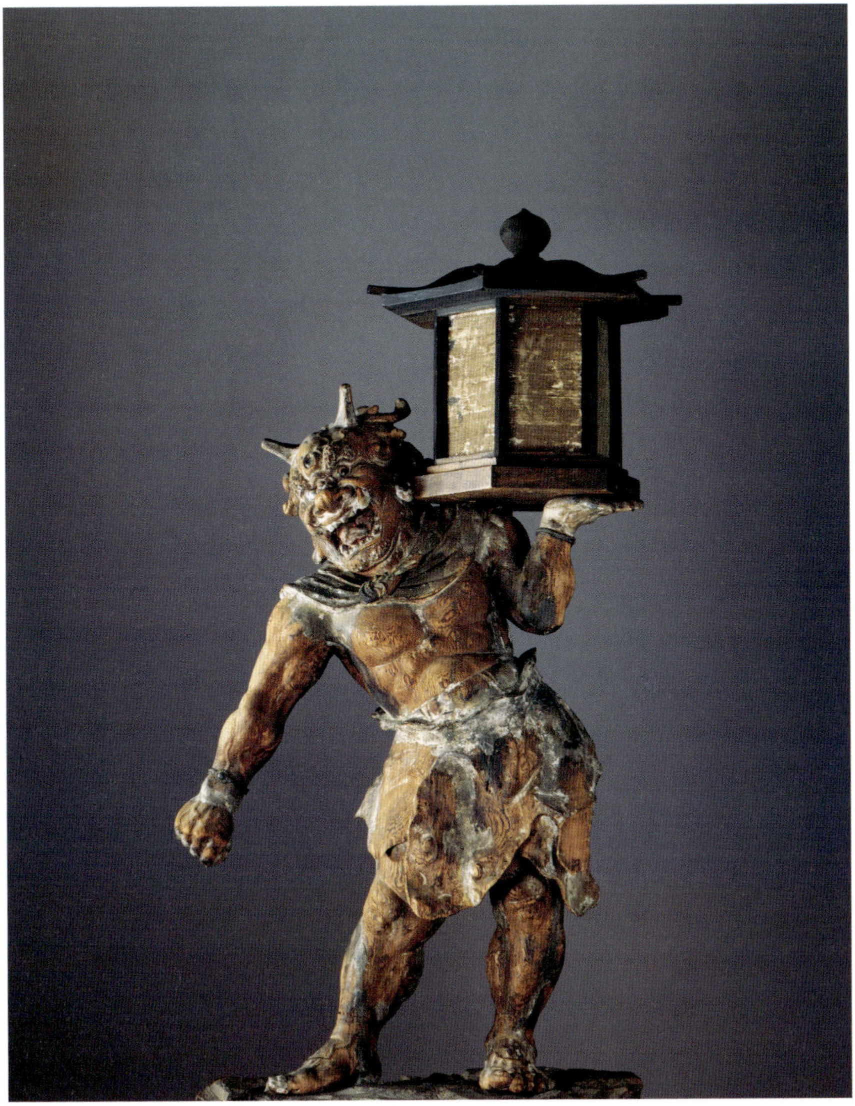

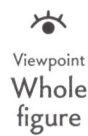

国宝 天燈鬼立像 興福寺国宝館所在
National Treasure. *Standing Tentōki*, Kokuhōkan at Kōfukuji

Let's examine the bodies in their entirety.

Each one of this pair of demons holds aloft a lantern brazier. One of the distinguishing elements that differentiates them is that one is open-mouthed and the other close-mouthed just as in the case of the Niō Agyō and Ungyō (The lantern braziers are Meiji-era replacements for the lost originals).

Ryūtōki, on the left, stands with two legs widely planted, holds the brazier on top of its head, and the left hand grasps the wrist of the right that makes a fist held in front of its midsection. The facial expression with its comically upturned eyes is unique. A dragon is wrapped around its neck like a scarf.

Tentōki, on the right, holds the brazier on its left shoulder with its left hand while the right arm is stretched down to the right. Its weight is balanced on the the left leg as the right leg takes one step forward. Tentōki has two horns on its head and a third eye in the middle of its forehead. The knitted brows, wide-eyed glare, and open mouth hurling invective are unique characteristics of its ferocious temper. The poses of the two statues, whose bodies overflow with energy, contrast stillness and movement.

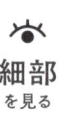

細部
を見る

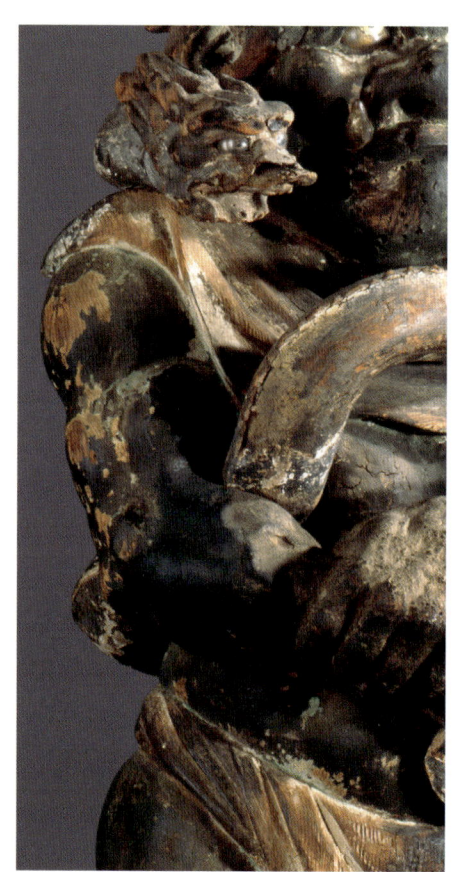

龍燈鬼立像
Standing Ryūtōki

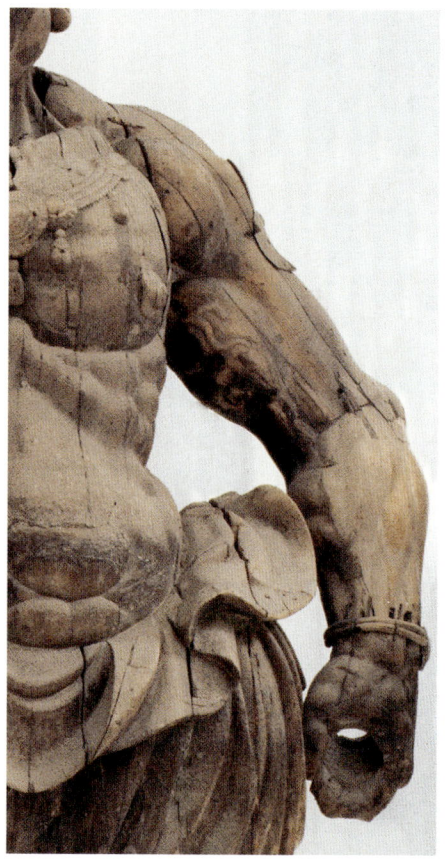

吽形
Ungyō statue

仁王像をよく学んだ筋肉表現

骨太の筋骨隆々たる表現は、大きさがだいぶ違うものの第2章で紹介した同時代の東大寺南大門の仁王像に学んだ感じが強い。

たとえば、龍燈鬼の右腕は筋肉が瘤状に盛り上がる。そのような表現は、奈良時代以来の伝統的な力感表現をとりいれたものであり、南大門の仁王像にも受け継がれている。南大門仁王像と比べると、吽形の左手のそれを、さらに肉づきよくした感じであり、両者共通の造形感覚に気づく。

天燈鬼の踏んばった右脚は、脛の骨が折れたかのようにねじれている。そのような力感表現は、南大門仁王像の吽形のそれに酷似する。

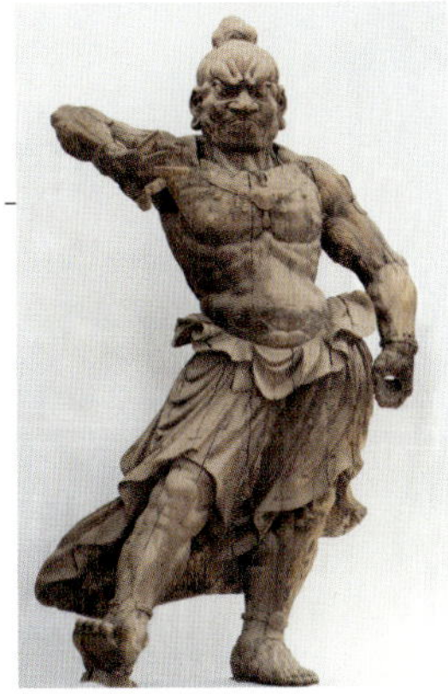

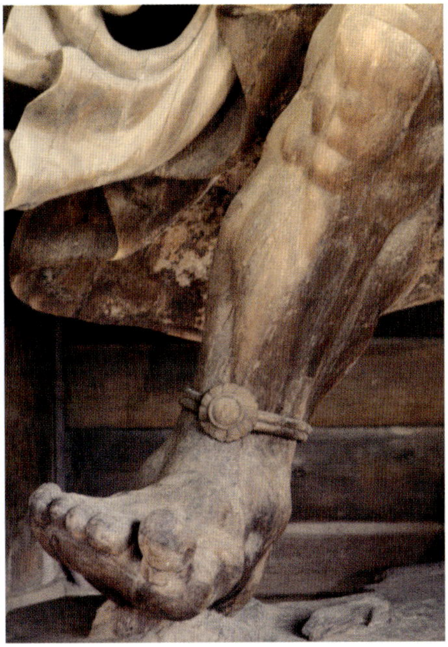

吽形
Ungyō statue

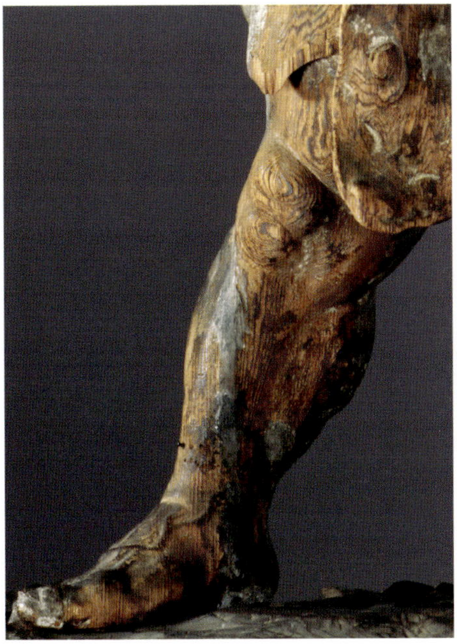

Viewpoint
Detail

天燈鬼立像
Standing Tentōki

吽形
Ungyō statue

The representation of the musculature modeled on that of the Niō Statues

Despite the difference in size, the artistic representation of the robustly bulging muscles and bones clearly seems to have been modeled on those of the Niō statues in the Nandaimon of Tōdaiji that were described in chapter two.

For example, in the case of the right arm of Ryūtōki, the muscles are formed by lumps of flesh. This manner of representation incorporates the traditional method of expressing strength that had been used since the Nara period, which is also preserved in the Niō statues in the Nandaimon. When compared to the contemporaneous Nandaimon statues, the left arm of the close-mouthed Ungyō statue has an even more muscular feel, and one realizes the two share the same sense of sculptural form.

The firmly planted right leg of the Tentōki statue is twisted to such an extent that the shinbone seems to be broken. This type of representation of strength is extremely close to that of the Ungyō statue of the Niō in the Nandaimon.

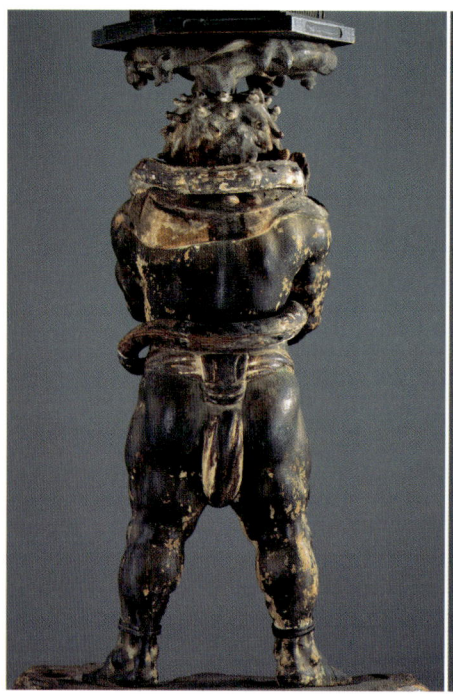
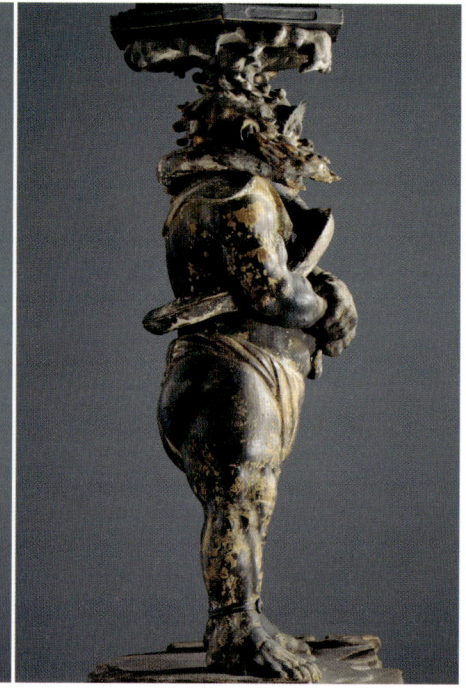

背面と
側面
から見る

龍燈鬼立像
Standing Ryūtōki

成熟した筋肉表現

南大門の仁王像では背面が見られることを考え
ていない造形だが、本像では背中、尻、太もも、
ふくらはぎの筋肉表現は仁王像よりも進展し、よ
り成熟した表現をみせている。確証はないが、
本像の作者康弁は南大門仁王像の制作スタッフ
に属し、実際に鑿を振るった1人ではなかった
かと想像をめぐらすのも面白い。それほどに力
感表現において両像はよく似ているのである。

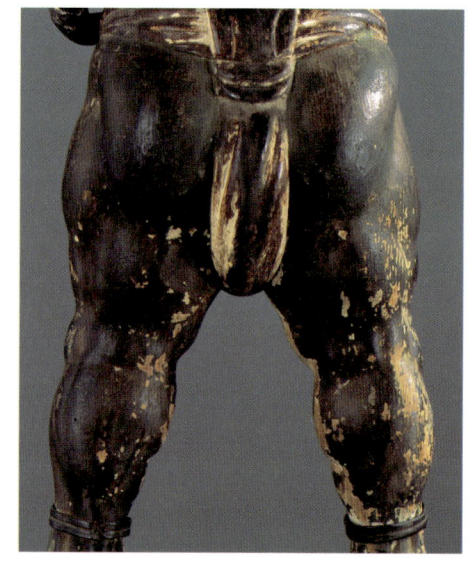

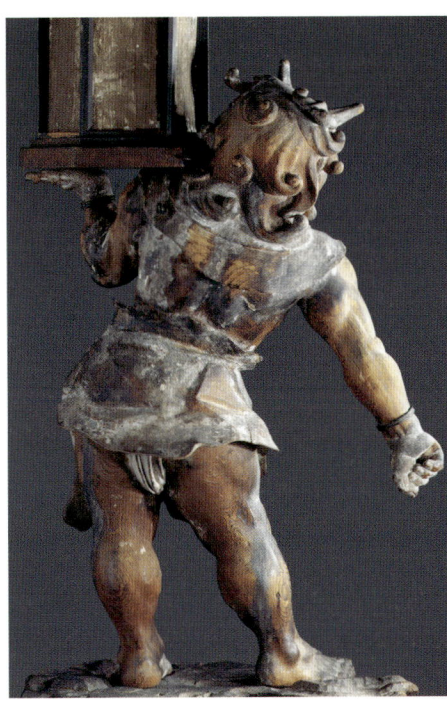
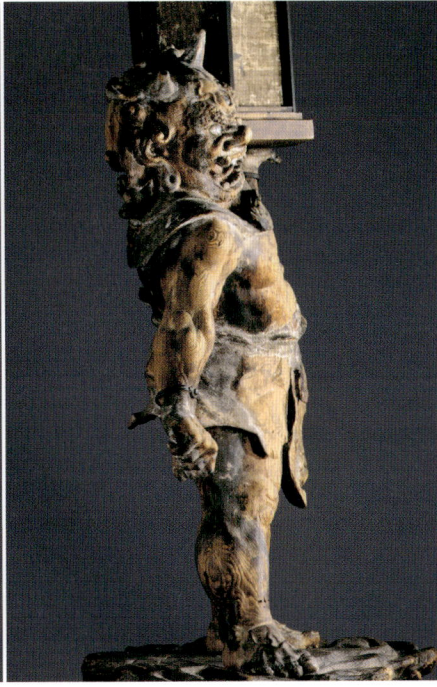

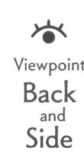

Viewpoint
Back
and
Side

天燈鬼立像
Standing Tentōki

The representation of fully developed musculature

Although the sculptural form of the Niō at the Nandaimon was not meant to be viewed from behind, the representation of the muscles and sinews of the back, buttocks, thighs and calves of the statues that you see here is more technically advanced, and the artistry displays greater maturity than that seen in the Niō statues. Although we have no proof, it is fascinating to speculate whether Kōben, the sculptor responsible for these statues, may have been an active member of the group who produced the Nandaimon Niō statues. In terms of the expression of the sense of power, the two pairs of statues are largely similar.

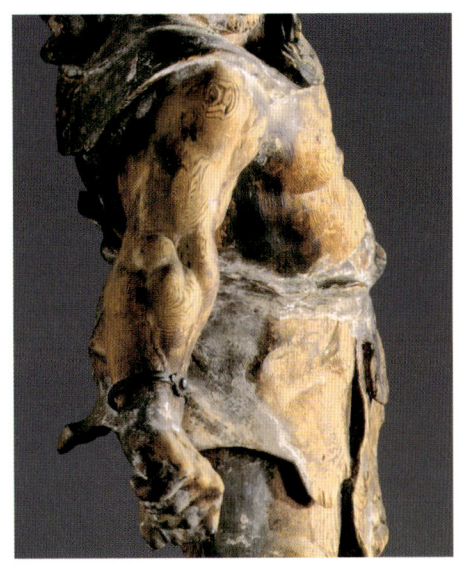

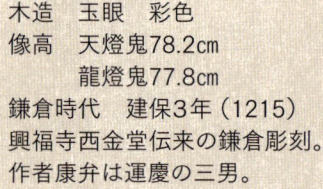

国宝 天燈鬼立像　龍燈鬼立像
興福寺国宝館所在
National Treasure *Standing Tentōki* and *Standing Ryūtōki*
Kokuhōkan at Kōfukuji

木造　玉眼　彩色
像高　天燈鬼78.2cm
　　　龍燈鬼77.8cm
鎌倉時代　建保3年（1215）
興福寺西金堂伝来の鎌倉彫刻。
作者康弁は運慶の三男。

Wood, Inserted Crystal Eyes, Pigments
Heights: Tentōki 78.2 cm.; Ryūtōki 77.8 cm.
　Kamakura period, 1215 (Kenpō 3)
These statues come from the Saikondō hall
at Kōfukuji and were produced by Kōben,
the third son of Unkei.

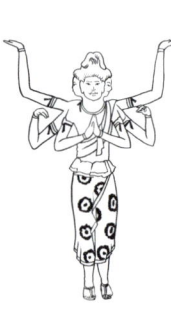

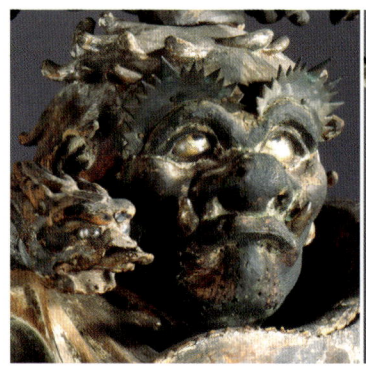

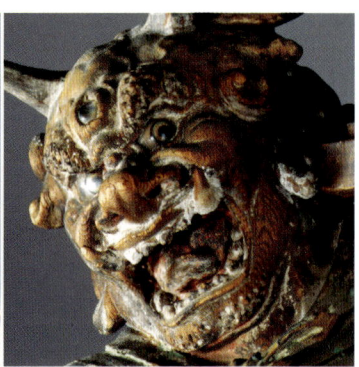

左　龍燈鬼の顔　右　天燈鬼の顔
Left: Face of the *Standing Ryūtōki*, Right: Face of the *Standing Tentōki*

この天燈鬼・龍燈鬼像は、あの奈良時代の国宝 阿修羅を含む八部衆や十大弟子と一緒に西金堂に安置されていたのね

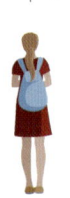

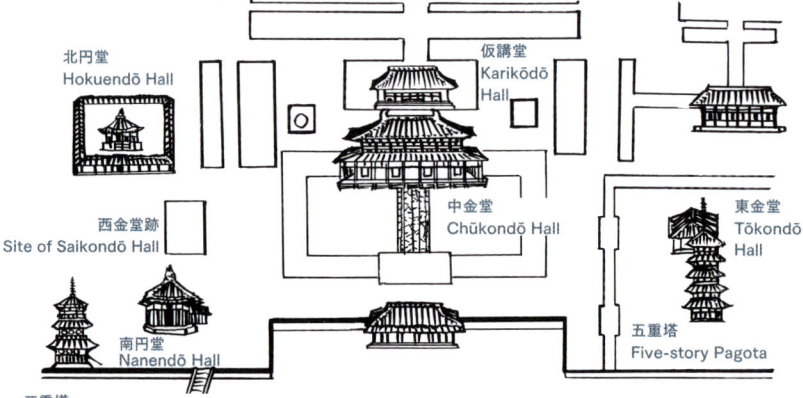

北円堂
Hokuendō Hall

仮講堂
Karikōdō Hall

西金堂跡
Site of Saikondō Hall

中金堂
Chūkondō Hall

東金堂
Tōkondō Hall

南円堂
Nanendō Hall

五重塔
Five-story Pagota

三重塔
Three-story Pagota

興福寺境内（整備計画中の建造物も含む）
Precincts of Kōfukuji (including building in planning)

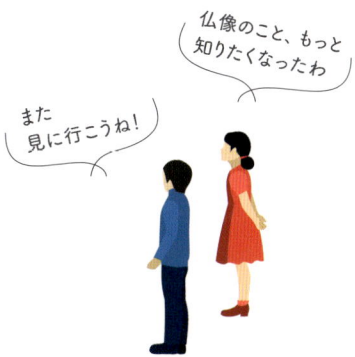

また
見に行こうね！

仏像のこと、もっと
知りたくなったわ

興福寺

〒630-8213　奈良市登大路町48
平城遷都（710）で飛鳥から移転したかつての藤原氏の氏寺。
南都焼討（1180）など何度も火災に遭うが、その都度「旧に復
する」精神で再興された。国宝・阿修羅像などの乾漆造の天
平彫刻、鎌倉初期の運慶らの鎌倉彫刻の名作が伝わる。法
相宗。中金堂が新しく再建された。
http://www.kohfukuji.com/

Kōfukuji

Nobori-ōji chō 48, Nara city
Kōfukuji, which was moved from Asuka to Nara when the capital
was transferred there in 710, was once the temple of the Fujiwara
clan. It met with disaster on several occasions including the burning
of Nara in 1180, and each time it has been rebuilt under the influence of the spirit of the "revival of olden days." The National Treasure, dry-lacquer statue of the Ashura from the Tenpyō period as
well as masterworks of Kamakura-period sculpture by Unkei and
Kaikei have been preserved here. The temple belongs to the Hossō
tradition. The Chūkōndō hall has recently been rebuilt.

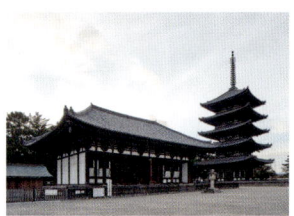

掲載作品
第4章
◉無著菩薩立像・世親菩薩立像
（鎌倉時代）

第5章
◉天燈鬼立像・龍燈鬼立像
（鎌倉時代）

Chapter 4
◉ Standing Muchaku and Standing Seshin (Kamakura period)

Chapter 5
◉ Standing Tentōki and Standing Ryūtōki (Kamakura period)

東大寺

〒630-8587　奈良市雑司町406-1
「奈良の大仏さん」と親しまれる盧舎那仏は奈良時代（752）の
造立。平氏の南都焼討（1180）と三好・松永の乱（1567）で
2度被災、江戸前期（1692）に修復開眼された。法華堂には
天平彫刻の名作が伝わる。南大門は鎌倉復興期の巨大建築
で、仁王像は運慶の作。華厳宗。
http://www.todaiji.or.jp/index.html

Tōdaiji

Zōushi chō 406-1, Nara city
The Great Rushana (Vairocana) Buddha that is known familiarly as
"Nara no Daibutsu-san" was built in 752 during the Nara period. It
has twice been severely damaged: once in 1180 when the Taira clan
attacked Nara, and then again in 1567 in fighting between the Mi-
yoshi and Matsunaga clans. Today's Great Buddha is the result of
the early Edo-period (1692) restoration. Masterpieces of Tenpyō-era
sculpture are preserved in the Hokkedō hall. The Great Southern
Gate (Nandaimon), which is a massive structure that was part of
the Kamakura-period revival, contains the Niō statues produced by
Unkei. The temple belongs to the Kegon Buddhist tradition.

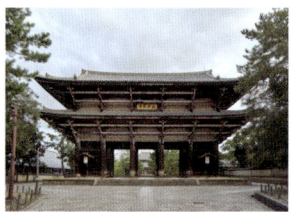

掲載作品
第2章
◉金剛力士立像
（鎌倉時代）

第3章
◉俊乗上人（重源）坐像
（鎌倉時代）

Chapter 2
◉ Standing Kongō Rikishi
(Kamakura period)

Chapter 3
◉ Seated Saint Shunjō shōnin
(Chōgen)
(Kamakura period)

奈良国立博物館

〒630-8213　奈良市登大路町50
1895年開館。初期は神仏分離等で荒廃した社寺の仏像の認知度を高める陳列で、仏教美術の殿堂である。戦後に始まった正倉院展は毎秋開催、人気度が高い。春季特別展は日頃の調査研究に裏付けられた企画展で学術的信頼度が高い。
https://www.narahaku.go.jp/index.html

Nara National Museum

Nobori-ōji chō 50, Nara city

The museum was opened in 1895. It was at first a hall designed to exhibit Buddhist art, displaying it to raise awareness of the Buddhist sculpture from the temples and shrines that were ravished by the anti-Buddhist movement. Annual autumn exhibitions of the treasures of the Shōsōin, which were begun after the WW II , are very popular. Special exhibitions held each spring are based on recent research that has been recognized as having a high level of academic reliability.

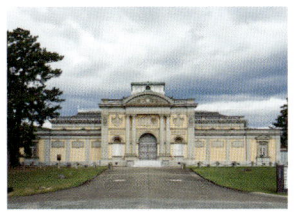

掲載作品
第1章
◎如意輪観音坐像
（平安時代）
如意輪観音坐像
（鎌倉時代）
◎十一面観音立像
（奈良時代末―平安時代初期）
◎十一面観音立像
（平安時代）
十一面観音立像
（鎌倉時代）

Chapter 1
◎ *Seated Nyoirin Kannon*
(Heian Period)
Seated Nyoirin Kannon
(Kamakura period)

◎ *Standing Jūichimen Kannon*
(late Nara period-early Heian
period)

◎ *Standing Jūichimen Kannon*
(Heian period)
Standing Jūichimen Kannon
(Kamakura period)

　本書は仏像をよく知るための入門書であるが、そのコンセプトは「仏像を対比して見る」ということであって、仏像の図像学、彫刻技法あるいは文化史的・仏教史的背景などを語る書物ではない。仏像の表現を十分に観察する力を養うことが、仏像をよく知るための本道である、ということを目標に掲げて、このようなコンセプトを提示している。本書を上梓するにあたり、学生時代に学んだ、美術史は様式論が王道であることを改めて噛みしめる思いである。

　仏像の美術書は「解説文が非常に難解だ」という声をいつも聞く。その大きな一因は解説した内容を示す写真や図解が、一緒に掲載されていないことにある。本書ではそれをクリアできるように、さまざまな角度からの写真や必要な図解を掲載し、また難しい漢字の熟語や美学的用語は避け、できるだけ日常のことばを使うようにした。写真掲載にあたっては東大寺と興福寺のご高配をたまわり、この企画が実現できる運びとなった。ここに記して感謝申し上げたい。

　私の仏像の勉強は奈良の文化財の現場が中心であるから、直観的で、若干舌足らずで、いささか言い過ぎたところがなきにしもあらず──といった現場主義特有の偏向があるかもしれない。しかし、何度も繰り返して恐縮だが、2つの仏像を対比して見ようとすれば、これまで気づかなかったところが見えてくる、といったことを経験するはずだ。本書はそのような読者の反応を期待している。本書で紹介した見かたをする仏像好きが増えてきて、古寺や博物館に足しげく通う人（リピーター）が多くなったとしたら、大きな喜びである。

　最後に、本書は編集部と私とのキャッチボールで出来上がったものである。論文調の文体が少しでもやわらいでいるとしたら、編集部の方々のお蔭である。また、長らく仏教美術の翻訳を手がけているマイケル・ジャメンツさんに翻訳をしていただけた。あわせてお礼申し上げたい。

令和元年（2019）10月

奈良にて　　鈴木喜博

This book is an introductory guide to help you familiarize yourself with Buddhist sculpture, and the basic principal behind the book is understanding Buddhist sculpture through visual comparison. I have avoiding talking about Buddhist iconography, sculptural techniques, and the cultural and historical background of the works. The goal of the basic concept of this book is to help you cultivate the ability to fully observe the expressiveness of Buddhist sculpture, which is the main path to a more profound understanding of Buddhist images. In writing this book, I was forced to reflect again on what I had learned in my school days, namely the claim that the study of stylistics was the royal road of the art historian.

One often hears the complaint that the commentary in books about Buddhist art is very difficult to understand. One reason is that the photographs and illustrations accompanying the commentary are not printed along side it. In order to make things clear and simple, this book uses photographs and diagrams from various angles. I have also avoided difficult language and aesthetic terms and have used instead straightforward simple language whenever possible. Both Tōdaiji and Kōfukuji cooperated in the printing of the photography in this book, and I would like to express my deepest appreciation for their assistance here.

As my study of Buddhist imagery has been centered on the cultural treasures of Nara, I may display some of the faults of a researcher who stresses fieldwork and relies too much on intuition, sometimes making my explanations too brief and at other times being too long-winded. Nevertheless, as I have continually repeated in this book, if you make a visual comparison of two Buddhist statues, you will undoubtedly be able to see things that you had not noticed before. I look forward to such surprised reactions from the readers of this book. I will be extremely pleased if those who use the technique advocated in this book become devotees of Buddhist sculpture and make repeated visits to the old temples and museums that house such works.

Lastly, I wish to note that the process of producing this book resembled playing catch ball with the editorial department. If the rhetoric of the commentary has become at least somewhat easier to comprehend, it is all due to their careful editing. I would also like to express my appreciation to Michael Jamentz, a veteran translator in the field of Buddhist art, for his assistance.

October 2019, Yoshihiro Suzuki, in Nara

鈴木喜博（すずき　よしひろ）

1950年東京生まれ。東北大学大学院博士課程後期中退。文化財保存行政
（奈良県教育委員会、文化庁）と展覧会等（大和文華館、奈良国立博物館）
の仕事に関わり、奈良国立博物館で退官。現在、奈良国立博物館名誉館員。
大学・大学院、文化講座・講演会等の講師を務める。奈良市在住。
主な著書に「檀像の概念と栢木の意義」（1992 講談社『日本美術全集5 密
教寺院と仏像』所収）、『仁王像大修理』共著（1997 朝日新聞社）、『宿院仏
師』（2006 至文堂『日本の美術』487号）、『日本美術史ハンドブック』共
著（2009 新書館）など。

マイケル・ジャメンツ
1948 年アメリカ生まれ。現在京都在住。日本中世文化研究家。大学講師。
翻訳家。

鑑賞ポケットガイド 対比でみる 日本の仏像

2019年11月27日　初版第1刷発行

著　　者　鈴木喜博

翻　　訳　マイケル・ジャメンツ
校　　正　鷗来堂
デザイン　林 陽子（Sparrow Design）
イラスト　芝田知佳（@shibatachi）
ベクター画像　Freepik.com（@macrovector）
編　　集　原 瑛莉子

発行人　三芳寛要
発行元　株式会社パイ インターナショナル
〒170-0005 東京都豊島区南大塚2-32-4
TEL 03-3944-3981　FAX 03-5395-4830　sales@pie.co.jp

印刷　株式会社 東京印書館

2019 © Yoshihiro Suzuki/ PIE International
English text © Michael Jamentz
ISBN 978-4-7562-5237-1 C0071
Printed in Japan